The Trials and Triumphs of Jessie Penn-Lewis

The Trials and Triumphs of Jessie Penn-Lewis

by

Brynmor Pierce Jones

The Trials and Triumphs of Jessie Penn-Lewis
by Brynmor Pierce Jones
ISBN: 088270-7272
Library of Congress Catalog Card Number: 97-73694

Published by:
Bridge-Logos *Publishers*
North Brunswick Corporate Center
1300 Airport Road, Suite E
North Brunswick, NJ 08902-1700

Contents

Acknowledgments

All the technical corrections have been patiently followed through and double checked by my wife Rosalie, my lifelong partner and friend, even while she was nursing me through a serious illness and lifting my spirits out of times of frustration. Thank God for her!

Grateful thanks to my publishers, Guy and Kitty Morrell of Bridge-Logos Publishers, who are also my friends and encouragers.

Thanks also to the Rev. Donald N. Carr for providing so many documents and for giving access to his precious set of *Overcomer* magazines.

Dedication

This dedication is to honor the life ministry of Captain John Metcalfe, now in his hundredth year. With his wife, Margaret, he gave half a lifetime in faithful service as volunteer helper, secretary (1943), editor, and trustee of the Overcomer Testimony.

Commendation

As the editor of *The Overcomer*, it gives me the greatest pleasure to write a foreword to this book by Rev. Brynmor Jones, whom I have known as a friend for many years. Jessie Penn-Lewis was truly a remarkable woman. Over these many years she has been an inspiration to many people. She was deeply involved in revivals worldwide and had the closest links with Evan Roberts and other Welsh revivalists. It was truly wonderful the way in which the Lord used her, in spite of constant poor health and much pain. It is still more wonderful that today her writings are so much in demand.

In past years, she also had links with the Keswick Convention and founded Keswick in Wales, and was the inspiration behind many other conventions. The basic emphasis in her teaching was the absolute centrality of the Cross—a teaching which, by and large, is much neglected.

This book is a must for anyone who is interested in a deeper spiritual life, and in the whole area of spiritual renewal.

D. N. Carr

Preface

In obedience to a God-given command to become the remembrancer of His mighty workings, I have endeavored to set out an unbiased history of the spiritual awakening in Wales and the world at the beginning of this century. Although I was urged on by the late Dr. Edwin Orr, I was hindered by heart attacks and other problems. Yet, I have been given sufficient strength to complete four previous books: *The King's Champions; The Spiritual History of Keswick in Wales; Voices From the Revival;* and *An Instrument of Revival,* which tells of the life and ministries of Evan Roberts. This fifth book, *The Trials and Triumphs of Jessie Penn-Lewis*, is built around a woman of great spiritual authority and her colleagues and prayer partners,

The first and only biography of Jessie Penn-Lewis, written in 1928, was compiled out of letters and journals and was centered on two periods of her life: 1890 to 1904 and 1920 to 1927. This current book has drawn upon newly discovered diaries of hers—and a number of letters she wrote concerning Welsh affairs, Evan Roberts, the American scene, the tongues movement, and post-1914 healing movements.

A major source of information is *The Overcomer* magazine; but for the Wales revival period there are also the valuable reports in *The Life of Faith* and *The Christian.* Also the many books and booklets that Jessie Penn-Lewis wrote provide glimpses here and there of her remarkable experiences, which took place in a period when few women were called to public ministry.

The few years of her secretarial work under the YWCA (Young Women's Christian Association) at Richmond and elsewhere, proved to be a doorway into an inward spiritual growth toward greater and greater consecration, and into an astonishingly active life as God's spokeswoman in Europe and America, as well as Britain. Her life was astonishingly active because of the threatening diseases within her frail body, and because of the occasional stumbles and falls in her long attempt to witness to, counsel, and win scores of girls and young women. There were trials as well as triumphs.

Surprisingly, Jessie Penn-Lewis was better known in Northern Europe than in Britain and was far more honored there. It is still hard to picture her praying with baronesses in boudoirs, teaching consecration at coffee-mornings, and riding with Russian and Scandinavian aristocrats in coaches and yachts. Hundreds studied her first books and booklets in their own languages and hundreds more heard her proclaim her four great messages in countries that were "white unto harvest." In this work, she was supported by praying bands of intercessors who understood that the day of opportunity would be short and that the seed sown would have to be buried deep in some countries.

The fifty or so books and booklets she wrote were a blessing to needy souls in many lands. As someone said, "Thousands came into the Life through them. Was not a woman like this under the seals of Heaven? Was she not tremendously endued and enriched?"

Her God-given task of recording and interpreting the revival in Wales and in many parts of the world needs no comment, but something has to be said here about her conflict with the early tongues movement. There did not seem to be enough time allowed to her to properly sift all the hostile evidence from so much of the world. Her correspondence shows, without doubt, that she wanted to find some middle-ground where the best qualities of the Pentecostal movement could be accepted, while what she called the "circumference," could be removed. It was not until 1912, when she published *War on the Saints*, that the whole atmosphere changed and any reconciliation seemed impossible.

Sixty years ago, the Rev. Nantlais Williams wrote about her fragrance and spirituality, but he also recognized the strong militant half of her nature that made her take up so many crusades and chase after Satan with great zeal. "If Satan was on the pathway," he said, "she assaulted him unsparingly." The price she paid was many wounds and personal sorrows right up to her last days. Perhaps she was engaged on too many battlefronts.

Without Nantlais Williams' testimony we would not know how she managed to serve the needs of Wales while living in Leicester. It was he who knew how energetically she had organized not only the Llandrindod Convention but several others. It was he who knew well how she had brought together the Welsh speaking ministers and English Keswick leaders in order to maximize the teaching ministry for hundreds of revival converts. Not even Nantlais, however, knew how deeply and humbly she had met the needs of the broken spirit and mind of Evan Roberts, and how she had brought spiritual solace and renewal to hundreds of weary or badly bruised Christian workers. This book attempts to show how important were the letters she wrote to troubled or perplexed workers all over the world.

All through this strenuous period of conflict, more uplifting spiritual books were coming from her pen. If she had lived a little longer she may well have provided Christians of her day with a balanced view of what were then new issues on divine healing, prophecy fulfillment, and the role of Christian women in Christ's kingdom.

But the Cross of Christ would still be at heart of her message. Thankfully, the Overcomer Testimony organization, founded by Jessie Penn-Lewis, has enshrined this.

Because a number of searching questions have been asked about the progress and impact of the Overcomer Testimony since the founder's death, the retiring secretary, Dr. D. N. Carr, has helped prepare a brief survey of the last fifty years, which is given in the last chapter. In it, I've attempted to assess the permanent worth of Jessie Penn-Lewis's teachings, the widespread outreach of this small movement, and to place it within the spectrum of evangelical thought and activity in this century.

Brynmor Pierce Jones

Part One

The Testifier

1

Down Memory Lane

About two years before her call home, Jessie Penn-Lewis had at last begun to dictate to her faithful secretaries the full story of her life. The only surviving manuscript, however, ends abruptly as she enters married life:

> I was born on July 28th, 1861, in Neath, South Wales. My father was a Civil and Mining Engineer and my mother was the daughter of a businessman who had married a girl of gentle birth. Her mother came from a genteel but financially broken family and had been adopted by a rich uncle who had her well brought up.
>
> My father's father was an eminent minister of the Calvinist Methodist Connection whose service was for the whole Principality. The Rev. Samuel Jones' colleagues were leading divines of his time. His main ministry was the building up of believers and his favorite theme was the Atonement. He was associated with intellectual leaders such as the Rev. Owen Thomas, Rev. Thomas Levi, Dr. Saunders of Swansea and the Rev. Thomas Phillips.

My father's house was a rendezvous for the leading ministers as they passed hither and thither on their Master's business. All my childhood memories are gathered around the great gathering of the Sunday School on the first Sunday in May and the coming to and fro of ministers. I was therefore brought up in the lap of Calvinist Methodism. My mother told me in later days that she had given me to God before I was born. She had ideas that children could be brought up without the knowledge of sin and it was a bitter shock when she found that in every soul born there was the old "Adam." When I first supported a nursemaid's lie, my mother fled to grandfather with bitter tears that their angel child had told a lie.

I walked without teaching and I learned the alphabet by myself and I had read from my Bible at four years old. The doctor bade my mother not to teach me anything because "Your child's enemy is an active brain which must not be roused." It was evident that my education had to be checked until about eight years old, after which I was sent for three months at a time to a Ladies' Boarding School.

The other months I had to spend in farms on the mountains where I could run wild among the cows and live a country life where there was no temptation to read. However at home my father had a library of books, being a great buyer of all classical works and standard books. I came to read the Waverley novels and Charles Dickens and Mrs. Henry Wood.

When I was about nine years old my father leased the Old Museum where his offices had been for some years. He turned it into a dwelling house for his increasing family. He retained the first floor as public and private offices, but the others were divided into rooms. Joined to the front building was a five story tower whose walls were three feet thick at the bottom. At the top they formed a room without a roof which was the old observatory, from which place could be seen all the surrounding country for many miles. This old tower was covered with ivy and was the home of thousands of birds.

Here in the old home many happy years were spent. An old attic with gable windows was our playroom. Our great delight was books. We used to sit on the floor in the midst of books and magazines of all sorts—reading-reading-reading. Four brothers followed me so my playfellows were all boys. In the garden we played cricket and climbed trees and had our own little 'Reading nests' in various ivy corners, or even in the branches of a tree. My father was devoted to us children and would walk six of us to chapel, being proud of his quiverful. How I remember walks with him as a child, when he would describe the geological strata of the rocks or we would hunt for fossils and remarkable stones. My father too had such high ideals of honour which have left their stamp upon us all through our lives. He would never allow a letter addressed to one of the children to be opened by another. He was very careful to teach his children the value of truth, not allowing careless promises to them by the servants, but insisting on truth in every word and tone.

In my tenth year a delicacy of constitution became very pronounced. Through a chill a swelling of the neck glands made its appearance and for many months I had to wear white bandages about my face and neck because of the discharge. When that stopped I was sent to a Boarding School at Swansea but my health was so poor that eight months was the longest I could bear. I well remember always being taken to church in a carriage and sleeping in the bedroom of the school's proprietors. I began to realize the restrictions of my body for I distinctly remember a bout of tears in the boot cupboard after watching the other children being sent out to play, while I had to stay indoors as it was an east wind. But even this kind care and discipline did not suit me and I had to be sent home again to be under my mother's eye.

About twelve years old my first bit of Christian service began. My mother was an ardent Temperance worker and at that time the Good Templar movement began in Neath. My mother was one of the first to join and I was eager also but alas! the adult Lodge did not admit anyone under the age of 12. The very first night after my 12th birthday saw me initiated into the coveted circle. I began my first crusade as a co-worker with my mother. Great was my desire to prove a good soldier in the Temperance cause. A Junior Lodge was formed and it was not long before I found myself Chief Presiding Officer over forty or fifty children. At 14 I was proposed as honorary secretary of the Adult Lodge. A Quaker gentleman who gave private tuition to twelve boys—including my brothers—undertook to teach me the secretarial work.

About a year earlier I had begun to attend the Sunday School at St. David's Church, though my parents were still members of the Calvinist Methodist Church. Their services were in Welsh whereas the younger generation were more and more making English their language. My parents were large-hearted Christians and on very cordial terms with the Rector so that they decided to let me attend the Church Sunday School and then to join the Church choir. I had no continuity of ordinary school life and the task of mastering French and German was of no avail. I continued as secretary of the Lodge by re-election quarter after quarter until I was compelled to give it up because of a great sorrowful blow which fell on our happy home.

My father had been ill two years through poisoning by sewer gas during his professional work. When I was sixteen he died, on April 24th, 1877. How well I remember the terrible day of the funeral when from a window I watched the sad procession, with two uncles behind the coffin and two fatherless lads on either hand.

> We were now eight children, the last being a three months old boy. My father was not a good businessman and disliked handling money and dreaded making a will or sending out accounts. He was consulting engineer to most of the Colliery Companies and was at the height of his profession, but outstanding bills and lawyers costs, etc., took all the means. My mother was compelled to start in business to maintain and educate her children, so the "Museum" was transformed into business premises. By skillful efforts my mother made an income sufficient to give one lad a course at Oxford, another training as a Civil Engineer and a third training as a Surveyor. This she did until all were on their feet. At nineteen I married—a genuine love match but I chose my husband for his character. Girl as I was, I reasoned that a man who never broke his word and never failed in an appointment was a safe one to trust to. (Her memoir ends at this point.)

Jessie's husband was William Penn-Lewis, and his bachelor diary has survived and shows him walking many times between Pontardawe, Pontardulais, and Neath just to take his future wife, Jessie Jones, on outings and sea-trips. It is possible that Will had already begun to be interested in sailing boats, which were a relaxation for him in later years.

In 1878 or 1879, William obtained a good position as an auditor's clerk for the County of Sussex, the first rung on the ladder of public office. His work was centered at Brighton, to which town he brought his young bride after their Easter wedding in 1880. Already the bride looked so small and frail that her uncle warned William that he was taking on "an invalid for life." Still neither partner knew how serious this problem was.

Although they learned early that Jessie could not have children because of her frail condition, their "love match" bore other beautiful fruit and their partnership in the Lord was to last 45 years. The story of those first years of conversion and consecration and witness is enshrined in her diaries and in her booklet, *The Leading of the Lord.*

2

Serving the Lord Together

During the second year of her marriage, Jessie Penn-Lewis went to a conference and heard messages and prophecies about the return of Christ, about which she had never heard before. She realized that she did not know the Lord Christ personally and that it was high time that she sought Him in earnest. About this, she wrote:

> My conversion took place away from any human help, but that day, New Year's Eve 1882, and that hour, has been indelibly engraved upon my mind. I used to take down my Bible from the shelf and read it occasionally. I turned over a page and my eye fell on the words, "The Lord laid on Him the iniquity of us all." By chance I turned the pages of the Holy Book and saw these words, "He who believes hath eternal life." Then I faced the question—Did I believe that God had laid my sins upon the Lamb of God on the Cross? After a few minutes of musing I saw that it was saying truly that I had everlasting life if I would believe simply on

> the Word of God. Then there was a sudden cry—I DO BELIEVE!—and one more soul had passed from death into life, a trophy of the grace of God and the love of Him who died. The Spirit of God testified unshakably and unalterably in my spirit that I was a child of God, and my soul was filled with deep peace.

Jessie had a deep desire to give her body and soul to the Lord's service. Sadly it soon became clear that her body would not be an efficient instrument. One friend said that she had already accepted that she would drag a frail body with her all the way to the grave—which refers indirectly to the onset of tuberculosis and other complications that she experienced early in her life. Yet, as she passed through many afflictions, Jessie was given the strength to endure and accept.

During the first ten years of their marriage (1880-1890), God gave William and Jessie several unexpected blessings. William became an effective Bible teacher and man of eloquent prayer, while Jessie reached new levels of usefulness and spiritual freedom.

Little is known about their first three years together when they were ordinary members of a parish church in Brighton; but Mary Garrard, her former secretary, found a half-sheet of note paper dated 8 a.m., February 28, 1884, which was Jessie's 23rd birthday. On it is the "Consecration Prayer" recited by Methodists, with these words added: "Keep my eyes fixed on Thee, ready to obey even Thy glance. Thou art my King, my Savior and my Guide. Take not Thy Holy Presence from me, but day by day draw me nearer, until that glorious time when I shall see Thee face to face, and faith be lost in sight."

The feeling that her end was drawing near at a young age seemed to urge Jessie onward spiritually. Often she would go to two or three meetings the same day, such as a confession meeting in one place and a holiness meeting in another. She took part in public testimony or some act of witness in July, 1884, for which she gave praise to the Lord. At a Watchnight service in 1886, she prayed, "I long intensely to be more single-eyed to His glory and that my will be more lost in His." The fruits of that deeper life were not always apparent, however, as her diary shows. A ruffled temper and hasty words often sent her to her knees to ask forgiveness and restored fellowship.

Up to about this time, Jessie and William had been unquestioning Anglicans, but events caused them to think again while at Brighton.

> When I was first married, my husband was attending a church where they had a confessional and I went with him, but we were the only two who stood up for the Creed. We held our ground there against everything of the Romanizing tendency until we found an evangelical church and withdrew. The Vicar, with his cassock and biretta, came to see me and begged me to remain, but I said no, for I had been brought up in the Gospel.

William developed links with informal house-groups and small prayer groups that resembled the Society of Friends meetings with which his Penn ancestors were identified. He and Jessie attended Primitive Methodist meetings and also went to "open house" meetings in Burgess Hill where they made new friends. Jessie noted in her diary on April 14, 1885, that Will had been to a meeting at a Mr. Head's and had come home very late, but "he said he had spoken there GRAND!"

In January 1886 in some hall, Will again, "spoke freely and splendidly for the first time for nearly ten minutes. My heart jumped. I could do nothing on my knees tonight except praise the Lord." How often had this young wife pleaded with the Lord for her boy, as she called him, to become useable? Now he was bold enough to speak often about his faith.

Jessie was happier with rescue work, but the most she could manage then were private talks with girls. Both of them prayed daily that their home would be the place where girls met the Savior.

For a few months, William was an itinerant auditor to several local government bodies. But ,by 1885, he had gone to work as the Borough Accountant for Richmond, Surrey, where they settled in lodgings on Halford Street. He had to spend long hours at work and his young wife would be without close friends unless she joined in a 'social round' (social circle) where she always felt "out of my depths." Almost in vain, she often reminded herself in prayer that Jesus was also lonely and that "if I would press on I must be content to be lonely too".

In her diary she continually rebuked herself for having, "a discontented grumbling spirit" or for feeling "depressed," by which she probably meant frustrated. She had such a high view of the Christian life as being one of "brightness and joy and the smile of the Lord," that anything less than that seemed like depression to her. She felt that shadowed moments shouldn't happen to her, even when her body was in agony. There are two entries in that diary that bring her very close to us:

> I feel too crushed to look up. Why is this so? Is it that I do not trust? Lord! Search me and show me myself.
>
> In all day. Was tempted much this morning and tripped. Satan came saying, "There you are. Down again." I flew to Jesus and looked to Him. Then I spent a peaceful time afterwards and wrote easily and happily in the evening.

During the spring of 1886, Jessie and her husband threw themselves into the Hammond Mission, a Church Outreach Mission, and a tract distribution program in the Kew and Richmond districts. There was a brief interval when she was called back to Wales to help her grandparents when Mr. Jones' serious illness began—he died at the end of that year. She also had to deputize for her mother in her Neath shop and was sent to inspect a family farm called LLwyngriffith in Aberdulais where she rode around on horseback as if she were a girl again. After this, it was time to settle down properly in the lovely town of Richmond-on-Thames, where the godly Evan Hopkins ministered.

William and Jessie simply drank in the teaching of Rev. Hopkins in Holy Trinity Church. He was the first to speak to Jessie about the way of victory over besetting sins, and he was the first to show William the rich possibilities of a Spirit-filled life. Sometimes the gentle pastor found it a bit difficult to keep up with the speed and energy of his new worker who went out daily to visit what she called "doubtful Christians." When they decided to surrender, she would take them to a special room in her house. After she was appointed as a Sunday School teacher/librarian, she devised a new syllabus for her girls' class in December 1886, and built up a select library of books and booklets on such practical subjects as consecration, service, clean living, etc.

It was during this time that she and William experienced a grave setback in the shape of a girl named Harriet from the church's Rescue Home. This girl often wandered out of their care, promised glibly to reform, spent nights with a soldier, and finally vanished. One night, they spent hours at the gate of Chatham Barracks looking for Harriet, but it was hopeless and Jessie was terribly cast down. Without the help of a Miss Hedley and a woman named "Edith," she would have cracked, especially as she had bouts of physical pain during June. The failure with Harriet was an agonizing learning experience for her.

Soon Jessie was told by her doctor to take a complete rest. Twice she ignored his warning and twice she was knocked out again. On December 14, 1886, "Dr. Cook came to sound my lungs. Says all right except for a weak spot at the apex of the right lung. Not active mischief but a weak spot."

Unfortunately, William was also paying for the strain and was now ordered to stop all work, even reading and writing, and to submit to having a pump applied to his temples to help his headaches. On July 14, 1887, Jessie wrote, "Will woke me at 5 a.m. and I nailed over every chink [to shut out light]. He was so sweet and patient in his darkened den. Next day he went down to a half darkened room. More light but with it a sick headache."

While her husband was sitting in semi-darkness and frustration for several weeks, Jessie went here and there to offer good counsel and to reconcile troubled young couples. Despite three bouts of pleurisy and neurasthenia, she became busily engaged as a counselor of the downcast. She was rarely free from callers who came looking for guidance, reconciliation, or hope. In the middle of this, they moved to a house of their own.

A second shock tested William and Jessie in 1888, when they were asked to deal with the turbulent emotional difficulties of a younger sister named Gladys. William tried stern lectures but these had no effect. Jessie felt that she was to blame because she had not prayed enough or because "I feel there are heights and depths I know nothing of." Gladys went her own way with her emotional problems unsolved.

One day, in June 1888, Jessie felt deeply troubled about her sad, restless husband who wanted to get back to work. She wrote "I felt no resource but God. Cried unto Him out of the depths. Dared not look at the future. Cast all care upon Him. Result: peace."

Though saddened by the plight of her husband, Jessie was still young enough in heart to share the joys of young people. She joined their boating expeditions on the river and did a bit of chaperoning and matchmaking on behalf of a couple she identified as "Edith" and "W. G." When this produced the expected engagement she wrote, "I cannot help rejoicing. It is all God's doing. He will smooth the way and the future is His. How can I help rejoicing about the two I love so much. God bless them both."

Perhaps because of her own constant expectation of a "final release" from her pain-racked body, she seemed to enjoy sitting up with aged Christians who would talk with her about their expected home-call.

Another dark cloud in Jessie's life was caused by a bitter quarrel between her mother and her brother. Jessie was deeply troubled when they both came to her home to tell their bitter grievances. This strain resulted in two weeks of asthmatic attacks and hypertension.

The year of 1888 ended with a wonderful convention service led by the Rev. Evan Hopkins who called for intensified prayer. A number of her friends were blessed and offered their gifts and service to the Lord. It is typical of Jessie Penn-Lewis that she made a special notebook of prayer reminders for each of her contacts. A small selection will show the breadth of her love:

> Prayers for co-workers, friends and the girls:
>
> For J. G.—that she may be brought into full blessing. For Miss King—that the Spirit may not cease to strive. That Miss W. be broken down and made willing to forgive. That a special baptism of love be given to G. W. so that he may serve and love the Lord in reality. That Katie may get through to the life of full surrender. That Edith may be deepened and softened spiritually and that she may enter into deeper union with Christ.
>
> Definite trusting about Nell. I have been carrying the burden myself. He cares for her more than I do. I will trust that she may come into full light and liberty.

By the close of 1888, Jessie herself had reached a new understanding. There had been time to read some highly spiritual books that delivered her. Her diary entries in the winter of 1888-1889 refer to two of these influential books: Andrew Murray's, *Spirit of Christ*, and Madame Guyon's meditational book, *Spiritual Torrents*.

The burden of Guyon's little book was that most Christians were content to remain in what she called "the way of light," where they gladly practiced discipleship and stayed faithful and true in God's service. But they could not break through to "the way of life abundant"—full union with Christ—because they were not prepared to see their secret faults and inconsistencies. So eventually they became dry and very discontented with themselves, unable to take pleasure in God. Only when stripped of the vestiges of self could they know an effortless spiritual life filled with joy, liberty, power, and fruitfulness.

In one of her booklets, Jessie confessed that she flung this Guyon book away and refused to let go of her own achievements, but then she heard the voice of the Lord saying to her, " 'If you want deep life and unbroken communion with God, this is the way. If you want fruit this is the path.' By His grace I choose the path of fruitfulness. It was dying not doing that produced the fruit."

Just as Madame Guyon had meditated and examined her own heart, so now Jessie Penn-Lewis decided to meditate and to carefully write down every important prayer need:

> April 4, 1888. That I may be consumed with intense desires that God in all things may be glorified.
>
> July 23,1888. That I may be meet for His use through helplessness.
>
> January 19, 1889. That I may be kept humble; I do so need this.

> February 1, 1889. That I may be kept from a life of "rush."
>
> February 4, 1889. That, for Thy glory and for Thine alone, Thou wilt, 0 my Savior, give me a conscious mind to my last moments.
>
> March. 8, 1889. For deeper understanding of SELF crucified. I long to be truly nothing.
>
> December 8, 1889. That I may be hindered at any cost from going forward in the YWCA work, if it be contrary to His will.

Solemn desires such as these were good for her spiritual discipline but, as Jessie would have said in later years, there was yet more ground to be claimed before she could sing with truth, "None of self and all of Thee."

3

None of Self and All of Thee

During 1889, Jessie had attended many meetings and committees of the Institute. An old photograph shows that this YWCA affiliated Institute was near the church-sponsored Rescue Mission. Once, Jessie was heard offering herself for work within days of a bout of pleurisy. In July 1889, she was coughing up blood and weighed only six stone (eighty-four pounds).

All through 1889, senior girls and some outside workers came to her house for prayer and reconsecration. Relationships with Matron Martin, who ran the Rescue Home, had at last improved to the point that Jessie was being pressed to take on greater responsibilities. The snag, however, was that for several weeks each year she was plagued with chills, migraines, and bronchial attacks, which left her too exhausted to think. But, true to her code, she would not break any engagement at the Rescue Home or the Bible class or the Mission Hall. According to her diary entry of March 19, 1889, there were times when she had not enough energy to sit down and compose an address and had to appeal to the Holy Spirit to give her a message.

In her autobiographical essay, "The Leading of the Lord," Jessie said that she had often felt like a defeated Christian until she came under the ministry of the Rev. Hopkins at Richmond: "I learned the secret of victory. It was not long before I proved the power of God to deliver from the bondage of sin through the precious Blood of Christ." She claimed that it was through Mrs. Hopkins that she learned about the rich possibilities of a Spirit-filled life. Perhaps it was Mrs. Hopkins who introduced her to Murray's *Spirit of Christ*, which had such a profound influence on her.

A special prayer journal for January to March 1889 shows the way she was moving towards a new phase. On February 10 she wrote, "That I may know more of the baptism of the Spirit and be more deeply taught of Him for I know so little." A month later she wrote, "Thank God for clearer light about the filling of the Spirit. May I yield continually so as to have my capacity daily increased." Another six months went by and she was still praying to be filled with the Spirit so as to be "lifted up above daily weakness, trials, and heaviness of spirit."

Three entries in her Diary sum up the effects of her prayers and reading.

Diary Extracts—February 21-22, 1889:

> a. Reading Murray, *Spirit of Christ* I came across these words: "To others it comes as a deep quiet but clear insight into the fullness of Christ as being theirs, and a faith that feels confident that HIS sufficiency is equal to any emergency." These fairly lit up to me and I saw that this had been my experience lately. I have never seen His power as I see it now. Reading paragraph 7 confirmed me. Has not Jesus been teaching me knowledge, love and obedience these last years? Have I not been entering into the fellowship of His death this winter as never before? Have I not been seeing the utter

> helplessness of the flesh and feeling keenly its insufficiency? Added to this during the past week I have just felt a "waiting for clearer light." THIS IS IT! The baptism of the Spirit is the blessing He has led me to. Tonight I see it and I praise Him.
>
> b. Same date. Had fresh light on the baptism and a conviction that it has come to me lately. My experience is according to Murray's *Spirit of Christ*, paragraph 5 and 7 and note A. I praise Him for his deep soul teaching.
>
> c. February 21st. 1889: Had such a lovely time in bed this morning feasting on 2 Corinthians 12:1-11. My text yesterday was, "Why tarriest thou? Arise and be baptized!"

Now Jessie was ready for a fuller ministry in the Institute, but first of all she had a "lovely talk" and a "little time together" with William, who had to accept her new calling and the demands it would make on her time. This was God's answer to her earnest prayer, "That he may be given deeper fullness from God and that I may be patient in the covering of love." Whenever her frail body would serve her, she did her round of training groups and workers' prayer meetings. She acted as secretary to various committees, helping with annual outings and celebrations. Towards the end of 1889, she began to feel again that something was missing from her work. She explained this in a later booklet, *Power for Service*:

> Truly the Lord did not fail on His part to give seed to the sower nor liberty in the sowing, but with no personal sense of the boundless liberty of the Spirit of God. No release from imprisonment in the vessel of the soul or being lifted to a position of dominance over soul and body.

It was in March, 1890, that Jessie commenced her full-time ministry as secretary of the Richmond Institute. This meant that she was now responsible for the welfare and spiritual state of the staff and volunteers. She probably conducted some kind of morning prayers for staff. She was expected to entertain supporters, engage tutors and instructors and even to interview a new Matron. She was immersed in the new round of singing classes, ambulance classes, flower groups, a consecration class and, of course, the vital Bible class meeting. In October of that year, it became necessary to extend the work and rent, what Jessie termed, "Upper Rooms," in Castle Drive. Throughout this busy time she did not give up her other task of leading certain senior girls and lady-workers towards holiness and confession of all sin.

Few could have guessed that Jessie was still troubled in spirit. Towards the end of 1890, she was given a strange little booklet printed by John Thomson of Glasgow. Its title was, *A Short Catechism by Madame Guyon*, and it was clearly intended to diagnose how far one was committed to Christ. It certainly challenged Jessie and filled her with new longings. Here are some excerpts:

> Q: By what are the children of God distinguished?
>
> A. Those who are children of God are moved by His spirit.
>
> Q. How does the Spirit move them?
>
> A. It dwells in them. They are separated from all not of God.
>
> Q. What means does God make use of?
>
> A. It is renunciation. It is to submit one's spirit by simple faith and to lose one's will into that of God.
>
> Q. Does it say that God dwells in the soul that doeth His will?
>
> A. Has not Jesus said that everyone that doeth My will, My Father will love him and We will come and dwell in him. Now he in whom God dwelleth is moved by the Spirit of God. Because, being God, He must

> command as a Sovereign in the heart where He dwells
>
> Q. What is it to love God with all one's heart, soul, and mind?
>
> A. It is to give all our heart to God and to give it so totally that we reserve nothing of it for ourselves nor for any creature. To love God with all our soul is to love without reflection, abandoning our soul to Him that He may do what He pleaseth with us for time and eternity. To love Him with all our mind is to submit our reason and all our spiritual lights to faith in God, the author and governor of our spirit.

It can be said that 1890-1891 was the time of Jessie's final search for the secret of self-abandonment. It was a time when almost daily she cried to the Lord for further blessings, despite the fact that she was being wonderfully used to help and counsel others. She became convinced that her new work in the Institute was not really bearing fruit because she had never known the special kind of power given by the Spirit. She wrote:

> My weekly Bible-class was a great trouble to me, for I had no power of utterance. Organizing work was much easier, but meetings were a sore trial. Self-consciousness almost paralyzed me.

Asking herself daily whether God had truly promised a full indwelling and outpouring of the Spirit, she began to read several more books on the subject but became very confused and certain that God could not use her to help others to obtain the blessing of the Holy Spirit. "All the people I could discover who were filled with the Spirit, I invited to Richmond. Everyone I heard of who knew anything about the Holy Spirit, I asked to come and speak to my girls. I was so anxious that they should get the blessing. I settled it in my mind that I was not the channel—that I was not the one to speak."

It flashed into her mind that she herself needed some kind of deliverance similar to that which changed Peter into a fearless witness. "I will not trouble about the words but I am after the thing. I want power for service," she cried. Somehow she felt that the more she prayed, the further away seemed the answer to her petition. She soon found that she was not the only one. Other women were passing through the same crisis in those same months. This moving of the Spirit began before an appointed "Woman's Day of Prayer," but continued with increasing force as Miss Soltau, Miss Nugent, and the Rev. Hopkins came to the meeting with solemn messages.

A typical case was a Miss Corke, who yielded her heart to the Lord on January 8, 1891, but who had a long struggle before giving up a certain relationship. Another girl was asked by the Holy Spirit to "lay her friend Birdie on the altar" and a third to "give your lips to the Lord." One ex-rebel came to say she had, at last, stepped into blessing, and two more called at Jessie's home to express their need of being filled with the Spirit. Eight put up their hands in one meeting and six in another and five on the third night. All were seeking more.

In October, 1891, three of her friends said they had found the full light and Jessie herself went to see Miss Soltau in search of a "fresh cleansing."

Before the final break came, there were more severe periods of self-examination, which had a slow but cumulative effect: "Why do I want this filling? For success with my work? If I were filled would I be satisfied? Would I accept if it meant unpopularity? Am I prepared to be without heavenly experiences? Am I prepared to walk entirely by faith?" About this process, Jessie wrote:

> The Lord waited until I came to the end of my own energy and strength. Then He began to break me and

> there came to me the terrible revelation. One morning I awoke and Lo! I beheld before me a hand holding up in terrible light a handful of filthy rags. A gentle voice said, "This is the outcome of all your past service for God." I protested, "Lord, I have been surrendered and consecrated to Thee for years. It was consecrated work." "Yes, My child: but all your service has been consecrated SELF—the outcome of your own energy and your own plans for winning souls and your own devotions. All for Me, I grant you, but your SELF all the same." Then came the still, small voice with one little word, "Crucified." What did this mean? I had not asked to be crucified but to be filled. Then as a little child I rested on the word ringing in my heart—*Crucified!* Then it pleased God to reveal His Son in me that I might preach Him. I knew the Risen LORD.

It was after this experience that the waters began to break out, just as Mrs. Hopkins had predicted. The Bible classes were now thronged and the once-dead prayer meetings changed and souls were won for Christ even at social gatherings. The final great change began on March 18, 1892, as Jessie returned from a meeting held in Wimbledon. This is her own account of the event that was as spontaneous as a revival experience:

> When traveling alone in a railway carriage from Wimbledon to Richmond it seemed as if suddenly my spirit broke through into the spiritual world and I was caught up. For some days afterwards I felt that I was as a babe lying in the Father's bosom, with all the world below lying in darkness whilst I was in light clear as crystal and so pure that every sin stood out in blackness. The morning following, the Lord stood by me and I clasped His very feet. That night when I entered the prayer meeting all the young women who were present

> were lying sobbing before the Lord. When I went to my Bible class the room seemed filled with glory and from this time broke out on the work the very river of life from God, which ever since has been flowing to the ends of the earth. It was my baptism with the Holy Ghost. For months I had been seeking it with intensity and crying to the Lord for a real Pentecost. I had asked also for that liberty of utterance which was given suddenly to Peter on the Day of Pentecost.

At one of the Wimbledon meetings Jessie had heard a Mr. Sergeant speaking about the Christian's freedom from fear of others, from which she had suffered for so long. But now, in one glorious hour, her entire situation had changed. "I SAW MY LIBERTY AND I WAS OUT IN FULL STREAM," she told her pastor's wife in a letter.

Mrs. Hopkins replied excitedly on March 25, 1892:

> I rejoice with you that you are fully in the stream and the stream in you. Glorious indeed is this anointing. Hallelujah! Where will it end? Waters to swim in and not a little trickling rivulet. "Ye have an unction." This is the positive power of the blessing The cleansing and weeping are only the preparation. I feel this is what so many need. The anointing abideth and continueth ever more and more if we do not hinder. May we never do so and then we may expect a continuous inflow and outflow. Oh! Is it not glorious that we have plunged in and are not standing on the brink any longer, out of the floodtide.

4

The Victorious Witness

In her letter to Jessie, Mrs. Hopkins wrote:

> Now comes the willing joyous giving out to others so that everything shall live whither the river cometh. May it be so ,dear sister. Isn't it lovely how He puts opportunities right in your path of passing on the blessing? No more "I can't. I can't. I can't." What a change! HE CAN! HE CAN! HE CAN! HALLELUJAH ! May the Lord bring many more to hunger for He only makes them hunger to satisfy and to fill. It's worth going through the hunger and the emptying and the "death" in order to get such a blessing.

In her diary, Jessie wrote, "The joy pouring into my soul is unutterable. In Christ! A vision of glory. A sweetness that made me feel almost sick. 'Turn away those eyes for they have overcome me' (Song of Solomon 6:5) I have had to weep for joy today. At HIS feet! No words can come—only *Master!*"

Six days after her day of blessing, she was thrilled to find that words of power had been given her, and that her sense of joy and victory was still present. This was not confined to her, but experienced by dear friends who had also needed deliverance. A wonderfully happy letter came from Miss Freda Hanbury on April 4, 1892. Freda's great fear was of physical suffering and she had to learn through difficult times that "Jesus is enough for me whatever may be done or ordered by the doctor." Now she was just praising the Lord who had enabled her to take in faith the offered blessing, as she wrote to Jessie:

> "I'll ask no more than I may see
> His promise is enough for me."
>
> This morning when we were on our knees it came to me that it was so dishonoring to the dear Master to be only able to say that one had asked Him to do it if He had not done it. It seemed that was too awful and by His grace I stepped out in faith there and then. And it is peace and joy in believing (not feeling). I knew what your long searching look meant and I longed to tell you then. The others were there so I could not well manage it. You will praise for and with me I know. Oh! How wondrous that our glorious Lord should fill His poor earthen vessels . . . Oh! The Lord has dealt wondrously with us both, has He not? Pray for me, dear one, as I do for you. Ever yours in His love and blessing.
>
> Freda

Jessie had always needed to be endued with power so that her fear of speaking would disappear. In a booklet called, *Power for Service*, she told how she came to that place where she could surrender even this problem to God:

> Peter was the pattern I put before the Lord. I saw that Peter was not nervous on that Day, and I felt

> intensely my greatest need was to be delivered from an overpowering nervousness, and a kind of paralysis in speech that fairly mastered me. I cried, "I want the deliverance that Peter got at Pentecost."

A few months of waiting and apparent silence were the final test of whether she could really wait on the Lord. Then the word of power began to come to her more and more often. On May 4, 1892, at an anniversary meeting, Jessie was asked to give a message. About it she wrote, "The Lord manifested His power and gave liberty. The minister was not pleased but it matters not."

She recorded in her diary on November 13, 1892, that the Lord had told her to throw away her notes and to put no trust in such. On November 18, she was told to arise, nothing doubting, and speak. On December 6, at a private meeting in Dynevor House, she said she felt quite restrained at first: "Then when my chance came, the Lord loosed me and I burst into a torrent and when I stopped there was such a silence, as if no one could speak."

Quite suddenly, Jessie was also released from the worst symptoms of her lung disease and people marveled at the power of her voice. She found herself well able to labor for the Kingdom in ways beyond all expectation. This lasted seven years, and the same kind of *remission* was experienced again during the 1904-1907 Wales revival period. It was accepted by her as a special blessing after she had asked for "power for service."

There must have been some comment when she boldly prayed for all the church leaders and the ministers of Richmond to seek and gain "the blessing." There was more public comment when "a good number trusted for cleansing and filling." In her long list of those blessed at the time, special mention is made of a Miss Everard who said she was hungry for fuller light, and a Miss Phillips, whose face lit up when she definitely trusted and who came in a day later "overflowing with the blessing." (All references from her diary entries in May, 1892.)

The small group of consecrated members of Jessie's YWCA branch were rather taken aback when Miss Soltau came to conduct another mission and said she would send back to London for someone to come and pray, "for this place is like a wall." Immediately the prayer intercession was intensified and there was a changed atmosphere. Within months there was a great change. Activity and entertainment schemes took a back seat in the Institute while prayer and Bible study were in much greater demand than the previous entertainment meetings. Jessie wrote, "We cannot compete with the world—we must win something far beyond competition and this is the presence and strength of the Holy Spirit. The number of members rose [increased] after the mighty wind of God blew through them."

A mighty wind of God was the only true way to describe what was happening day after day. The second half of 1892 saw a miracle. To some extent it was caused by events at the annual Keswick convention. Some of the Institute workers went together to the 1892 convention and came face to face with special teachings about the Cross. This is what Jessie Penn-Lewis wrote in a terminology that was all her own:

> There came a gradual cessation of the heavenly experience and a time of drought. I began to dread the loss of my experience and to seek anew an experience which seemed to be slipping away from me. At this point, by the mercy of God, I was shown the path of the Cross and the wisdom of God in withdrawing gifts from the soul in order to rest entirely on Him and not in ecstatic communion which made me spiritually self-absorbed and apart, pitying others who were not on my plane of

> life. I only wanted to be left alone to retire within for Communion with my Beloved. The physical being was not involved and the ecstasy of delight was purely in the spirit, keeping me away in a realm far above the earth, so that I moved among others and did my daily duties as one in a dream. When I saw that the loss of this spiritual delight and ecstasy meant FRUIT through death and a life in God Himself above His gifts, I gladly chose the path of the Cross and consented to walk by faith to that goal where God would be all in all. Through depths upon depths of fellowship with Christ in His death would the Lord lead me in succeeding years, to see that Calvary was the very pivot of all things and was the one great supply to the needs of the child of God in every aspect of his spiritual life. I saw that the baptism of the Spirit which I once thought to be the goal of the Christian life, was really meant by the Lord to be the beginning of a path which should lead believers into a fellowship of the Cross and, through the death of the Cross, into union with the ascended Lord in the bosom of the Father.

When Jessie and her companions entered the Keswick convention tents in August, 1892, they found that others, such as Dr. F. B. Meyer and Mr. and Mrs. Albert Head, had already been deeply stirred and were seeking. One day, F. B. Meyer testified to a personal blessing in a meeting and prayed in a rush that could not be stopped. The twelve sessions of uplifting Bible expositions at the convention—plus news of revival in Australia and a special Tent meeting to intercede on their knees for general revival—had a dynamic effect. They all returned to Richmond with great joy and gladness, magnifying the Lord, and on September 28, 1892, Jessie sent a report to the *Life of Faith* on the results in her Institute:

> There were just ten of us for our time of prayer on Thursday. We waited on the Lord until 11.30 p.m. It

> was a wondrous time. He did appear among us and reveal His glory. All were melted at His feet and every barrier broken down. We cried to Him for a very baptism of fire and fearlessness and told Him we were willing to be anything or nothing that He might be glorified in us. He then gave us such blessed promises and let us do some big claiming. One girl claimed her whole workroom, one girl claimed an outpouring for her chapel, one girl claimed every member of the Institute's "Ready Band" to be broken and filled with the Holy Ghost. We knew that all the promises of God are "Yea and Amen in Christ Jesus."

When it became known that these prayers had been answered, there were more prayer and praise meetings and more of the staff members and workers were changed almost overnight. In her diary, Jessie wrote about some of the things that happened:

> August 16th, Miss Pettit broke down and surrendered.
>
> August 18th, Nellie knocked, broke down and fully trusted for cleansing.
>
> August 21st, Freda fought out the battle and had the victory
>
> August 24th, Dear Agnes Longland came in for a blessing and was quite ready and drank it in, praising God.
>
> September 4th, Rhoda seemed to fully yield for "none of self and all of Thee." Hallelujah! My cup runneth over.

One report in the *Life of Faith* mentions an outing to Hampton Court, when the girls got together in the bow of the riverboat and sang songs of salvation: "Choruses and hymns kept bursting from our lips and one theme [the Cross] was always the foremost." At least one bystander was converted.

Jessie then testified how she herself had changed:

> I feel ashamed to think of how I have limited Him in the past. I have thrown my reputation to the winds and I am trusting Him for utter fearlessness and the boldness of the Holy Ghost. I will be wise and prudent no longer.

That mood lasted until October when she felt once more a loss of power and liberty and searched her heart for the cause.

> Found that since my little talk with Mr. Hopkins I had doubted on the death of self and lost the measure of liberty. But the Lord loosed me today (the 11th) and I must go on with Him at all costs. Mr. Hopkins' sermon on Achan's loss of power was a picture of the last fortnight. I had taken a step down through fear. After dinner had an hour with the Lord and told Him that I could not live a moment without His smile. I felt an intense drawing unto Himself with all the world and its people left behind. Joined in one Spirit. Oh my King, my King!

The last weeks of November were astounding and here we must include Eastbourne as a place of blessing, also:

> There were twelve consecrations on Sunday; sixteen on Monday; forty on Tuesday—all surrendered and claimed the baptism of fire.
>
> Great brokenness on the 27th, and several decisions for the Savior two days later.

The thrill of those two weeks stayed with her till she returned to her house. There she found that four more ladies were waiting to yield and claim cleansing. On December 10, she wrote triumphantly:

> The view of things prepared for us made us almost breathless.
>
> My soul filled with glory. The Lord whispered such blessed words from Scripture that it was a time of soul ravishing.
>
> Numbers of God's own children entered into an experience of the in-filling of the Holy Spirit never known before, resulting in a closer walk with God and a keener desire to win souls.
>
> (From *The Centrality of the Cross*)

It was typical of Jessie that instead of looking only at groups, she looked at individuals who were blessed. As before in 1889-1890, she wrote case notes about those who had reconsecrated themselves. We end the 1892 report with examples:

> K. C., August 8, 1892. Could not see at all. Left the room of the prayer meeting because not in true depth of conviction. On Sunday she came again and shut herself in a room, not to leave until it was settled . . . Peace and power.
>
> N. L., August 19, 1892. Convicted at night she came up in the morning and fully trusted for cleansing and took real hold. Went back to Suffolk claiming that God would use her, and we heard of blessing through her afterwards. A happy testimony to the keeping power of Jesus, she broke off from her young man.
>
> Miss Brodie, [a close friend of Jessie's] October 14. Could see that she was getting a longing at all costs. She told me she had come up every night this week hoping the Lord would clear it up. Said that every time she came made her more hungry. Felt she must be OUT and OUT to show forth the love of Christ. Evidently a deep hunger.

> N. G., Eager for blessing and not subject to morbid introspection. Got to talking against the teaching and she stayed away. On October 7th sent a note asking me to forgive. Came with tears on the 13th and owned that she had done wrong. Then made an utter surrender of self to be buried. VICTORY!
>
> Miss Williamson, Leader of a Woman's Class—came to our anniversary and afterwards said she must have the fire for service that she saw we possessed. On October 29th in class she broke out into earnest prayer for the blessing and then wholly yielded unto death and claimed the anointing. She told her class she would not rest until they were through.

As we move into Jessie's last four years at Richmond, her words should cause us to examine ourselves and see whether we ourselves have taken hold of true power:

> Two years I had labored in my own strength without the anointing Spirit, and for four years afterwards I was permitted to watch what He could do, when we consent to be crucified and to give Him right of way through our souls.

5

The Last Institute Years

The last years at Richmond on Thames are well covered by the Institute's annual reports, which showed a steady expansion. Those for 1893, list the seven forms of activity they had at that time: the Ready Band for evangelism; the Junior Branch; the Support Band for overseas missionaries; the Flower Mission for sick-visiting; the Home Mission for help to distressed families; the Singing Band; and the Prayer Band.

Gradually there was a change in spiritual emphasis, however, which can be traced to a private meeting in the spring of 1892. About it, Jessie wrote, "A small band of us were led to wait upon God for an outpouring of the Holy Spirit upon the Institute. After many weeks of heart searching and waiting upon God, this was graciously vouchsafed."

The 1894 annual report said this new vision and spiritual force had given birth already to a Ten Day Mission, a Tract Mission, and some Gospel services. There were also new ministry groups called "Rescue" and "Fishers." A page in the report was devoted to testimonies, and another page listed the Christian work of ex-members of the Institute who were now on active Christian service. A third section describes the special blessing or calling of people such as an Edith Phillips who wished to serve in China, and Nurse Naomi who said she was overflowing with joy after she had heard God's clear call.

Jessie was interested in visions at this time and entered in her journal the experiences of a "Miss Ada" who dreamed she was walking in Christ's footprints until she came to Calvary and shrank back. The two ladies agreed that this signified some kind of rebelliousness, and Ada then took the step of full consecration. A few days later a Miss Easton claimed to have the same vision of Calvary and the tomb and herself buried there.

At a meeting on April 29, a man wept loudly and said, "I see Thee, Lord; I see Thee." Jessie felt a strange prompting to sing and preach, and she suddenly realized that it was the first anniversary of the night on which "I was thrown on the Lord in agony of prayer and He answered me, 'Rejoice! I have found my sheep.' " Now she was no longer reluctant to share her visions with others.

In the second half of 1894, Jessie began her public preaching at some YWCA meetings in Eastbourne. But far more wonderful things happened at Swansea and at Neath where she had helped to found new YWCA branches. It was at a Swansea meeting that she claimed that, "A girl in any house who lives in Christ will cause a revolution. A woman filled with Christ will touch her home, her business life, her service and all her friendships." She believed that every YWCA branch could be the handmaid of the churches because it would train girls and women in prayer and service.

This kind of thinking can be seen in her annual reports from 1893-1896. She stood out firmly against anyone who doubted these ideals and was supported by the editor of the

YWCA's magazine. In Wales she gave unlimited help to those who were founding the YWCA and a Rescue Home in her hometown of Neath.

Some missions undertaken by the bands went so well that she wrote that Christ was soon going to manifest Himself. One night twenty-five girls were in the upper room praying to the Lord to come. Sometimes Mrs. Penn-Lewis was asked to speak to men's meetings and felt not a twinge of nerves. Such outreach work did not go unchallenged, however, and she described one terrible day as "the Day of the Fury of the Oppression" because one girl got drunk, and one was arrested by the police and was accused of stealing. The only time she could relax was when her fond husband came down and took her off to the seaside at Brighton or Eastbourne.

In November 1894, Jessie and Miss Jackson were asked to conduct a week of mission at Neath and they went as "humble instruments." At the very first meeting, she reported, there was an outburst of weeping and five souls surrendered. This happened every night so that on the last evening 150 people stood up, scores went to the inquiry room, and large groups were praising God. She noticed that many girls were oblivious of each other as they prayed. Many girls could not sleep at all because of conviction of sin.

Jessie wrote, "At one shop where one girl had stood alone, all the others were now saved and the cry went up, 'Shop on fire!' " Girls in groups were singing on their way home about the wonderful Savior. On Friday the workers sang in the street, "All hail the power of Jesus' Name" until 10:20 in the evening because they were full of joy. The minister split the converts into bands of six to visit every court and alley in Neath. There was also a Rescue Society meeting attended by sixty ladies.

One particular event shook the town. The story went around that Mr. Joshua and his friend Mr. Perry had been kneeling at a bedside on November 14 beseeching the Lord to give them power. They had one candle between them, and one of them opened the Bible at Zechariah 4:1. Soon they were overflowing with joy and confidence. Wrote Jessie:

> On the next Sunday morning as Mr. Perry was preaching at another Mission, people were coming to him with streaming eyes. Mr. Joshua also had a blessed breaking down and then he told how the Lord had shown him they must be set to work and he asked for volunteers. With weeping, the people poured their names in. Blessed be God . . . In the afternoon the Rev. Caleb Joshua said, "I am really hungry. I am not satisfied. I want power and I mean to have it." We gave him Acts 1:8. Then the Rev. Seth Joshua said that he needed it but he was silenced. The Baptist minister was receptive and said, "God has taught you." Something like this happened also at Swansea where a minister called Rowe Evans said, "You have upset all my sermons and I cannot go on preaching abstractions." Also a minister's wife named Mrs. George shut herself in a room and prayed for a baptism of the Spirit. Others gave open testimony as to how they had been delivered at Calvary or how they had been emptied and cleansed.
>
> The whole town was talking and many said they had been forced to make a bolder stand for Christ. God was even moving the Town Council. On bad days God silenced them and gave me opportunities throughout the town. There were 45 meetings in 28 days. Altogether over a hundred came forward.

In the first months of 1895, Jessie continued to minister to her own workers such as Lucy and Miss Kemp and someone she identified only as Miss S. She also witnessed to people even on train journeys. She took mission meetings at Hammersmith when she should have been in bed, and then she went off to Wales once more on her way to engagements in Ireland.

In her diary she hints that something devastating happened at the next Keswick Conference. It seems to have been bitter rumors about her unorthodox views that caused such pain. A Mrs. Hatt-Noble told her that she had expected upsets and had been surprised that any blessing came. At the general meeting Jessie spoke on the "necessity to be imbued with the power of the Holy Spirit before going forth because it is He who emboldens for witness and sanctifies for service." Some women objected and she had no support from other speakers. Wrote Jessie, "I staggered to Miss Soltau who was not in. I was shaken through and through. She took me to her room and I sobbed out on her bed, then I rested and had tea and went to a meeting where Dr. [Andrew] Murray spoke on the theme, 'Can you drink this cup?' "

She next went to Dublin to address a YWCA conference. She was invited to take public meetings in Belfast and more extensively in Armagh where ladies such as a Miss Irwin and Miss Eustace longed to take her around their branches because, "You were so sympathetic to all who spoke to you that I feel you will understand even if you cannot come." Miss Marrable, a noted temperance crusader, also invited her and offered the use of her hall for any further meetings. These ladies were worried that some YWCA members had joined a new Pentecostal League and were holding separate meetings when they needed to be one in order to combat widespread indifference.

Mrs. Hatt-Noble also asked for intercession and it seems from a Miss Ewart's thank you letter that they had a real blessing. In January 1897, Miss Ewart described how they had been kneeling in prayer with a Miss Franklin who was called to missionary service soon after Jessie issued the challenge to go out in faith. Some of the Overcomer circles met to discuss her pamphlets or letters—or the testimony letters of others, such as this one:

> I have an ever deepening sense of the work of the Lord Jesus and a rejoicing in the liberty of entering into the Holiest. What a change after fourteen years of Christian life! You understand perfectly well what it is to desire earnestly to press on and yet at the same time to be perfectly satisfied in God first and God only. It's a foretaste of the time when God shall be all in all. I thank God that you came so sacrificially in such weather and you so ill. I will thank God through time and eternity that you were willing at any cost to be obedient. May God bless you and keep you in body and spirit.

Jessie's diary entries for the spring season of 1896 show that she knew that her work at Richmond was coming to an end because her husband had received a new appointment to be Treasurer of the City of Leicester. They gave sad farewell to all the co-workers on March 4, 1896, and went from there not knowing what the Lord had prepared for her. Two months later she was launched upon a new ministry that was soon to take her abroad. One night she wrote in her diary, "The Lord has shown me what is His purpose for me."

One fruit of her services to the YWCA in Richmond was that from time to time she agreed to turn her discussion and instructional notes into booklets that were soon translated into many languages. A later chapter discusses the significance of this.

Part Two

The Traveler

6

Scandinavian Journeys

Jessie went on a tour to Northern Europe as a recognized spokeswoman of the YWCA in Britain to address the first Scandinavian Conference of YWCA. Yet it gradually became a much wider mission as private invitations poured in. She was able to revisit three countries—each time, as she put it, "wearing a new hat." It's fortunate that the original journals of the visits to Copenhagen, Stockholm, and Helsingfors still exist.

In those days it was unusual for a married woman, especially one with such a bad health record, to be able to spend so much time away from her busy husband newly launched on a good career, and with plans for their own household postponed. But William and Jessie consciously and prayerfully made a sacrifice each time it was decided that she could spend two or three months abroad on the Lord's work. There was also a lovely understanding between them that they would be full prayer partners in this ministry and would use private prayer-telegrams whenever either of them needed prayer.

In a letter to a relative, Jessie wrote of their burdensome, yet joyful, vision:

> How little did I think that He would knit with me in blessed oneness of heart and fellowship, my beloved husband, and give him to see me as a trust given back by God from the grave when, humanly speaking, I should have been with Christ which is far better . . . How can either of us rob God and appropriate for our own selfish use the trust given for His own special purpose? How we bless God, my husband and I, for the opportunity in the little while of counting all loss for Christ. We feel how little it is and how brief the time. We covet that our God may do the most with us in our short lives. Think you that we shall regret any sacrifice. When we look in our beloved Master's face, shall we regret giving our home and our lives for Him? Oh the joy now! What will it be then?

If they needed any confirmation that they were walking within God's will, it came in the form of letters and telegrams that poured in saying how they longed to meet her. Not until 1899, did William press her hard to come home and really rest.

Jessie's Travel Journal: 1896

> I want to write—as I am able—a brief story of God's leading and dealing in my Swedish visit . . . I left London on Friday, May 29th. Dear Miss Soltau and Edith Pacey journeyed with me to Tilbury and were able to come on board the "Thorsten" for a few minutes to see my cabin and to stand with me in silent prayer as we looked up to God for His blessing on every step of the way. It did not seem like going alone, for there is no loneliness when Christ is all in all and it was only a great privilege and

joy thus to be sent forth by Him.

It turned out to be a rough passage and all the passengers ill except one gentleman—nothing to do but lie on our backs and keep quiet. I do not remember how the hours passed—only that I had one anchor "My Father is at the helm." Toward the evening of Saturday I had the assurance that I should be well at Gothenburg and then had a very good night, waking up well and fresh. . . . After breakfast I went on deck and enjoyed the sunshine with my Bible. Then I turned nursemaid and rocked a Swedish baby to sleep and had a chat with the mother.

On shore I was led to an English clergyman and his wife who said, "You are to stay with us. Here is a letter for you." Found he was the English chaplain and his wife is a Russian lady. They seemed overjoyed to have me and longing for Christian fellowship. They said they might be entertaining angels unawares and I did not take long to find out their eager souls. The little wife saying, with tears in her eyes, "I am hungry, hungry, oh so hungry." I felt overwhelmed with God's wonderful planning. Here was a beginning.

I found they reckoned the *Christian* and the *Life of Faith* their greatest treasure but had no spiritual fellowship here at all and little work, yet longing to be used. God's "Arabia" for both of them. We plunged into spiritual things at once. We took the sixth of Romans and read it together—God revealing and doing His own work. This morning she was waiting on the stairs to tell me that God had done His work. She saw that it had been consecrated SELF eagerly at work for God; now it was to be Christ working through her.

Evening meeting at the Gothenburg YWCA: 60 or more came though it was only given out on Sunday that I could hold the meeting. First they sang "Come to the Savior" in Swedish. Then the YWCA President prayed and, afterwards, turned to me. I felt lost for a moment then I said, "Tell the girls to bow their heads and everyone say, 'JESUS, speak to me.' " Miss Dickson interpreted, but at first it seemed impossible. I told them what Jesus was and could be to every heart. I told them about our Richmond work and prayer meetings. Tears were in every eye and all seemed grateful for the Word. We could only talk with our eyes.

Next morning. I am having a quiet time writing and my hostess is rejoicing in her "secret" as she calls it. "It has made everything new," she says.

Wednesday. My little hostess took me upstairs to meet a Gothenburg worker and we had a good time together. She is telling everybody her new secret—her housemaid, then her cook and then a German governess who came in. We had a Bible Reading and then went out shopping. I left Gothenburg for Stockholm (14 hours) stopping at Halsberg for food and seeing the natural beauty and also the politeness of people. I heard some Swedish men singing hymns and I used my Bible and theirs to converse about receiving the Spirit. On Thursday I had a private meeting with 40 Christians but the devil kept telling me I could never grip a meeting by interpretation. I threw myself on God.

The next day it dawned on me that I was to ignore the problem of interpretation and speak exactly as I would in England, letting Him be my voice. The interpreter prayed and I KNEW with the first word God was there—perfect liberty. God was here and took hold of every heart. Then we went on with silent prayers and we rose to separate but nobody moved. There was a deep hush and awe upon us all. I asked for questions and answered them. I asked those who wanted God's best to say YES (Ja) but still no one would move. So we went back to prayer and there was great liberty and it was blessed. After two hours we moved and one lady whispered to me in English, "It has been a revolution in my heart this morning." Another whispered, "I see it all but I don't know it." I felt overwhelmed at this—our first meeting. God is evidently going to do great things and the great relief was that interpretation, in God's hand, was not going to be a fetter.

After dinner the President of the Swedish YWCA came to see me and thank God for bringing me and to say how they longed for blessing. At 7.30 we had a public meeting—another time of liberty—and then had tea again and they still didn't want to break up so we gathered together again. We took up the petition before God for a great outpouring of the Spirit upon ALL THE BRANCHES.

I said we needed the spirit of utterance and liberty for there is a great deal of dumbness and stiff conventionality to be broken down. Politeness had become a barrier and the strong national prejudice against women speaking had helped to freeze meetings. But God has broken this already. I told them the Holy Ghost would set them free. On our knees we went and there was a stream of ceaseless prayers. God is most evidently moving mightily; hearts are ready and God's tide is already bursting and God's army of women are awakening and Sweden will know it. When God gives the Word who can stop it? One by one they have been stepping out. It seems to me that in this first conference we shall reach high tide. The interpreter said, "You have had Swedes, Norwegians, Finns and Russians here," and I said, "How like Pentecost! Now we shall have an outpouring upon the daughters."

In the morning a lady came and said, "I want to be a new creation. New altogether but I cannot get at it. It seems to slip me." The Lord gave me the word that Self was longing to be new and Self was struggling for blessing and Self wanting to be used and Self wanting to get spiritual riches. She saw it—and then entered into rest.

Friday at 1 o'clock I went to the Training Home for Nurses and the Matron interpreted. An old saint was

> there who had raised money for Homes for different purposes. God used me to tell her a little of the deeper walk by naked faith and she was truly one who knew God. One lady there was a Russian princess who had to leave Russia because she and her husband had been converted and would not have their children baptized in a Greek church. She asked for a private meeting at her house where she could call in a few gentlemen.

Although Jessie was taking matters into her own hands by having these special talks with people in need, she didn't get into real trouble with the conference officials until she told them at a meeting that God had given her the text of a "new translation" of Psalm 68:11-12, 24-26, which implied that God's army of women had proclaimed the tidings. About this, she wrote:

> I did not know how women in Sweden were fighting a battle for freedom to speak. Let your women keep silence is a strong word in Sweden. Strong prejudice existed against handmaidens prophesying and this was based on misunderstanding of Paul's word of rebuke to the chatterers of his day, the women who would persist in asking questions at the wrong time in the wrong place. Yet he instructed them how to prophesy.
>
> I did not know this was one of the subjects put down for discussion. It was just like Him to meet the need and strengthen their hands by taking my mouth to show them how when God gives the Word, the women who publish it must needs be a numerous host. Surely Psalm 68:11-12 (RSV) must have been a prophecy for these days but it was repeated and confirmed in Joel, "Your daughters shall prophesy." The pastors are strongly opposed but there is a movement among the Christian women which cannot be stopped.
>
> In the Baroness Lieven's drawing room on Monday we had tea served by liveried footmen and the guests

were each introduced, including the wife of the Danish minister and then the Russian princess and finally Princess Bernadotte. I could only feel that they were souls. How solemn it was to speak to them. God kept me in His hand, perfectly at ease. I had to talk to them of sin and sinners in the sight of God, and of peace with God through the Blood of the Cross and of rest and satisfactions the world could not give, and the blessed life of Jesus lived in our earthen vessels. The hush of God stole upon us and heads were bowed and tears flowed and Jesus Himself drew near. We went on our knees and our hostess sobbed out a broken prayer. How rarely have they heard of the real Christ. One after the other thanked me and I gave them "The Glorious Secret."

. . . We talked of all seeing how Christ satisfied and of being drawn to Him. Truly our God is a wonder working God. . . . How wonderful an opportunity and privilege He has given me!

After this I went to hear the Conference discussions. Women have long been too timid to discuss but God has heard their prayers and a large number have come and there is great freedom and keen discussion of vital subjects. Praying souls are looking on and wondering at God and praising Him for doing exceedingly abundantly. On Sunday at 1:30 about 400-500 people gathered—from the highest to the lowest—factory girls and conference delegates, fashionable ladies and military men. The Princess brought Prince Oscar Bernadotte. An exhausting meeting. God manifestly moved and I know that numbers were weeping. I spoke on the work of the Holy Ghost in converting, cleansing, sanctifying—which they had heard little about. I went to the door and numbers came to thank me. I was told the Prince wished to see me and he said, "I do long to give up more. I have thought much of the power of the Holy Ghost this winter. I have the Spirit but I need more." I told him the secret and how it came to me and tears filled his eyes and then his wife came and talked of full surrender.

The Tuesday meeting was the most blessed of all despite the incongruous surroundings. Some young men came from the YMCA, one of whom is of the royal house of Russia. The Lord's presence was melting and I saw one young man brushing away the tears behind his hymnbook. I used Philippians 3, "I count all things loss to win Christ—I count them but refuse." I told how Paul had surrendered and how Moses esteemed the reproach greater than treasures in Egypt. The Princess was summoning people to come and see how to find Christ more fully.

Next evening was the Foreign Missions meeting and I gave the closing address on "How shall they preach except they be sent." A lady put a gold chain into a worker's hand—for China. After Communion Service in the Finnish church, we had an 11 A.M. meeting where God simply smashed souls. I spoke on the fire of the Holy Ghost and the fire did fall. It is blessed to see the hush of God but it is still more blessed when He works so mightily that they are utterly broken down. So it was then. In one room there was someone weeping, "Oh He never had one so hard as I. I am an utter failure. He will have to do it all." Just a word and she entered into rest. In a side room another sobbing on a couch, and I could only give her a loving touch and leave her to God. No one will forget this day.

How they are all singing with joy about their first conference. To God be the glory. I am perfectly well and carried in His divine life. My interpreter and I are perfectly one in the Spirit. The last meeting was again one of great simplicity and liberty. Then there was the gentleman's meeting where I spoke on Romans 6, and they drank in the story of deliverance from death. Souls were too eager and time too precious to stop for most were going where there would be no human help. After dealing with sent-in questions I was besieged and dealt with soul after soul right up to 2 p.m. The next meeting waited while a Countess from Norway begged for prayer and then she clearly decided and "died."

At the 2 p.m. meeting before the Prince and the Pastor, I spoke on "Characteristics of the Christian life" and they just hung upon the word. I answered questions and then asked any who wished to leave, as we were going to wait upon God for enduement of power. Only six moved and I had that mass of souls waiting and purposed to meet God—it seemed incredible. Against custom they knelt to pray and spoke short, low prayers separately and then two or three together. I couldn't believe my eyes and ears! The whole meeting broke into prayer, everyone in his own language dealing with God. It rippled and rippled like music and I could have laughed and cried. The low murmur ceased and I could hear petitions again and the old pastor broke out twice. I could only stand and look, amazed at the beautiful harmony—everyone praying in complete oblivion of the presence of the others. This was Pentecost. Then a final cry to God for an outpouring of the Spirit upon Finland, Norway and Sweden. It was past 4 when I got from the meeting.

Even as I left by train, one lady gave a first class ticket and others sought my prayers. 14 meetings in 7 days and a ceaseless stream of souls yet I was not a bit tired. Now it all seems like a dream to have had such fellowship with God's children and to see His work go on gloriously in such a short time. O magnify the Lord with me. Even on the voyage home a gentleman working for YMCA came to me and opened his heart fully whilst a lady worker was broken down and went to her cabin to settle it with the Lord.

BLESSED BE THE LORD WHO ONLY DOETH WONDROUS THINGS. ALLELUIA!

Jessie had been away from home three months and took quite a time to catch up with letters she had received while she was gone. All the letters were answered faithfully—even a hurtful one from some lady who later apologized for listening to suggestions that Mr. Penn-Lewis was a neglected man. Closer friends knew better. Early in 1898, William paid a very brief visit from St. Petersburg over into Finland and was able to introduce her translated booklets on the "Pathway" theme. Later, she made her own way there—in January when every river and lake was frozen over and her best friends unrecognizable in heavy furs. The chief excitement was meeting and saluting the Empress as she drew near in her little riding coach on her way to one of the fairy-like palaces. The brief visit convinced her that there was an open door there and she must eventually reach that land. Meanwhile, she was persuaded to stay a while in Copenhagen and again in Berlin to address special drawing-room meetings. As usual she sent a letter of apology to her waiting husband, but assured him that blessing was coming to Denmark.

"There is little doubt," Jessie wrote in a Circular Letter to the prayer-helpers, "that God is making preparations for some mighty movement that the near future holds. Those of us who are sent quietly and silently to the preparation of the future instruments may thank God and take courage."

Sweden and Finland's turn came again in May 1898, after another brief visit to her disciples in Copenhagen where she met both the outer "circle of witnesses" and the "inner circle of seekers" who wanted to know still more about the *Way of the Cross*, the *Way of the Resurrection* and the *Way of the Throne*. She was delighted to discover that they had translated some of her booklets and had studied the "Pathway to Life." They all wanted to act as "Buried Seed" in their society and culture and they longed to follow the guidelines set out in "Pathway to God." There was only one major public meeting in Copenhagen, where she had the joy of seeing many respond. Public meetings at Malmo were equally responsive but she had to remind herself that she had a very full program.

After these brief engagements, the party had to go on up to Stockholm and found that the famed Dr. Charles Inwood had already been giving Bible readings on Jessie's favorite themes: the "Spirit's Entrance," the "Indwelt Life," and the "Divine Call to the Cross." One of the public meetings of the conference got packed with a mixed audience that fell silent as she told them about the Spirit longing to take possession of their entire lives. "Channels only, blessed Master" became one of their treasured songs.

The following week she addressed one private meeting in Prince Oscar's house about "The Call to the Cross" and suddenly there was a breaking and a melting and a clearer light shone upon faces. A man who watched this happening said, "This is what Sweden needs. We have been waiting." The Swedish churches seemed to be ready to absorb it because they had been waiting already for the message of the Cross. Wrote Jessie:

> The Holy Spirit has been preparing for it and we MUST have it. When shall we learn that there is a need in the hearts that only the Cross will meet and that the Holy Spirit can make simple the deepest majesty of the Cross to the youngest believers. Let us not withhold GOD'S secret.

In theory, these were YWCA meetings, but every meeting was packed with people wanting to know how best to become God's prepared vessels. She was convinced this was being accomplished by the constant preaching of the Cross as the power of God.

One unexpected pleasure for Jessie was a yachting trip on the Baltic, followed by an important private talk with key people who had just begun to learn about what some called "the Applications of the Blood of Christ." She also greatly enjoyed the voyage across to Helsingfors (now Helsinki) in Finland, though she did have problems there with extremely hot weather and also with a lack of proper interpreters, which was a matter for urgent prayer. Looking back afterwards to those days she wrote with astonishment:

> I never quite saw how much the Lord carried me until I was side by side with interpreters. As I gave forth the Word of Life, I seemed to get more vigorous whilst they seemed to flag and grow weary. This is the difference between the "power of His endless life" to quicken, and our natural resources.

Why the Free Churches' Conference was without a properly qualified interpreter is never explained, but she marveled that five languages were needed at each meeting. (While we are considering interpreters, it is noted in her journal that she was approached by a Professor of English at the University who wanted to translate all her works into Swedish.) It seems that her main theme at the conference was relatively uncontroversial—"Life in the Spirit." But the last session was devoted to soul-winning, after which the forty delegates went to their own fields of service.

Jessie planned, as at Stockholm, to hold informal meetings where she could give her other teachings. It was decided to throw all meetings open so that " those who were seeking a deeper knowledge of God would come."

There appear to have been three of these public meetings. Her messages were, "Fire of the Holy Ghost" and "The fire of the Lord," followed up by an afternoon study of Ezekiel 1:5, "Born in the midst of fire." The Tuesday night service was attended by a large mixed audience. The same thing happened twice the next day, and Jessie realized that God wanted to work among these people before they dispersed all over

Scandinavia. After this conference, Jessie was invited to rest at a house called Mon Repos (home of Baron Nicolay's mother), but she could not resist slipping over to St. Petersburg before she went home in late June.

Somewhere in her journal of the visit to the Baltic countries there is a remarkable account of a meeting that surely was a forerunner of the Welsh revival ten years later. This is how she described it:

> The morning meeting merged in the afternoon and the afternoon into the evening and nearly everyone forgot coffee time and mealtimes because they were so eagerly asking questions. Then in the evening, when an opportunity was given to pray, there was a great sound of murmuring and then a sound never heard before in Baltic lands. A sound of joy and perfect harmony as the people prayed in a dozen languages. An overflow meeting ran on till 7 but then it was time to entrain for Gotheburg.

A year or two later, Jessie paid a flying visit from St. Petersburg through the lake land and the forests into Finnish Karelia where she managed to fit in three well-attended public meetings, full of people who seemed to be hungering for the same truths. The only work done during such a short stay was to arrange the publishing of her longer works in Finnish and Swedish.

Twelve years went by before Jessie set foot again in Finland in 1913. She stayed at one of those huge mansions that were burned down during the soon coming war. Bible studies were held during the planned forest rides, and the whole discourse was about "walking after the Spirit." There was a quiet conference for Christian workers at Ruvaniemi and three major public meetings in Helsingfors. The high spots of this brief stay were the free praise meetings at Ruvaniemi. The low point for Jessie was the unexpected departure of Miss Volkoff.

Miss Volkoff's place was only partially filled by the Baroness Kurke of Rynge, whose group had taken a kind of crash course on "Spiritual warfare" in order to equip themselves for the battle for Sweden's soul. When the Mission Societies, such as the Russian Missionary Society, opened up again in Baltic Russia after the war, they found that the Gospel witness was still there. They had proved the truth of Jessie's last message at Stockholm about God's abundant power to deliver and keep His own. After lengthy and emotional prayer-meetings, she had managed to deliver that final word of exhortation in order to strengthen them for the coming battles, both spiritual and physical.

> Now unto Him that is able do abundantly more than we ask or think, according to the Power that worketh in us, unto Him be the glory in the church through Christ Jesus—world without end. Amen!

7

The Beginning of Her Writing Ministry

Whenever Jessie returned from her various journeyings, she found herself face to face with four quite different responsibilities. Three of them were the several counseling interviews every day, speaking at business meetings of various Mission Societies, and a round of visits to her YWCA girls, whom she loved with a faithful and prayerful love. She did all she could to keep in close touch long after the girls were "diffused like salt of the earth" through missions, orphanages, hospices, and other ways.

The fourth and heaviest responsibility for Jessie lay in the stacks of letters that her secretaries had set aside for her personal attention. Some of these were proposals for new conferences, others were discussions of projects that were close to her heart—such as the setting up of an International League of Prayer Intercessors, or a Christian literature ministry to Russia and Scandinavia.

Jessie protested to her friends that she was not a literary type and that she had no inclination to write books. Yet she felt she had to find some avenue to take her message to Britain and Europe, especially after giving up full-time YWCA work and also withdrawing from Keswick's "Ladies Meeting." This happened in 1897-1900, when she discovered that several Keswick leaders, including her own Vicar, distrusted her teachings as "too subjectivist."

Her first books were published at the request of those who had heard her brilliant expositions at conferences. They were skillful collections and collations of the key biblical texts that showed Satan's existence and intentions and his modes of action as the tempter and accuser of believers. But the last sections set out every verse that assured those same believers that they could overcome satanic attacks and enjoy a degree of security because of their special relationship with God in Christ, and because of the great victory of the Cross over the powers of evil. These words reinforced many a missionary in times of direst need, yet her work was sharply criticized in Britain.

Some form of opposition inspired her to write a very important letter in August 1897, which explains why she was so totally committed to whatever special message or task was entrusted to her. Isolated more and more from former colleagues, she felt that the Lord was calling her to publish her messages as a top priority. In a letter to a friend on March 10, 1897, she wrote:

> It is very deeply on my heart that God would have me do more writing but I find the sitting at one desk very exhausting. Will you specially ask for abundant life for this and for His hand mightily upon me for writing? Yours in the glorious Lord.

The entire story of the *Pathway to Life*, which she first wrote in 1895, and revised in 1898, is truly remarkable—not the least the fact that 75,000 copies were distributed and that it was translated into several European languages as well. It was 32 pages of packaged study of the developmental side of the Christian life, every stage supported both by the Scriptures and by up-to-date examples. The preface to the first edition stated her clear purpose:

> The booklet has been written to interpret in some degree the death with Christ on the subjective side of the Holy Spirit's dealings with the soul. There is no desire to dogmatize or systematize but only to show in the main the experimental pathway. The Holy Spirit is not bound and will lead souls along this road in a thousand different ways. The writer earnestly prays all to whom the booklet is not of PRESENT use, to put it aside until God, in His own time and way, becomes His own interpreter.

Much of the theory of spiritual development was based on personal experience of change, yet there is some internal evidence that she had been influenced by Fenelon, who wrote two mystical treatises, and those pietist writers in whose meditations the direct work of the Holy Spirit and the applied work of the crucified One received equal and parallel treatment. Jessie wanted Christians in her day to understand that the combined effect of the Passion and Pentecost was a radical change in personality and relationships. Slowly one reached the goal of "continuous dependence on Christ the Living One." It was no longer a question of effort or feeling or even faith, but a restful abiding, a being "hid with Christ in God" (Colossians 3:3). "To abide in God is the key to an anointed life and an overcoming life," she said.

In her humility, Jessie sent proof copies to her own pastor and to the Rev. E. W. Moore, a Christian editor, who wrote warmly and generously about the book's potential. He said,

"I cannot criticize it. Let it go forth and may God bless it. He has led you in His own way. You must tell on the house-tops what He has taught you in secret."

But her pastor, Rev. Evan Hopkins, wrote to her in a different tone:

> Many thanks for your letter. I should like some day to go thoroughly into all the teaching with you when an opportunity offers. That there are dangers in the path of the closest fellowship, the Lord has shown me clearly. That we should not be ignorant of Satan's devices, is a duty He has deeply impressed upon me. Of course this does not in the least make one afraid but it keeps one from thinking "There is no danger now."
>
> People have often asked me about you and I should like to be able to tell them with certainty that I have the greatest confidence as to the views you hold. But to tell you the truth I am not sure what it is you hold in the matter of sinlessness. I have seen nothing in what you have published to lead me to suppose you do hold unsound views on that point. But it would be nice thoroughly to go into the whole thing with you so that I might be able to speak with confidence. God has greatly blessed and used you, but it is for this reason I am jealous of my Master's honour—you understand.
>
> The danger comes very often through a misinterpretation and a misapplication of texts of Scripture. It is then that I don't feel quite certain about your teachings. I do not believe for one moment that you are heady or obstinate about this. I am glad you have written to me candidly and I will certainly be open and candid with you . We both desire the Master's glory. I am very sorry I cannot possibly get away at the time you name. I am really overwhelmed with work at that time. Yours.

There were numerous letters of appreciation that Mrs. Penn-Lewis kept and used in her second, much revised edition. This time the *Life of Faith* gave it a very warm welcome because it dealt with an important aspect of sanctification:

> The very valuable part of her teaching is as to the detailed individual working of the Holy Ghost in the soul of the surrendered believer, holding it firm, guiding it in thought, feeling and action; reaching down into its secret sources.

The truth of this verdict can easily be illustrated by a few examples of the letters sent in by grateful readers:

> Pastor Blocher of Paris thanked her "for this new spiritual experience which, through the grace of God, I owe to your words. I have seen the Cross of our beloved Savior in a new light. I have, of course related our talk to my wife who has read the booklet *Pathway to Life in God.* To her also it has been a new and wonderful vision of the Cross."
>
> The Rev. Langley Hall of Jerusalem said, "I think the Lord has enabled you to put very deep and precious truth in a condensed simple and fairly clear form—enlightening and helping God's children."
>
> Miss Helen Davidson of the Ceylon and General Indian Mission said she had met Christians in Madras and elsewhere who had had blessing channeled to them through these exposures of the self-life and the revelation of the Christ-life.
>
> A Mr. Smeeton, who later went out to Algiers to work among the blind beggars, confessed, "I have been utterly powerless to speak to souls and my life appeared to be a failure but your *Pathway* has given me the key and my prayer is and has been 'Lower, Lord, Lower still!' I find that I have been waiting for a resurrection

> experience that does not come by waiting but by faith."
>
> Another lady, Jane Pollock, wrote, "He has brought me where I can walk in the Word alone apart from emotions and manifestations."
>
> And a Mr. Arthur Evans wrote from Pimlico, "I have been through your pamphlet, most of it on my knees with Bible open; and in simple faith have been taken through the Gateway. I have spent several hours at Calvary and I do believe that I am 'dead with Christ.' Not just the old sinful 'I' but the saved 'I' is dead with Christ. Yes! The consecrated 'I.' Now I am trusting in Him to keep me 'nothing' that Christ may be all in all. I do not yearn for Pentecost now but am quite content to see no fruit yet, if only it be His blessed will."

The *Pathway* became a study book in many spiritual classes at home and overseas and it went through many editions. What had begun as an address to missionary workers became a valuable tool to set free scores of Christian workers who would then more effectively bear the seed of the Word wherever they went.

Three of these letters inspired her to think of further writing. A Miss Trevanion asked for more copies of all her writings because "God's spirit is speaking to many souls through these books, all around me, with the result they are being set free in a wonderful way hitherto unknown."

A Miss Lucy Vaughan's letter, written in May 1897, contains similar news but was also a personal testimony to deliverance from backsliding. She said she had lost heart "until I read the little book the *Pathway*, which encouraged me to press forward. Last week the precious Lord's own messages came through to my soul. I am very conscious of having not a blessing but THE BLESSER, not a help but God Himself in greater fullness within. By His grace I have clean done with everything not of Him. Oh! What a Saviour and what a dear tender Father! Oh! What a Comforter possesses even me! Praise be to His holy Name! He is all in all to me! I am so glad to be stripped of every perishable element. Forgive all this."

Is it any wonder that Jessie Penn-Lewis longed to present the same message to dozens of groups in Europe and Asia. If any further proof were needed, it was the response to the fourth and fifth of her books, which she began to prepare while still abroad. After her return to Leicester in May 1897, she found a large number of requests for her writings had arrived from Australia and the United States, as well as from the lands she now knew so well. An especially urgent request came in from Sweden.

In August, her generous friends, the two Countess Volkoffs, were with her on holiday in Switzerland. Her Russian friends did everything possible to make her comfortable and well entertained during their stay at Interlaken. She could sit out on the balcony of the top story and write or pray or talk quietly with new friends. She kept an exquisite holiday journal that pictures the scenery and the house and the lake land, the cascades, and even the storms. But there was serious work to be done—the editing and translating into Russian of her *Pathway to Life,* and the first-stage preparation of two little books. After they moved to an austere guesthouse near Abendbeg, way above cloud level, they discovered a German Christian couple, named Buckhardt, who felt they had been led to wait there and pray. They were overjoyed at having this privilege to translate her writings into German.

What a time of fellowship this was, except one or two days when they chose to go alone and meditate on the golden slopes of the Alps. In her diary for August 10, 1897, she says, "I went off to a lovely spot and reveled in three hours with the Lord alone."

Before they parted company that week, they had a Bible reading session in German, which was their only formal meeting. Then she moved down to Vevey and sat alone by the lake with the waters lapping at her feet. By the time she was back at Leicester she was ready for a new round of meetings in Swansea, Rothesay, (Scotland) and Manchester. She could hardly wait to travel abroad again; not to Scandinavia this time, but directly to Russia where her various visits were marked by great spiritual victories—and serious physical troubles.

It was out of Russia that the seed-thoughts came for her major work, *The Cross and its Meaning*. But the book would never have taken the form it did without the special vision that Jessie had. The vision inspired a Good Friday sermon, but it did something more enduring. About it, she wrote:

> On Sunday night the 27th of March, as I was going to bed, there suddenly flashed upon me the "Message of the Cross" with every chapter marked—the whole scheme, every heading, chapter and title. Next morning I arose with every bit of it printed on my mind. I went to my study—locked the door—took each passage and wrote it as rapidly as it was possible—the first chapters. I arose at 1 p.m. and said, "I have not had a revelation like this for many a long day. Will the devil leave me alone over this?"

So she locked the door and wrote nine chapters in three mornings. Her diary continues:

> On Saturday I went back to an empty house to complete the written message in two days. I felt everything else must stand aside so that God would speak through it. I was able to bring it down to London where the last chapter came to me—the vision of the Lamb in the midst of the Throne. The next weeks meant ceaseless labor in proof correcting and the detail of issue ere I went abroad. But then the battle was over.

Considering that it took only a month to compose and six weeks to print, Jessie covered many important aspects of Christ's death on Calvary, which she described as *The Gateway to Life*. She told her friends that God had revealed to her that the book would be greatly used. It was translated into the major languages of Europe and reached thousands of anguished souls who knew that they were in sore need of deliverance.

By 1904, it had become clear to many thoughtful people that this book's chief effect was to prepare many minds to accept that there would have to be a return to Calvary before the Lord would send world wide revival. There is evidence in correspondence to Jessie that it was being studied more and more on the very eve of the Great Awakening in 1904.

Somewhere in this same period Jessie issued, by request, her conference notes on the experiences of Ezekiel, Job, and Moses. Two of those, *Face to Face* and *Glorious Secret*, were translated into three or four European languages at the turn of the century. Rather different was her *Studies in the Song of Solomon*—the most mystical and the richest work she ever compiled—which was finished off in St. Petersburg in 1899, just a month before her almost fatal illness. In letters to her husband, she pictured herself as working six hours a day and feeling such peace and joy as the theme opened up.

> God is pouring light upon it and my pen is running without halting. The light is so full and the bubble-over of life so strong, that I can hardly lay it down. I get up in the morning and scribble notes with a pencil and even dress with the Bible open. . . . This will be my first book written with delight.

When she was at last free, in 1901, to finish off *Job*, she had a similar experience of "deep peace and an assurance of being very specially in a definite place. There has been such a lighting up of the message. He has brought me here for this." Two months later ,the book was done and the selected extracts from other writers had been approved. The printers, Taceys of Leicester, moved fast and scores of copies went to India and to the missionaries in China who were passing through a time of great suffering and personal loss just when the book appeared. The intention and significance of the book can be seen even more clearly in the Preface and the Appendices. She said that she was writing *Job* for all who walked in integrity of heart and obedience, yet were in fiery trials whose purposes were not yet clear.

> I ask all who read this little volume to take for themselves only the portion that commends itself to them as "from the Spirit of God for their own heart's need"—and to leave the rest for His use to those souls for whom it may have been given.

This kind of request can be found at the start of several of her more controversial books in the post-revival period. But the old reluctance to write had vanished and the only time she got agitated was when her brief autobiographical account of her spiritual journey in 1889-1892 appeared on a publisher's list.

During the strenuous revival period, she confined her time and energy to a hundred or so essay articles. After the revival, for nearly twenty years, a stream of Christian literature flowed from her gifted pen in the form of pamphlets, booklets, and a few substantial books that traveled the world for fifty years.

8

The Russian Aristocrats—St. Petersburg

Towards the end of 1896, Jessie was asked to go to St. Petersburg where she found a circle of active evangelical Christians won over in the days of Ambassador Lord Radstock. One or two leaders were already planning to form a new type of outreach. The significance of the group contacted by Jessie is that they formed a spiritual link between the pre-1890 group of converts and the larger groups won over by the Fetler brothers about ten years later.

This winter journey was quite an adventure for a lady traveling with only one companion. After a sea-crossing to Flushing and a long train journey via Hanover, she arrived in Berlin in wintry weather and stayed at the Hotel Continental. With a new lady companion, identified as Mrs. C., she journeyed to Warsaw on an antiquated train. Together they learned the art of dressing and undressing in very narrow sleeping accommodation. They were taken for their meals and rest to the Emperor's suite, always kept for him at major stopping places. By courtesy of Countess Stakelburg, the daughter of the Governor-General of Poland, they passed through customs and the frontier controls "like royalty." Once in Warsaw, the ladies were taken to elegant chambers, which also turned out to be the Emperor's reserved suite." For a few hours they were driven around in the Governor General's carriage, procured by the same Countess.

In her travel journal, Jessie details much of the trip:

> I decided to make a call upon Mr. Titterton, an old Richmond curate who was now a missionary. He asked us to take a meeting if he could get police permission. He feels that there is a definite awakening among the Jews who are losing faith in the old Rabbinical teachings. He is the only English pastor authorized to baptize in Russia, and the Jews prefer his type of baptism. What an opportunity to deal with souls and tell them the Gospel and insist on heart surrender and faith. He gets on with Russians and Germans. He is wholly cast upon God. I visited the Bible Depot for Jews and had a straight talk with the one in charge. The Countess came and said she would obtain police permission for the following Sunday in Warsaw.
>
> On Monday night we left Warsaw for St. Petersburg in a wide-seated carriage, traveling through miles of snow—vast tracts of snow—a great barren land with very few rough-built peasants' cottages. We tried to prepare for the Russian meetings—translating things for the hoped-for prayer-circles, using cards and YWCA portions all written by hand. Before we began we had a morning drive on the frozen River Neva.
>
> Our first meeting was in a classroom attached to the British and American chapel whose minister, Mr. Francis, gave me full freedom to speak. He said they had been praying for revival. God had sent a messenger who had not been disobedient to the heavenly vision calling her to a distant land. Two Scotsmen, who were

members of the Prayer Union of the Faith Mission, greeted me. A brother from Finland, with the stamp of Christ in his face—said in English, "I knew the Lord's voice tonight: His voice always arrests." He asked me to go to Finland and I said I would if God said "GO." Then came the agent of the Russian Bible Society who was making more arrangements. Our days are likely to be full.

We visited Russian teachers out in the villages, who said they would appreciate a monthly letter to link them with the Christians in St. Petersburg. But printing is very difficult here. Then our first Russian meeting—in the house of Princess Lieven, which was packed with ladies and gentlemen and five other princesses. God gave me a clear message on "All things new." How they listened and how many surrendered all to God that night! One lady said, "I have waited many years for you." That night, at the close of the meeting, I asked all who felt convicted to say so aloud, and a majority of the meeting broke out and cried for full surrender to God, so that the old things might go. In my closing prayer there came spontaneous murmurs of response, saying "Yes, Lord."

On Friday, Baron Nicolay called to offer help in writing papers for the new YWCA. We got into talk about the enduement of power and he described clearly the path which the Lord had led him last year. He saw his soul dying and could not help himself but cried like a sinner, "Just as I am without one plea." He had not heard teaching on life with Christ in God. That afternoon I held a meeting with Princess G., Princess L., and Princess O. and also Baroness Wrede, who for fourteen years had been visiting Finland prisons, using a cell at certain months in order to see seven hundred prisoners individually. She is given entire liberty by the government and is the only one allowed to visit. Her face was an inspiration. Three other ladies stayed to talk about their souls.

At an eight-o'clock [evening] meeting for Germans, Finns, and Swedes—God mightily present and a wonderful weeping response.

A morning visit to an Institute for Girls and an afternoon visit to Baroness Kruse and several countesses and princesses—including a lady in waiting to the Dowager Empress. I spoke on "The place called Calvary," and God was very present. I spoke also in the entrance hall just as the men servants were drawing on their mistresses' snowshoes.

God is truly working among "Chief women not a few." We drove again to Princess Lieven's where I spoke by translation about the "Self-Life." I went to a discussion group and threshed things out among them—personal things with the princesses. These women are the chief Christians in St. Petersburg. Their position covers them and their names protect the Christians gathered at meetings under their roof.

At another Princess's house the young princesses—girls of 14-16—were talking intelligently about Christ, whilst young Prince P. was evidently a true Christian. After dinner and a lie-down, I was driven in a sledge under magnificent furs over to Madame Tcherkoff's where we had another large meeting in her dining-room. Poor and rich together, countesses and peasants, the butler and footmen. I spoke on "The Lord looketh upon the heart."

On the Monday I spoke at family prayers and at the school in the grounds. I then had an interview and then a meeting in the English chapel before the same ladies. Then two more interviews before retiring. The next morning I spoke with two ladies who were seeking the baptism. Later on there was a meeting in a poorer district—the people truly as sheep without a shepherd. I was simply pressed upon for interviews but had to leave. What a time of reaping we could have if we were free!

After a sightseeing morning, there was a meeting with Dr. Nicholson and the Rev. Keen of the Bible Society. Then a public meeting after which a Prince interviewed her, the first hostile interview. After this there were several more interviews—one with a Jew who wanted to know how to enter the Kingdom of Jesus, Son of God. On Friday morning there was another drawing-room meeting with Madame Kruse. Next came a large meeting for Germans at Baroness Nicolay's, and then a meeting with Sunday School teachers and deaconesses. After that meeting a group stayed on to talk about spiritual matters—until 11 p.m. Then, on Saturday, there was a vigorous meeting of leading Christians about Pentecost and the Fullness of the Spirit. Jessie ends this travel journal with this statement, "If these souls get the Spirit so as to have power in prayer, this is the only key to the condition of things in this great land."

On February 4, 1897, she was escorted by a governess down to Moscow for a brief holiday. Groups still clamoring to see her in St. Petersburg were told that she had a tired husky voice and couldn't go on. The one semi-public meeting that was held was filled with power. Then she was on her way once more. As she left Moscow, she was given expensive presents and was treated with great respect by the American vice-consul. But she was unable to take any meetings and wondered if her visit had any further purpose. When she returned to St. Petersburg, she was told by the Volkoffs and Baron Nicolay that the blessing was continuing both to groups and to individuals who had been seeking. She was welcomed everywhere as Christ's messenger and was able to set up intercessor bands to "wait on God every week for an outpouring of the Spirit on the Russian Christians." What glorious faith!

On Wednesday evening, in the British-American chapel, in the presence of the American ambassador and his wife, she spoke on Romans 12:1-2. Then, at 2.30 p.m., she faced a little group of German workers and spoke of their need to seek an outpouring of the Spirit. The Princess G. asked for a private talk and spoke joyfully of the witness of the Spirit given to her in Colossians 3:3.

On Thursday, the German workers met again and then a lot of YWCA ladies met for two hours of prayer. It was a tiring schedule that went on until Jessie's final day in St. Petersburg when Baron Nicolay had arranged a "men only" meeting to discuss "The Anointing." Later that morning, there was a special meeting for the young people, where several people were praying at the same time and the whole meeting was broken down. This was followed by a final address at the German Institute on "Vessels." That was followed by an evening public meeting attended by all three language groups and by several social classes. Jessie said about this unusual service, "Our God was present as a consuming fire."

The last page of her St. Petersburg journal is unfortunately badly faded, but it seems to refer to a number of private interviews with ladies; and to a farewell service held in the chapel pastored by Mr. Francis, who was soon to be debarred from letting her use these premises in any subsequent visit. She wrote to friends at home about her need for more of the supernatural life to carry her onward because "these dear people are making the most of their opportunity."

Jessie also describes the excitement and dignity of her departure, but when she wrote to her husband, she confessed to a sense of relief because she now dreaded the public meetings and felt far safer in "little sanctuaries in a strange land." She confessed to a sense of fear and said she badly needed the reassurance of her morning reading—"Ye shall not go out with haste nor by flight. The Lord shall go before you and the God of Israel be your rearward."

This is what she told her husband about the increasingly restrictive attitude of officials:

> You will understand that the work of necessity be spread out. We cannot go on in the same place. There are many adversaries. If it could be public and free there would be a wondrous reaping of souls. Alas! It cannot be, so that to meet the needs here takes much longer than a few days in England. God overwhelms me with wonder when I see Him make strangers do such things for me.
>
> The dear things are so hungry—so utterly different to the stolid indifference in England. The days were so full that by Sunday night I wondered how I should hold out. Although I saw the tremendous need I hardly dared to commit myself to say that I would stay. I began to find myself flagging and needing a breath because the atmosphere here exhausts you much more than the free air of England. It is awful to live under the feeling of restraint.
>
> Well! I shall not be home on the 12th, but I am hoping to get to England by the 20th. I can only tell you that God's purposes are marvelous in this visit and that you will not regret every possible day I can give them. Souls are being touched that no one else has touched, and I stand in awe.

Madame Astronoff and Madame Kaminsky accompanied her to London, but all plans to prepare literature in Russian were blocked by a government ban on their distribution. She wrote to her circle of close friends in order to ask for more discretion:

> I have been compelled to suppress all names of places of the work in St. Petersburg. All that it has meant you will know in eternity but, until then, the greater part of the work must remain as the Lord's secret. All the glory is His—I did nothing but watch His work. I had only to be "not disobedient" to His readings. May it encourage us to launch out.

> Most of you know the difficulty of all Christian work in Russia. May I then beg you not to let this journal pass on to any but those whose names are on the list, and not speak of its contents to others. I have ventured to share with you a part of the Lord's trust and you will not be unfaithful in revealing it to others. It would have the most serious consequences if it were to get into print.

Briefly, there were two other visits to Russia about which the letters and diaries speak. When they were on holiday in the Gower near Swansea, they were visited by the Volkoffs and Kruses who pleaded for help. They might have learned from former ambassador Lord Radstock, in a private talk on November 5th, that things would be more difficult. Despite all setbacks, she told the prayer-circle, "God is now going to show you His plans for your life and He has linked you with me for some wondrous purpose. Look to Him to show you what channel of blessing is for your fellowship."

In December 1897, Jessie was actively engaged in preparing a supply of booklets—mostly in German—to take with her to Berlin, Warsaw, and St. Petersburg. Friends were distressed that she was so weary and thin, but she was determined to go ahead with her travels. One long letter describes the drama of this journey—a collision in the fog, an encounter with icebreakers in the Baltic, and yet another collision involving troikas and sledges. This time no details of meetings could be given and no one used personalized visiting cards any more. She was in close contact with the Volkoffs and especially with Baron Nicolay, who afterwards sent a warm letter of thanks to Mr. Penn-Lewis for "letting your wife come at so considerable sacrifice." It was the beginning of a strong friendship.

The Russian correspondence is as interesting and informative as the Russian journals. Some of these letters failed to get through and others were sent to Miss Flora Hanbury's house in Richmond so that some friend could take them up to Leicester. The earliest of these letters was from the Volkoffs, the Kruses, and Miss Kaminsky, who told their new friend how she had met their need.

> While we were yet speaking the Lord had heard. He knew previously what His children needed and He gave through you exceeding abundantly above all we could ask or think. The hearts of many of us are now praising Him for the new light that has shone upon some of the blessed truths of His Word . . . He who gave you grace to obey the heavenly vision and, leaving country and kindred and house to venture, not knowing where you went. He has branded the name of this country on your heart. May He give you grace to fulfill His priestly charge enabling you, as co-worker with Christ, to raise up the foundations and "repair the breaches and restore the paths." (Isaiah 58:12)

Madame Astronoff also wrote about how she was learning to reach hearts by bold witness. She asked for prayers for her planned religious concerts in which gifted Christian performers could reach people's hearts. Then a Miss Zass wrote about obeying God's call by persuading her Young Girls' Union to come out of their shells and go seeking other girls on railway stations and in hospital wards. Lastly she wrote, "I thank the Lord for all that He gave me through you, that He showed me the Father and that the Holy Spirit filled me and taught me to understand that Christ in me IS the hope of glory. I thank you again and again for your prayers for Russia and for all your love given to us."

The fourth and most soul-stirring of the letters came from Baron Nicolay. It raised a number of important issues:

> It is strange to tell you that my mind is daily occupied with one or another part of the message which you brought us. Yet I have not thanked you for your very welcome letter and your Circular Epistle to the Church at St. Petersburg. I did not want to write in a hurry and I put off and put off according to the fashion of the world. Alas! There are other people here in the same plight as me, I hear. Do not think of us as cold and forgetful.
>
> The seed that God made you sow has gone deep in many hearts. It has been like a revelation to many. I believe that many, like me, are digesting it. The notes I took will soon be all copied and will recall to memory much of what was said..
>
> On the whole there is another spirit in our circle—more meekness, peace, harmony and unction. Much seems to have been melted by the fire. Several praying groups have originated. The Young Men's meetings are blessed and a new member, Prince Galatzin, has appeared. On Sundays some of us meet regularly but there is a blank somewhere. I want something to come out of us—not to go warming and warming the water once or twice a week and never getting it to boil. I suppose we are not hot enough ourselves.
>
> I am so afraid that with some there be sins which keep them from advancing. For them I wish that some work could be found. I feel I ought to know more about the lives of some of these young men; otherwise they may be rotten underneath.
>
> On Thursdays Miss P. and I go to the dear working-men believers and God has blessed this.

Baron Nicolay probably had many court duties to perform and also held some kind of public office which gave him very little free time until the hottest month of the year. Then he dedicated his sailing yacht to God, filled it with books and visited various homesteads on the Finnish isles. He enjoyed his new friendship with Mr. Penn-Lewis (pen-name, Vassili Vassilovitch) who was also a keen yachtsman. "Vassili" actually paid a private visit to St. Petersburg and took part in the Baron's welfare work. One of the Baron's most interesting secret letters to "Vassili" was written in November 1898. It gives a bird's eye view of the evangelical groupings such as the White Cross Union for young men, the missions in Courland and Estonia, and the work of the Mennonites in South Russia.

Jessie was keeping very close contact with the two Volkoffs and Miss Kruse, whom she had discerned to be quite fearless for their newfound faith. Profiles of the most useful Christian ladies were written in a little brown notebook alongside a list of her preaching topics while in Russia. These notes are our only guide to the visit in 1898. The journal talks about sea-fogs, collisions, bumpy, slow trains to Warsaw, and lost tickets for the train to St. Petersburg, where Miss Olga Volkoff became their escort and guide, but says little about the private invitation meetings—one for the Russians and one for the Germans.

When Jessie returned from her second tour in March 1898, she continued to write long letters to the Volkoffs and to "the circle." They linked up again in a Danish conference and again in Keswick and again in Davos in Switzerland. She constantly reminded the Russian group that the oppressions they experienced were part of the wider battle of the "hosts of darkness" against the "hosts of light."

At home in Britain, she constantly urged the Intercessor Bands to pray that Russia should have religious freedom. Seven long-suffering years later the Czar granted full liberty of conscience and there was a respite until 1915.

The third of Jessie's visits to Russia was a near disaster. There were hardly any meetings now and she spent a great deal of time writing. Then, in March 1899, she was ravaged by pneumonia and pleurisy. The entire Russian circle were engaged in almost continuous prayer for her recovery. When she got home to Leicester, she sent a monthly letter to the circle who, in turn, wrote regularly to their "Beloved Malenky," as they called her. There was no more talk after 1900 about traveling to Russia .

The happiest postscript to all this can be seen in the *Life of Faith* in the Spring of 1906, when Mrs. Penn-Lewis was at last able to write "Glad Tidings from Russia," in which she described Pastor Fetler's praise meetings. Fetler's seven essays in the summer and autumn of 1906, followed on with even better news. Jessie herself had the special pleasure of announcing *Revival in St. Petersburg.* Full harvest at last!

9

In the Valleys of Humiliation

For eighteen months, beginning in the late autumn of 1898, Jessie Penn-Lewis went through several valleys of humiliation and had to put a sudden end to many of her plans and cancel her engagements. She had to learn how to sit in the shadows, wait until she could understand why she was set aside, and then accept the chastening of the Lord.

One of the contributory causes was the failure of all her efforts to deliver and restore "Nursie Laura." All means were tried—physical, emotional, spiritual. But despite her prayers and her most spiritual teachings, Jessie found no way to stabilize this strange woman whose schizoid nature, combined with alcoholism, led her into states that looked like demon possession.

Nursie Laura had been one of the many who came to Jessie's home in 1892-94. She had professed to accept Christ and to be a seeker after sanctification and such blessings as would enable her to witness to others. Yet she slowly relapsed into superstition, addiction, and quite irrational willfulness.

No job that was found for her lasted long. In September 1898, Jessie Penn-Lewis had to nurse her through three weeks of delirium and put up with two more weeks of eccentric behavior. Suddenly Jessie ran out of steam herself. She wrote in her diary:

> I suddenly felt as if all my nervous powers ran out and I was strung up to the highest pitch. I saw Dr. Johnson at night about "Nursie." He turned to me and said he thought that I was in the worst condition, and that I ought to stop two months. I was in the most overstrung condition.
>
> I fled London by the 6 p.m. train and was feeling as if I should swoon, with the tingling of my nerves.

Three days later she unwisely challenged Laura and thought that she had brought her round, until she fell into raging and cursing. Laura was now openly stealing her friend's personal things and then sitting piously in the front pew wherever Jessie was speaking. The falling about and screaming were bad enough, but these exhibitions were worse. Jessie now understood that she had been deceiving herself with false hopes, and her husband sadly agreed.

On December 4, 1898, she made this sober entry in her diary:

> In bed all the morn—broken and wounded unto death and could not shake it off. The revelation of Nursie's heart deceit was so awful. I saw her at seven o'clock and burst out and told her my spirit seemed bleeding to death and she was killing me with her sins. In prayer I saw Calvary and the two crosses besides His with the words—"saved and lost in sight of Calvary." I felt this was her last choice. I told her all I could and left her to go and deal with God.

Only seven days later, Nursie was wandering around threatening to strike Jessie with a stone she had placed on the kitchen table, if she did not let her go. Jessie told one of her friends, "God showed me that the end had come and I could not see her again. I have left Nursie to God's judgment."

To rest from her ordeal, Jessie went into a nursing home in November, probably in Eastbourne. She received many anxious letters from her Russian friends who thought that her strenuous work had caused all this. She had not told them anything about Laura.

There is no diary at all for 1899. A handful of letters alone help us to reconstruct that year. A January 1899 letter that she wrote says, "I must have complete cessation from active service. I feel the pressure on my fragile vessel to be eased as I go abroad. The cause is a baptism of suffering through over-caring for a wandering soul. My residual energies have broken down. Someone other must deal with her." Now it can be understood why a circular letter, dated February 28, 1899, refers back to 1898 as, "the year of fellowship with the Lord's sufferings"—a year of "stress and conflict."

Jessie announced to all her faithful friends that there would be no more circulars and no more talk about small matters. "Let them stay out of sight until the Spirit orders otherwise. I will write only if I can I be of use to you on spiritual matters."

Months later she produced an explanatory letter, "My New Position in Christ." The gist of it helps us to understand why she turned from many tasks, except writing, and took a long rest, if only for the sake of coping with enormous changes.

> On New Year's Day the Lord told me this was to be a year of "Solemn rest unto the Lord" (Leviticus 25:4-5). He reminded me of His word to Israel, "In the seventh year release it and let it lie fallow." The Lord's release

> was proclaimed and I could with a quiet heart go and rest awhile. I had forgotten that I had concluded six years of action and ceaseless service on the Canaan side of Jordan. After this blessed word from the Father's heart it was with a thankful heart that I went abroad.

She felt far less stressed when she returned to Keswick Convention but she refused all invitations to meetings other than engagements already fixed. "The mere seeing of people seems impossible. There has been hesitation as to whether I want to be well. I feel as if I can never get in. To go and be with Christ is very tempting. I would have asked it but I did not dare."

Six weeks later, after holidaying in the Channel Islands with her husband, she wrote a letter in which she sounds a little more hopeful:

> I am getting free from the shrinking and am better able to do things like going down to the dining salon. I want to do "JOB." I am going to buy a little tent in order to be out of doors.
>
> I am becoming a baby for I seem to cling so helplessly to those who have gone through the fire with me. Now it comes back to me all that you did for me. What you have both been to me. I seem now to be gradually awakening from a dream and everything is becoming natural again. I marvel that I could have caused you such suffering.

Such frank confessions have at once cleared up the mystery of how Jessie quickly responded to the needs of someone like Dr. N. L. of Chicago, whose successful daytime evangelism was being undermined by nighttime horrors and delusions. For months in 1899, this noble servant of God experienced days of success and delight, and nights of terror when he felt corrupt and damned. In such bondage he lay until a friend and his wife got him to write to Jessie. A few months later he testified to complete deliverance and to a new lease on life. A year later, he was running evangelistic missions at St. Louis, Detroit, and Toronto. He wrote again to Jessie about the obstacles to his hopes, "I believe God is going to give me as it were a new chance. Pray that he may give me great wisdom. I want to win all the ministers and Christian workers that I can, without compromising the truth." In response, Jessie's group of intercessors upheld him until he had the total victory.

Soon Jessie was receiving a score or more of letters beseeching her to tell them how to overcome some collapse that was threatening their witness. In Western China there was a pioneer missionary who would surely have gone under without her spiritual guidance and encouragement.

Another fruit of her time of testing was that when she came to Keswick in the summer of 1900, she was listened to with respectful attention at a Ladies' Meeting. The keynote of both her addresses was absolute confidence in God's provided Mediator of the Covenant, and absolute confidence in the "Immutable counsels of God" (Hebrews 6:17-20), which are like sheet anchors for our souls. The longer she spoke the more vibrant became her whole body; "As I stood up my voice went out like a trumpet and the power was intense."

Perhaps it was at that same convention that she told them about her near fatal illness in the spring of 1899, when she caught pleurisy after an ill-advised trip on the River Neva. Russian friends nursed her devotedly but without hope. Even so, she demanded that someone purchase her passage home to England because the Lord had work for her there.

On October 10, 1899, she at last felt wonderful and wrote a happy letter that described her recovered liberty and fruitfulness. Now she believed that all these testings had been a preparation for a life of poured forth service more than ever before.

Most of 1900-1902 was trouble free, accident free, and weakness free. The visit to the USA was planned for 1900-1901, but she kept looking over her shoulder at Russia and had to be warned not to visit any cold lands in the winter again.

This then were the valleys of humiliation into which she had to descend more than once in 1899,1900, and 1901. It was during these years that two fine books were created—books which clearly reflect her personal experience of suffering: *The Message of the Cross* and *The Book of Job.*

Jessie's secretary, Mary Garrard, believed that the theme of the *Message of the Cross* was born out of a discussion during her stay at the Bridge of Allen Convention, when she was called upon very suddenly to address the main body of clergy and laity. However, Jessie said that it was in a Convention in Edinburgh that she had been touched by the appeal of a Mr. W. D. Moffatt, who had urged her to proclaim every aspect of the Cross and back it up with every possible Scripture. At the next Convention she addressed, she found that this new message had a strangely solemn effect. Because of these experiences she could claim even more dogmatically, "All aspects of the spiritual life could be shown to have as their basis—Calvary—and that all spiritual truth radiated from the Cross."

Some of Jessie's Russian diaries suggest that she had been thinking on this theme long before this, probably because Christians there were beginning to suffer greatly once they chose to identify with the Cross and its shame. Whatever the deeper reasons, we know that by the middle of 1898 she *knew* that under the Spirit's strong compulsion she was going to write as well as preach about the Cross. Only her own description of this guidance can be relied upon—the best starting point being diary entries in the winter of 1898-1899.

> Three days before I turned homeward there came a cold chill as from the tomb. Looking up there stood a great shadow—the shadow of the Cross—dim but real it stood. The heart fainted at the consciousness and certainty of a pathway of the Cross that this foretold. It meant surrender. As He said, "Are you willing to drink of this cup?" There could not be two thoughts as to the voluntary acceptance of His Cross, whatever lay in the path beyond.

Back in England that winter, there followed three weeks of tossing in a troubled sea. Toward Christmas, the path grew darker and the New Year opened watching a soul under the power of the evil one for the first hours of the New Year. Again a foreshadowing of what was to follow. Jessie wrote:

> A soul who had deeply sinned was brought to me and, as I sat by her and she told me of it all, I suddenly began to feel pressed and burdened. My head fell on my breast with heavy breathing and for some time I groaned heavily. Then God spoke, "He who knew no sin was made sin on our behalf." I felt as if part of myself or a member of my body was corrupt and loathsome. It was part of me and tied to me by life and I could not be separated from it.
>
> Thus I knew what it meant for Him who knew no sin to be made Sin, to have identified with Him and the accursed ones, corrupt with the fallen life and yet joined to Him their Redeemer. For a week I walked so strangely under ceaseless condemnation. All I did seemed wrong. My conscience void of offense seemed to become all offense without a cause.
>
> Until the Lord gave me an interpreter who had been prepared by a similar experience, I knew not that the devil's object was to get the soul to accept what he put upon it, and thus sink into defeat. The lesson was that it was all permitted of God to teach me how truly the Pure

> and Holy One suffered as He became SIN on our behalf.
>
> It was a fellowship of Christ's sufferings in the one sense, that it lets one understand His agony as the sin-bearer. Yet one cannot do what Christ has done, that is take the sins of another upon yourself. None can share in His atoning sacrifice. This was the first deep knowledge of the Cross.

During the first weeks of Lent in 1899, she was again prostrated in mind and soul and felt quite unable to go on with her studies. This state went on until she was almost due to speak on Good Friday about the Cross. Now she experienced "the first touch of the Nail-Pierced Hand"—healing and delivering, "One day I realized that Christ had nailed everything to the Cross, and had rested on His word and dropped the miserable old body with all its groans and symptoms and exhaustions."

In a letter of March 12, 1899, to one of her prayer support groups (nicknamed "The Philippians") she told of two strange events:

> I resolved to take it all to the Lord's Cross (Colossian 2.19) in order to get the victory over an exhausted body. Now He has taken me to an old saint at Nottingham who said, "I have been told to pray for you that you may fulfill your mission." A message came to me from another "child"— "Her flesh shall be fresher than a child's; she shall return to her youth."

On March 20, it was revealed to her that there was a spiritual link between her painful thoughts and the sufferings of Jesus:

> I went to God about 4 p.m. and, as I knelt, I was suddenly within the veil. It seemed as if I and the Lord

> were one. He stood before the Father holding out His pierced hands, but it was I who stood there, too, in Him. He was saying "Father I have died," but I was saying it, too. Calvary seemed far away down on the hillside.
>
> This was the Risen Lord with marks of the wounds, in the presence of the Father—and I was there. I saw Calvary within the veil. My whole being was melted. I knew the Father must answer such a plea.
>
> In a dream I arose and went downstairs and sat alone far away in the vision. A voice came to me from the glory, "From henceforth let no man trouble me for I bear branded on my body the marks of the Lord Jesus." The knowledge was unspeakable. . . . The succeeding days found me looking to the Lord for His special message for Good Friday.

It was in these ecstatic and mystical states that Jessie gave her Good Friday message that was seed for her new book, *The Message of the Cross*. Friday morning began badly, with someone announcing that she was going back on her repentance from sinful paths. Into her mind came the suggestion that she was not the right person to go down to London and preach. The Lord showed her that place in Psalm 22 where there was no answer from God in Heaven when the enemies mocked Jesus, "He who had trusted in the Lord they mocked and said it was all in vain."

In her own account Jessie described what happened next:

> My heart got rest. It was enough to be like Him. As I knelt before Him there passed before me a clear vision as to His promise that the message of the Cross should go forth to the very ends of the earth and carry with it the power of the Cross for seeking souls. The storm was past and I arose and went inside and sent off to my friends saying I would follow them alone.
>
> I left Leicester for London at 9.30 p.m. and I seemed

> like one walking in a dream. On Good Friday morning I went to the meeting and my heart fell as I saw the crowded hall. There were leading workers there and the temptation came to me in my shattered condition that it would be awful to hand it over to them till I remembered that the devil hadn't thrashed me for nothing. I rose to my feet but couldn't look at the people—I could have sunk before them. He gave me power and ere the meeting closed that night the glory of the Lord had been revealed and all had seen it together.

She said nothing about her vision during a much-blessed conference in the Paynter house at Stoke Hill, Guildford. The conference had been suggested by Dr. Andrew Murray as the best way to bring all teachers of holiness together "to wait unitedly on God for the outpouring of the Holy Spirit, cementing His people in love."

All the first session was to be devoted to humiliation and prayer before they discussed deliverance from sin and self, the gifts of the Spirit, and "the place of the human body in redemption." Jessie walked by herself and walked with God until, on April 19, she at last confided her secret in a letter to her husband, who was away at the time:

> This is a message that He gave me Himself. It is a vision of Calvary from inside His heart. Your letters are unspeakably precious and I long to answer but I cannot. Shall I ever be able to tell thee all that is in my heart?

Six weeks later, writing to close friends in Sweden and Denmark, she said:

> Putting the Good Friday message into print has meant much labor. I had to give up everything for God who has guided me. OH! this message. It is a book of tears and it has been baptized in the valley of weeping.

The much larger *Job* book also bears the stamp of her experiences in the valleys of humiliation. First conceived while she was still in Russia, it had to be set aside several times during 1899, when Jessie was battling with pneumonia. It was still in rudimentary form when she crossed the Atlantic to speak in Canadian cities and in New York and Chicago.

In February 1902, she was very shaky once more. Once she scalded her leg severely and had to send for her mother to nurse her because her husband was also down with lumbago and flu. She fell into deep depression because she had to postpone or cancel visits to Scotland and Denmark. But, by the end of April, she had rebounded a little and wrote to her friends saying, "This is a new spiritual experience and a new principle—not seeking but abiding, not asking but accepting."

Convalescing on the South Coast, she managed to write a little more, but it was not finished until she was in Davos once more, writing at a little desk on the balcony of the Belvedere Hotel. On December 6, 1902, she wrote to all her "precious Sisters" about the last stages when she had definite assurance that God had brought her to this place of "light":

> *Job* is being lit from end to end and I see now how I have been qualified for being the channel of the message all these last months. Now it all lies open—the mystery of the suffering which will be a message for the church in its final stages on the eve of the "Translation."

The lessons to be learned were that you can overcome suffering by deliberately caring and praying for others. Above all, the suffering must be accepted not just as chastening, which leads to maturity, nor as an affliction, which leads to fruitfulness, but as a definite training-ground.

> Thus does the Lord of Hosts, wonderful in counsel and excellent in wisdom, patiently teach His loved ones His varied ways of working in their lives.
>
> The end of all His dealings with His loved ones is for their eternal good.

While Jessie was at Davos completing her work on *Job* and another book, her husband was devoting his energies to moving house—this time to a large country residence in Great Glenn, about five miles from Leicester. When she arrived home, she cut out many visits and committee meetings and seemed determined not to confide too much in close friends. Bessie Porter received this curiously stiff letter:

> God has shown me that we are to stand detached with one life and soul but with diversity of work and interests. In God we must leave each other. We are to meet every soul as God's mouthpiece as we are to minister His Word. We must not allow any conversation about others in our presence. This is the only way we can act as God's mouth. In my deepest heart I have been sealed. So do not speak for me but leave it all in God's hand.

The reason for this self-isolation may also have something to do with the long passage which she quoted in *Job* from a book by G. D. Watson. The passage discusses "Heart-Loneliness":

> God intends to unite all holy souls in a divine unity and fellowship. Before that is accomplished, He must take each devoted soul in a private manner off to itself and detach it from all things and creatures and the threads of instinctive natural attachment. . . . These threads must be snapped and the best natural affections circumcised.
>
> Not that they are sinful, but the soul must be islanded

> away out in the ocean of God, that it may learn in solitude with Jesus how to love as He loves, and be attached to all things and beings as He is, in the order of God's will. Hence the soul going through this process of interior isolation must suffer pain.

The first month of her 1902 holiday in Switzerland passed swiftly by before Jessie could record proudly in her diary that she had managed to walk uphill. Six days later she was admitting sadly that she was strained and exhausted and "after dinner I quite broke down and I cried and I was unnerved." At this crisis point, a Lucy Butterwick read out a verse from Genesis, "You have dwelt long enough on the Mount. So Abraham went forth into the Plain of Mamre." This seemed like a signal to move on, and other daily verses seemed to confirm this, but it was the medical verdict from a consultant that brought this holiday to an end, as Jessie recorded:

> March 3rd: Dr. H. has found a large cavity at the apex of the right lung. Pleurisy pains are coming from sacs left in the pleura. Any rundown in health will awaken the tubercles. It is possible to winter in England but watch! Bronchial irritation is likely at your age to become chronic and troublesome. Davos is too cold for this.

Jessie's writing makes it clear that Dr. H. wanted her to cancel plans to stay on when there was obviously no physical improvement. However, the whole party hung on for a week or two in chilly weather at Zurich, which cost her ten days pleurisy. The rest of that year was lived more quietly and there are few details of her activities until her visit to Egypt and her planned program of visits in India.

The Lord was very gracious to her after her return from

India and her launching of two significant books. She turned in simple faith to the Lord and He gave her a verse, "In the Name of Jesus of Nazareth rise up and walk." In later years she would refer to this event as her way of understanding divine healing.

After just ten days of convalescence on the South Coast, she felt fit enough to take local meetings once more. News from Wales urged her onward to prepare for the first Keswick in Wales, which took place in 1903. She trusted the Lord to take her through the Bridge of Allen Convention in Scotland, and suffered no ill effects. On June 23, 1903, she wrote a friend, "The enemy said I should die if I went to Scotland but I went and did a full work and took the Cross at every meeting and I came home much better. I am not afraid."

A few weeks later, she was in full spate at Keswick where she met with no difficulties. Indeed, her diary for the second half of 1903 is quite amazing, and so is her correspondence. She was able to take part in the parent Keswick in England and then go straight on to the infant Keswick in Wales, where she had a multitude of duties. She stayed remarkably fit until a November visit to Salford where a chill laid her low again and she endured a mild hemorrhage. This may be one reason why she accepted invitations to go to Egypt for a warm winter break.

Even there, she had times of testing that sorely tried her patience. But now she knew the secret of casting every burden upon the Lord and seeing with joy how His grace was sufficient for all.

The days of her humiliations were almost over and the Lord completely healed and restored her just a few months before the outbreak of the revival in Wales. An amusing letter from old Dr. Cynddylan Jones in July 1904, says, "I don't know quite what to make of you. Grace, or something else, has so altered you that you are not the little girl whom I knew.

To me you are a mystery. We would like to hear more about this work of grace."

Perhaps no one realized at the time that because she had passed through the valleys, she was far more fitted to be a helper and counselor to hundreds of people who experienced the sharpest of sorrows as the 1904 revival visited the land. Her special ministry during those crucial months was blessed. The long months of weakness and pain, of frustration and seeming failure and loss, were not wasted.

From the missionaries in far off Africa, India, and China to agonized souls in Wales, Ireland, and the Americas, words of thanksgiving came that they had found someone who had passed that way before them—and so could enter into their "Valleys" and show them the Light of God.

10

Doors Opening in North America

During the last years before the outbreak of the great revival in Wales and the world, Jessie Penn-Lewis was granted a rare opportunity for a woman speaker—rare, that is, in those days. She was invited in 1900-1901 to address meetings and conventions in Canada and the great northern cities of the United States. This visit combined semi-private drawing room meetings, public services, students' meetings and a few rallies—all sponsored by different religious leaders. The impact of her visits has never been assessed, but to hundreds who attended, she remained a friend, advisor, and faithful correspondent for many years.

The first invitations to America may have occurred in the summer of 1899, when the Moody Bible Institute launched an Extension Bible Course in London. Groups met in Morley Hall, Exeter Hall, and the Mildmay Conference Hall. The American leaders whom she met there also attended the Keswick Convention that summer. They admired her addresses and enjoyed her conversations, and some kept in close touch with her. She wrote letters of encouragement to a professor in the Moody Bible Institute, who was so grateful that he took steps to have her books distributed in Chicago. He said that one booklet alone, *The Message of the Cross*, had helped him greatly and that he hoped she would soon have closer contact with his various Bible classes. Several months later, Jessie let him know that she was coming to the United States, so she was promptly asked to include Chicago in her provisional schedule. She wrote back, "There is a fruitful field here now. The ministry in May was one of much blessing along the lines of 'identification with Christ,' and the power of the cleansing Blood. Many have found liberty."

Long before the Chicago project bore fruit, Jessie found herself involved in a different ministry under the auspices of an unusual group. Her close friend, Miss Brodie, had been a guest speaker at a place called Fieldhome in Peekskill, New York; these were informal meetings on what they called "Quiet Days" or "Waiting Days." She told the leaders that it would be good for them to invite God's better messenger—Mrs. Penn-Lewis—especially as she herself would not be available again. The De Peyster Fields, whose many-roomed mansion in Peekskill had a dozen or so servants, invited Jessie to come over and speak at this country house. A second series would be held at another "House of Rest" in New York, which had some connection with the Young Ladies Christian League.

Mrs. Field had studied the writings of Stockmayer, Simpson, and Torrey, but when she read some of Mrs. Penn-Lewis's booklets, she became convinced that this was indeed a messenger of God. She called her "a special channel for the communication of the life of Christ." Mrs. Field was an energetic, determined, and wealthy Christian lady who generously invested personal money in this project, which she made her own. She preferred such meetings to be private gatherings, yet she fixed it so that about thirty people could stay in the huge house, and an equal number travel in daily in hired transport. Mrs. Field had promised a large degree of flexibility, but it didn't turn out that way because the dear lady was hustling things along and wanted all the preparations done in double-quick time. Once or twice Mrs. Field apologized that she was taking too much for granted. She apparently was miffed when the whole thing was postponed for three months.

In her replies to Mrs. Field, Jessie stated quite firmly that she would decide the pattern of invitations and that she had to have some kind of public "Convention for the Deepening of Spiritual Life." Eventually they agreed on some degree of latitude, but Jessie was still not satisfied and wrote, "If you are the Lord's steward, wouldn't you feel that He meant it for the service of the whole church of God as well as for gatherings specially entrusted to you?"

Mrs. Field finally accepted a postponement to the autumn, but clung on to the idea of small-scale "Days of Waiting," using both Fieldhome and a city center house called "Hepzibah." Jessie sent an important letter to explain why she also wanted to take some meetings in New York where many had as yet no understanding of their calling in Christ Jesus.

A second letter to Mrs. Field, dated March 19, 1900, asserted her special status as a messenger of God, but she did now concede that there could be arrangements for small Bible Reading Groups only at Fieldhome. She also accepted Mr. Field's offer of hospitality because of her urgent need "to go forward very quietly with God, to abide in His anointing and to be fit for use by Him." She repeatedly asked for "breaks for waiting upon Him" but, instead of speaking frankly about her personal problems and stresses common to women of her age group, she told everyone that she needed to avoid all "rush or pressure in these days of feverish activity."

More tension developed, however, when Jessie told Mrs. Fields she had accepted an informal visit to Canada and had allowed herself so much time there as to constrict Mrs. Field's program. She justified this by describing her vision of Canada's need and said, "I dare not lose one precious opportunity to give His call." Mrs. Field, quite naturally, stuck to her guns and maintained that she too had been guided by the *light*, but Jessie retorted in militant fashion:

> I dare not take one step on what you believe to be His light. It must be given by Him directly to me. All that you write I lay before Him and you will fear lest you touch His revealings to me in the least degree. Will you bear with me if I beg you not to have any preconceptions for the work nor plans for what He intends to do? He invariably upsets them and I have had to learn to go forth like a little child and let Him have His own way.

Two paragraphs later she was already talking quite openly of ways to meet other circles of believers. Once again she was seeking special guidance, and she told the conveners of a proposed New York Conference, "I have as yet no light and I will continue to look to the Lord for guidance in this matter. I am expecting letters that will show more clearly His path for me, but so far as I can see I do not think that the Lord intends for me to be involved in any convention work."

A different kind of meeting was envisaged by Jessie, one on the same model as those held in Europe. This plan involved the help of ex-Ambassador Breckenridge's wife and two or three influential YWCA leaders, such as the President of the Harlem YWCA. She wanted Russian-style drawing room meetings with specially invited ladies to whom she would teach full surrender.

There was no more talk of depending upon Mrs. Field's strict program, and one of Jessie's letters says that Mrs. Field had raised a wall of prejudice by her attitude. There seems to have been growing conflict, and her diaries and correspondence of that period say very little about the Fieldhome and Hepzibah meetings. Mary Garrard's account records state that there was a blessing at those meetings. There is also a letter from a Mrs. Christy of Albany who said the meetings had "planted my feet at last on sure foundations. This is the one message that satisfies my heart and soul, yet it is the one that I have dreaded above all else. I know that it will mean suffering with Him but He will keep. How little I had dreamed of the new truths that God had in store."

Jessie once described Mrs. Field as "holy but hard," but the various meetings changed all that. A year later, Mrs. Field wrote a testimony of how she had now experienced deliverance from self and from disobedience to the Lord. She stopped resenting the many changes in plans. It is a regrettable fact that Jessie was not prepared to change her own attitude. She somehow misinterpreted Mrs. Field's well-meaning efforts and wanted to reject even her generous gifts. Mrs. Field's surviving letters are humble in tone and tell Jessie and her prayer circle a great deal about plans to develop Hepzibah House and form a new prayer league. In her last letter to Jessie, she wrote, "I hear quite frequently of the blessed results from the messages God gave through you. I think that He is truly stirring up, making straight and making new. Our responsibility is to let His mind be in us and not to hinder."

The Canadian tour deserves mention. As usual, Jessie compiled a travel diary for her adventures in Canada and in Chicago. Five letters sent to relatives also throw a brilliant light on her as a very human being. Can one ever forget the little pen portrait of a service aboard the Swedish liner where she somehow gathers together the crew and conscripts a passenger who can interpret her message—then puts on her fur coat and Russian boots because it is so chilly—in August?—before she begins to speak from an improvised dais.

It was the same on their trip from Montreal—where Williams had joined her—to Ontario. They took a side trip to Niagara Falls, and, while viewing the falls, Jessie protested his suggestion to take off her furs and wear something more suitable to withstand the spray from the falls, until some young attendant volunteered to fetch towels to wrap round her neck. The falls and the local fauna become materials for several parable sermons. She is naively surprised that she felt much stronger and was enjoying porridge for breakfast and solid food for other meals. She wrote, "I have forgotten all about odds and ends between meals. I have not felt the traveling a bit too much."

After a couple of meetings at Kingston, Ontario, the Penn-Lewises traveled by train to Toronto, taking their ease in special lounging chairs provided by the railway company, as advertised on the tickets. They were invited to stay at the Missionary Home of the China Inland Mission. For a blessed two hours before any visitor arrived to greet her, she was left on her own, sitting in a rocking chair on the lawn and just thinking. This was the only respite during that tour. There was just time to visit an aged Welsh exile before they departed for a long journey via the Hudson valley, Poughkeepsie, and Westhill—all in New York state.

Jessie's letters speak about the sadness of seeing her husband off to Britain, but the truth is that in her heart she wanted to extend her stay because she was so sure that there was a divine purpose. Before she began her main meetings she sent a rather excitable letter to her prayer intercessors in Britain, "I desire your supplications for the King's service in Canada. The burden is in my heart here—'Prepare ye the way of the Lord.' Surely the time is short."

About the second group of meetings held under Mrs. Field's auspices, Jessie notes that she was presented once more with a detailed timetable. Her secretary's account speaks of many women being blessed, but Jessie's only written comment is, "I felt it well worth the strain for they had been met with by the Lord. I am very tired but I have been truly strengthened for four days of ceaselessly going on."

Just as she had dreamed long before, Jessie was invited to Chicago and made a great impression on students at the Moody Bible Institute, where her lectures had standing room only. According to her own enthusiastic Circular Letter about the lectures, she spoke first on "The fire shall try every man's work." She was then asked to address men and women students together on the theme, "The grain of wheat sacrificing itself for fruitfulness." Afterwards a number of students came to her for interviews on spiritual matters.

She also visited Northfield Hall, spoke to scores of girl students in the presence of Mrs. D. L. Moody, went to see the great preacher's grave on "Round Top," and traveled in Mrs. Moody's buggy to Mount Hermon College. Four hundred students heard her applying the words of Paul, "I will not be disobedient to the heavenly vision," and comparing those words with their lifestyles and life-plans.

When Mrs. Field escorted Jessie into bustling New York for the last time, she found that not only was the Nyack Missionary Convention in full swing, but there was a rather rowdy pre-election series of mass meetings involving William Jennings Bryan, William McKinley, and Theodore Roosevelt.

Her first public meeting was the occasion of what she called "a severe message," which she didn't want to give. On October 15, for the first time, she addressed 150 quietly expectant people who were packed into a double drawing room. She had been given two messages: "Our God is a consuming fire" and "The Man with the eyes of fire." By Wednesday, the rooms were so packed that a third room was prepared. Her messages were: "The Sacrifices of God" and "God forbid that I should glory save in the Cross." More rooms were opened up on Thursday and she spoke on, "Life from the Heavenlies to the Kitchen." Finally, she had to give the challenge to "Consider Jesus," and the choice, "Shall it be the Cross of Jesus or the world?" Spontaneously many broke out saying, "The Cross, The Cross."

Over the next two days, she addressed eight meetings at the Nyack Institute in two-hour intervals. Off then to nearby Jersey City and Philadelphia. The final address was given to a conference of deaconesses, after which she concluded, "We were not touching the fringe of things but the vital centers." Those who heard her were writing to her long after she returned home.

After her return voyage to Liverpool, she found letters awaiting her from the students of the Moody Bible Institute. A Miss Emily Strong wrote to express appreciation that Jessie had undertaken to pray by name for the girl students. Her February 1901 letter told her that the name of Jessie Penn-Lewis had become a household word and that her books were in great demand. There is a first urgent plea that Jessie will intercede for all those who are being accused of being fanatics. Then a final request that she pray for Miss Strong herself, who feels she has many defects.

There is also a letter from a Pastor Newell—a Bible teacher and evangelist attached to the Moody Bible Institute. He believed that the whole land needed "a movement towards Christian Holiness on Pauline lines," and that could only follow upon "a great awakening and a real breakdown and a separation of thousands from all over the world into a life of victory and holy service."

It was 1907 before these dreams were fulfilled, but the story is well worth printing at this point. The magazine, "Revival News" published in Kingston, Jamaica, informed the Christian world in 1907, that the fire had fallen upon the students of the Moody Bible Institute after a small group had prayed for this for four years. Excerpts from the report were published in the *Life of Faith*:

> There was no lecture and no dinner. All order was dispensed with and instead there was public confession of wrong doing and sin. Sometimes there was a dozen students on their feet at once, whilst others were going about settling difficulties with one another and asking forgiveness—getting right with God and each other. Some would be praying for pardon, some were singing and some asking for the Baptism of the Holy Ghost and others for Healing.

This blessing spread to the Nyack Institute in Nyack, New York, where there was confession and self-humbling and the end of all criticism. Presumably, it was Jessie Penn-Lewis who put in the "Life of Faith" the glowing report of the coming of the fire from heaven:

> The faculty are of the same mind that we must not take up any ordinary duties until the whole body of students are persuaded that the time has fully come to return to work. We must be equipped for service. As we get into the deeper conflict with the powers of darkness, I cannot write about it. No man interferes. It is blessed to see how hands are kept off and the Holy Ghost shows His power and control. . . . We are still waiting on God. He is doing, and will do, a new thing.

For many years after her remarkable visit, Jessie kept in close touch with certain people in the United States right up to the time of the Second Advent movement and the war against Modernism. There were contacts with the Bosworths and Jacksons and Hodgsons in the mid and far west, as well as the Nyack people and Hepzibah House in New York. Despite many pleas from these people, however, she declined to go again to North America.

11

Doors Open to the Orient

During the very cold winters of 1902 and 1903, Jessie Penn-Lewis obeyed the advice of her physicians and went to warmer climates where her weakened lungs could hold their own. The 1903 visit was confined to the western provinces of India, which included Bombay, Bangalore, Madras, and Coonor.

During the voyage on the S. S. Persia, she befriended a J. D. Lewis of Massachusetts who was the official representative of "Twentieth Century Pledge Signing." He escorted her through Port Said's shopping area and drew her attention to the dark Sinai ranges and the camel caravans as the boat moved through the canal. She also met up with five lady missionaries who arranged deck services. She got deeply engaged in talks with a Miss Kinsella who had drifted from the faith into some kind of personal disobedience. She was saddened to find that no one else was approachable because they seemed to be absorbed in card playing, dances, and concerts of various kinds.

After four days of meetings in Bombay, mainly for the Europeans, Jessie moved on to Bangalore where she stayed in a unit belonging to the Soldiers' Home. By means of Bible readings and public services, she presented her "Message of the Cross" to pastors and mission workers. One of these was a V. C. Matthew, who told her that he was willing even to give up wearing European clothes for the sake of reaching souls. She herself showed a startling humility in asking to speak to the goldminers at their actual place of work. She avoided the genteel Poona and Amritsar, and asked native pastors to take her to such places as the Blacktown Mission and the Orphanage. After one of these meetings, she had a long talk with some Indian leaders. Afterwards, on February 19, someone called Appajee Amrit wrote a long letter beseeching her prayers for a demon-possessed woman to be exorcised, for a caste-conscious hospital assistant to be humbled, and "for me that I also be directed. I ask for guidance for He is calling me."

The city of Madras held a peculiar fascination for Jessie, who described, in minute detail, the matting beds, the punkah (fan), the huge zinc bath, and the violent methods of the dhobi wallahs down by the well. She did not seem unduly worried by the outbreak of plague that eventually caused their hosts to send them off to a place of safety. One Sunday, she was driven to Royapuram Native Church and spoke to them about the precious Blood of Christ. The next day she went out to Orphan Homes run by a Mr. Israel and his native helpers. They were greeted by the strident music of the church band playing "cowjahs," and by rows of salaaming children, one of whom hung a garland of red and yellow flowers round her neck. She had a good reception at the special native teachers' meetings, which for some reason used the Tamil language.

One day, she was persuaded to look at a primitive "Mission school" run by a ninety-year-old named Andrew.

To her great amazement, she found that he was preaching the same message of total identification with Christ crucified. Still more amazed, she realized that "the presence of the Lord at times was almost overpowering and the meltedness and brokenness very evident."

Despite the short visit, Jessie told her prayer partners in Britain that she had been treated as God's special messenger and that she had found open doors everywhere. Writing to them from Coonor she said that the object of her coming to India had been accomplished. The proof she offered must have surprised her friends when they received this letter, dated February 17, 1903:

> Glory be to God for leading me to a writer who has come into the blessing—a man of influence who has read every book of mine. He has endured great agony of soul over his sins, seeing his own loathsome body on the Cross. He says that I have the clearest purest truth about God that he has ever read.

Then in a letter written on February 18, she said:

> A gentle, greatly blessed head of a large publishing house has told me that all my books must go into Indian languages. He has a printing press for five dialects. This is the biggest thing that the Lord has yet done.

In her diary she wrote:

> Dr. Rudeshill has told me that God showed him his press should be used for the message of the Cross. He had seen someone coming in shining armor covered with precious stones and this being was filled with God. Someone said to him that this being was commissioned by God and that it was he himself.

Before Dr. Rudeshill's work was brought to a standstill by certain religious authorities, he got into circulation a series of Jessie Penn-Lewis's booklets in various Indian dialects. Probably the best known of the translated tracts was, *The Pathway to God.* Yet the impression that is given by Jessie's open letters to her prayer-partners is that it was her other booklet, *Word of the Cross*—a compendium of key verses—that was most urgently needed; and that Dr. Rudeshill had been given to her for the task of getting that little book printed in a hundred languages.

A translation of this booklet somehow reached Tibet and Burma. At the same time, a Mr. Hogben of the "One by One Band" undertook to distribute copies systematically throughout Britain and all the colonies. It was followed up with translations of the longer *Cross of Christ and its Message,* in 1903, which was acknowledged by many spiritual leaders as a book that played its part in preparing India for the great Revival in 1906.

There was a sadder side to Jessie's visit to India. Somehow she got involved in the first pre-revival splits among missionaries. Already there were some who stressed the need for some kind of difficult self-crucifixion and there were those who were saying, "No! you must trust entirely in the finished work of Christ for your salvation and sanctification." At one stage, the dispute got so bad that missionaries who had worked together for years began to openly criticize each other. Jessie's last letters to India spoke sternly about the missionaries' hardness, confusion, bondage, and negativeness. They were terrible words to utter, but how she longed for them to find spiritual freedom and victory by passing through the Cross, the gateway to life.

One of the most confused was a Miss Maud Olebar of Madras, who described herself as tactless and impulsive by nature until a deeper work had happened in her heart at Madras.

Now she was inquiring how to become an instructor of other fellowships, but the forewarned Jessie Penn-Lewis held back. Soon another letter from Miss Olebar arrived asking for the gift of prophecy "so that I might be able to teach them clearly." After another week of wrestling like Jacob, Maud Olebar had decided she was now fitted to cope with anything.

But Jessie discerned the danger and longed to re-unite the Olebar group with those at Coonor. She asked Mr. and Mrs. Walker to beware of division caused because one party was off balance. "There is too much about dying and too little about Christ's work," she wrote. " I am pained and grieved. God forgive this over-emphasis on the negative instead of on Him who is All in All."

On the same day in March she sent this disturbing rebuke to Miss Olebar:

> My only sorrow is that you and I have not been brought into that fusion that is His will for all who know Him. It is not a question of will or heart or vision. I feel that the experimental side has hidden the power of the Divine side. I have seen the disastrous confusion and despair produced by preaching an experience instead of preaching the work of Christ. I can only cry to God to lift your eyes to His side, to lift up Christ.
>
> For hours I have watched and prayed and sought to see the error; i.e. preaching experimental death and not death as the fruit of Calvary. He has given me 2 Corinthians 11:3. I beg you to take it to the Lord.
>
> Let Christ illuminate your mind and give you a deeper sympathy with God's people instead of putting bondage in others' souls.

In a letter to Jessie on April 9, Maud Olebar still justified her special messages as the new truth that the Lord had taught her directly. She wrote again in August saying that she was "Commanded" to take her teaching to Pondicherry and beyond. (We shall meet Maud again after the 1905 Revival had spread through parts of India—followed closely by the "tongues movement.")

On balance, the visit to India had many blessed results. It became evident, in 1905 and 1906, that many Christian leaders in India regarded her as the best channel between the main awakening in Wales and the new spiritual stirrings that began to move churches and missions in their vast subcontinent.

Visiting Egypt

One more international mission came Jessie's way without plan or intention, only a few months before the outbreak of the revival in Wales. Her medical advisers had told her never again to risk going to very cold climates. Instead of Switzerland, she was to go to some Mediterranean country. So she chose Egypt, where she had contacts through a missionary council. After the usual tourist sight-seeing, she met up with a Mr. J. C. Logan, who was very persuasive as he spoke of the need of that country. In her diary entry of August 18, 1904, she wrote, "I felt great pressure on my soul and a burden of prayer for Mr. Logan and for Egypt."

For a while, she enjoyed holiday fellowship with Christian publisher, Richard Cope Morgan, and his wife, who tried hard to persuade her to meet with them again at the Hughes Hotel at Jerusalem. Another person begged her to come over to Sivas in Turkey. Somehow she felt constrained to stay with the Logans in Egypt, and was a bit upset when nothing spiritual seemed to happen. A long letter to her husband shows how she gradually sank into a new kind of depression:

> I was crushed before and could get no relief for my spirit, I was in net and could not see my way out. I know now that the pressure was of God and that the ceaseless restlessness was a true sign that He was hindered. You know I can always rest when He wants me to, but no enjoying myself is possible when His spirit is grieved and quenched within me. I spent hours in prayers and with tears seeking His will.

In a later letter to William she wrote:

> When I am ill I get down and lose my poise of judgment and get into mess after mess somehow. I could do nothing properly and I have made some stupid blunders in words. I lost my clear path and have floundered, and left them thinking I am inconsistent. But God has helped me not to go under altogether and I must trust Him with consequences.

She appreciated the Logans' sympathy, friendliness, and nursing care, but she got more and more upset as Mr. Logan dallied and failed to make up a working program for her visit.

Meanwhile, an American named Bradley wrote to her and urged her to come to his mission place at Belbeis. It was he who provided her with an open door into the real Egypt, and what a difference that made to her. By March16, 1905, she could send a circular to her friends announcing, "Now I feel in myself no tiresome imaginings. I have been to Assiou and addressed 560 men students and 200 in the Girls' School." She had meetings in Cairo for American students, in Alexandria for staff workers, and, finally, a meeting for field workers in a place called Ramleh.

An account of her journeys was printed in the *Life of Faith,* in which she praised each pioneer missionary, and enthused about the scores of men and women who were attending Bible classes and preparing to serve their fellow-countrymen. She wrote, "The altar is built; the fuel is laid; the Word of God has been carefully implanted in their mind and heart—NOW all is ready for the fire."

Watching the people repair the channels through which their strong but burdensome "shadufs" conveyed water into the waiting fields from the unceasing Nile, Jessie Penn-Lewis had a new vision:

> So may it be that the pure river of life flowing from the Throne of God and the Lamb may break forth and fill all the prepared channels made ready by the patient labor of these, our brothers and sisters. Pray for more laborers thrust forth by God Himself. Pray for the river of God to break forth and fill the ditches. Pray for those in the battle here.

Many years later, Egyptian leaders of a growing work were still corresponding with her and teaching many of their lessons from her books. But, in the meantime, that prayer for the flood of living water was to be answered in Wales first, and then throughout the world.

Jessie refused invitations to Australia, Germany, and the United States. No one but God knew then that He wanted her in Britain to report and interpret the wonderful things the Lord was about to do. Very soon now there would be hundreds of newborn souls who needed guidance and care. People most ordinary and people most special were equally willing to share their fears, perplexities, and pains with one who had already learned how, in God's loving but mysterious purposes, one could be "hard pressed but not crushed; perplexed but not in despair; oppressed but not abandoned; struck down but not destroyed" (2 Corinthians 7:17).

From 1904 onwards, Jessie stayed at home in Leicester; yet, in another sense, she and her books were always abroad as she became totally involved in the worldwide revival and the ensuing missionary movements.

Part Three

The Witness and Interpreter of Revival

12

Special Correspondent of the Revival in Wales

Throughout this short account, the term *correspondent* will be used to mean both a journalist and a person who corresponds with others. Jessie Penn-Lewis was recognized and greatly used as a journalist to send to newspapers and magazines reports of Revival scenes, many of which were based on letters sent by ministerial and other friends. She was also a special correspondent to several of the men most deeply involved in the Revival, who found it hard to confide their personal hopes, fears, and opinions to anyone else.

The first time that Jessie contributed revival news to the *Life of Faith* was on November 9, 1904. It was inspired by a single prophetic letter from the Rev. Seth Joshua—one that was soon more than fulfilled. "The cloud as a man's hand" quickly became the massed storm clouds of revival. Three weeks later she informed the same newspaper that "God is sweeping the southern hills and valleys of Wales with an old-time revival." Almost immediately, she was asked to undertake a news and comment column every week. Few were more intimate with the workings of revival, few were in such constant touch with the chief instruments and their prayer-partners, and few were so well-known abroad that their reports of miraculous events would be believed and responded to. No one could imagine how those reports would affect people in other countries until visitors began to flock to Wales.

Jessie had always been a prolific letter-writer, but in 1905 and 1906, the stream became a torrent. Much of this correspondence shows that she was acting as an encourager, wise counselor, and intercessor for a number of men who were at the heart of the revival in Wales.

From time to time, during 1905, she received reports from Emlyn Davies, the celebrated opera singer and soloist, about his partnership in missions with R. B. Jones. Very thrilling news came from the pastor of Holton Road, Barry, who saw 236 people confessing personal faith in Christ within a week. More came from a Mr. Davies from Swansea who thought she would love to know that there was a blessed transformation in the YWCA, whose weeknight Bible Classes had turned into revival prayer meetings in March 1905. One of the Aberdare ministers wanted her to know about a new Band of Christian Workers of the type that she herself had suggested.

It may well have been the Rev. Cynog Williams of Heolyfelin Chapel who first told her about the way that women were now taking a principal part and were plunging enthusiastically into Christian work just as she had foreseen. Cynog Williams and Rev. Owen M. Owen shared her vision of still greater things to come. They wrote, "We believe that the revival teaching has created a desire in our churches for a higher spiritual life. A great responsibility has fallen upon us ministers. If we are filled and clothed with the Spirit we can discharge all our responsibilities to the glory of God."

Amongst the many correspondents were several ministers and evangelists who had found themselves in difficult situations. The Rev. Thomas Francis of Loughor wrote happily about the brightness in the village—in faces, homes, and communities. But then he asked her to pray about a serious dispute that was attacking a Loughor church that had been at the very heart of the revival. The Rev. W. S. Jones of Tonypandy shared with her all his worries and sorrows as his church resisted the revival. Pastors counted on her prayer support and sometimes turned to her for counsel. The earnest, young Rev. Owen M. Owen was much shaken by his experiences at Llangollen where the townsfolk seemed to reject his revival mission. He cried, "The Lord has laid the burden of their indignation upon my soul." He also sensed, but could not understand, the growing anti-revival feeling in all North East Wales as the aftermath of Evan Roberts' visit to Liverpool. (See *Instrument of Revival*, published by Bridge-Logos Publishers.)

Several people wrote to Jessie to ask her advice on the subject of Evan Roberts' odd ways. One of these, M. B. Phillips, commenting on the revivalist's sudden disappearance from Briton Ferry in late February, asked her, "What shall we do with this boy?" A collection of Jessie's jottings entered into a black notebook seem to be reminder notes of all those public statements Roberts had made about supernatural things, many of which had puzzled and distressed people.

When Jessie heard about the *Cambrian News* reports of his unbalanced behavior down in Newquay in March, 1905, she tried to intervene personally as soon he came back to his home. She wrote many letters asking him to come over to Leicester and accept counsel and prayer before he broke down altogether or fell victim to some kind of demonic attack. He did not reply.

The experienced evangelist, Seth Joshua, wrote to her for prayer support when he was in difficult situations. On April 8,1905, before he began a campaign at Merthyr, he wrote, "A very hard fight is going on with the forces of darkness. Nearly every error under the sun finds root in this place. The Spiritualist Society, the Ethical Society, the Agnostic Group, the Christadelphians, the Seventh Day Adventists. The last importation would be the "Pentecostal dancers" who are drawing a strong following at Dowlais. . . . It is dangerous these days to speak too freely. Never was Satan so on the attack."

Two months later Seth was asking for prayer support for hard and unresponsive people in a Cardiganshire chapel:

> These churches are full of nominal Christians whose lips have never been opened in prayer and testimony and who believe that assurance of salvation is not a possible human experience. They lack vital religion and they lack knowledge of personal baptism.

He confided in her that he had been shunned and misunderstood by others after some special joyous experience of refreshing had changed him greatly at the last Keswick. "My crushing is inward. I am becoming a lonely man but He is leading me into the wilderness."

There is no trace of direct correspondence between D. S. Jones of Bridgend and Jessie, but his close friend, a David Evans, asked her and her prayer group for prayer cover for D. S.'s much criticized work among the down and outs and tramps.

The public image of the Rev. R. B. Jones as a bold, stern, indomitable warrior would have taken a sharp knock if people could have read his six letters to Jessie Penn-Lewis. On April 7, 1905, he had written to her, "I am persuaded that after this present excitement has to some degree subsided there will be a unique opportunity to emphasize long ignored truths. The judgment of Isaiah 6:9-10 is to be lifted from all our people."

Yet, suddenly he had a spasm of doubt about his fitness to do this work when he was called to Liverpool. In fact, he was sent home ill and exhausted from that mission. Only a week later, he is appealing to her for comfort, "I feel guilty in having to lie down. It must be SELF that prevents the extension of trust in God's willingness and power to sustain His servants."

Later he wrote to her, "I feel that my church is not entirely with me in this revival work. He has kept me on my knees." Such moods ended after a serious interview with Jessie in Llandrindod in 1906. When she wrote asking him to help Evan Roberts, she reminded him of that time when she had been used by God to lead him into a new understanding of how to obtain victory over all defeatedness through the Cross.

Using the very same proof-texts that she had shown him, he had preached with new authority at Cardiff and Llanelly congregations in September. He spoke so boldly about renewed revival that forty-six people stood up to reconsecrate themselves for service. "Now I see what is my work this winter," he wrote. "The fire is to burn in the direction of more enthusiasm and sacrifice." He launched a new series of preaching conventions and never looked back again.

These examples of Jessie Penn-Lewis's intervention are all the more remarkable when one realizes that the men who wrote to her were regarded everywhere as giants in the faith. Great Bible teachers such as Dr. Inwood and Dr. Pierson were as eager to talk and pray with this city official's wife in Leicester as were Dr. Simpson in New York or Pengwern Jones in Bengal.

All through 1905, Jessie supplied new information about the Wales revival to thousands of readers in England, Europe, and the mission fields. It is highly likely that she did not come down regularly to the numerous meetings, most of which were in the Welsh language. But she had no lack of trusted ministers and church leaders who could send her detailed eyewitness reports that she skillfully knitted together into "Spiritual Tapestries." It may be of greater value for us to read what these informants actually said than to print here the carefully edited columns from the two Christian magazines.

Reports of Revival

On January 10,1905, Jessie received another report from R. B. Jones that contained sections of his diary of his mission tour in Anglesey.

> Day 3. At 8 p.m. I went to the chapel. A prayer service was already in progress and soon the chapel was filled to the doors. Many had to stand for lack of sitting accommodation. The singing was slow and lacking in fire and spirit. The place seemed pervaded with an air of curiosity. Many were there for the purpose of witnessing unusual sights.
>
> Day 4. There were signs that the previous night's service had told upon the people. The Spirit searching their hearts had brought into view weaknesses and defects. Yet there was again lacking the note which bespeaks definite decision.
>
> Day 9. It is quite impossible to adequately convey a work which reaches deep and wide in the lives of the people. They are exulting in new discoveries of what is their inheritance in the salvation wrought for them and in them by the Lord Jesus. Best of all the pastor (D. Lloyd) has been led to a crucifixion of self, in order that the life of Christ may be made manifest in and through Him. He seems mastered by the Spirit.

Jessie was thoroughly informed of every revival event that affected Anglican churches. Friends had supplied her with copies of *Church and People* (January-March, 1905), the magazine of the Church Pastoral Aid Society. It printed remarkable reports from its twenty-six linked parishes in the dioceses of Llandaff and St. David's. For example, on February 16, the Vicar of a Welsh-speaking parish sent this report via a Mr. Matthias:

> Some few weeks before Mr. [Evans] Roberts began his meetings in Loughor, some of my people came to me and asked me and the clergy of the parish to conduct a week's mission. Soon afterwards we started services of a revival character in our Mission Room at Gorseinon. Night after night the people thronged together and we gave an address and then threw the meeting open. The people readily took part and the clergyman in charge of the service would walk up and down the aisle, exhorting the people, many of whom acknowledged the Savior.
>
> Now I hold an after-meeting at one or other of the churches every Sunday evening for those who care to join. Some of my people do not care and do not believe much and some of these are my best people. They do not discourage me in holding after-meetings [however] and they all acknowledge a transformation in the lives of the people.
>
> I remember one New Year's night that eight were praying in the Parish Church the same time in English and Welsh. I thought some of them were really off their heads so I stood up in the aisle and began singing a well-known Welsh hymn.

This revival report was in a letter to the magazine from Elim, Penydarren, in March or April 1905:

> We have now completed ten weeks of prayer meetings. Though many souls were gathered in, I felt all the time that the church had not yet received its

> Pentecost. One Monday evening a fortnight ago the church appeared, to many present in that ever memorable prayer meeting, to cross the line to Pentecost. The Lord had led the church time after time to the line but there they stopped and continually fell back without going through to the promised land. But this night, several crossed the line and, during the week, the church had her Pentecost. Some men were literally drunk with the Holy Ghost. A great love for souls took possession of many hearts. Many made public confession of sins and consecrated themselves to the Lord. 150 souls have confessed Christ up to the present time. There are undoubtedly several more to follow.

Here is a brief excerpt from one of the two finest reports of this kind, which are too long to be included in this book. It's from the Rev. Thomas Francis of Gorseinon who looked back in October 1905, at what the Lord had done in his community and his church:

> The rushing of the mighty wind is passed but the breeze of Calvary remains. The heavy showers have ceased but the waters of life flow quietly. Converts we take not in a net but by line and rod. Compared with what it was here before the glorious visitation, it is very pleasant. The hearts of believers are enlarged. The atmosphere of the Church is charged with love. The spirit of prayer and praise rests on the people. Spontaneity and intercession, twin graces of the revival, remain with us. Many souls who were once indifferent are laboring fervently in prayer.

The other lengthy report was from the Rev. David Evans of Bridgend. It was unusual in that he didn't want Jessie Penn-Lewis or anyone else to go on insisting that the Lord was blessing places not visited by Evan Roberts, because he felt such reports were unintentionally doing great dishonor to the young man who had been anointed by the Lord.

Jessie's regular reports were commended by a wide range of church leaders because she tried impartially to cover the remotest parts of Wales and because she paid attention to different forms of the outworking of revival. It was not only the leaders but a hidden, humble, band who appreciated her role. Two sisters, Kate and Jessie Leach, wrote to her in December 1905:

> Because He has made you a watchman for Zion in this glorious Day of Visitation, we want to tell you that this little circle is pressing on and is praying that, though the powers of darkness are very real, they will become sham powers when faced through the Blood of the Lamb.
>
> . . .
>
> God has in a marked way led us to see that He is calling His children for definite intercession not only for individuals but also for Bridgend at large. Prevailing prayer in union with our risen Lord will bring down upon the town conviction of sin.

Those words would have been music to Jessie's ears since they agreed so well with her own understanding of the need. She was not content to produce excellent accounts of revival events but aimed at stirring up the saints to still greater expectations. A little magazine called *Bright Words*, distributed from Rothesay, Scotland, ended one of its special revival reports in January 1905, with a lengthy quotation from a Jessie Penn-Lewis essay:

> All that we read of this work in Wales must awaken a great longing in many hearts for such a movement of God all over Great Britain. Oh that individual churches would suspend ordinary services and appoint gatherings

> for prayer until the same Holy Spirit breaks forth in their midst! Does this seeking unto God in prayer not correspond to the ten days of prayer by the hundred and twenty before Pentecost, until the Holy Spirit came?

Her third aim was to discover the spiritual forces that lay at the back of the revival and of Evan Roberts' amazing work. Jessie's published history of the Awakening (1907) was undoubtedly factual, but it was also selective. She described herself as "on the watchtower watching the movement of God." True!—but it is sadly true also that even the best watchman can only interpret what he can see in his particular sector of the city. From the tower where she stood on the "Mount of God," Jessie could see living springs rushing out from a number of "Prayer-pools" and endorsed the old tradition that revivals were close-linked with more definite and fervent prayer among churches—that such prayer was the reason revivals came.

It seems to the author, however, that Dr. Edwin Orr's post-war interpretation makes better sense. He stated that this bursting forth of prayer was *not* the cause or pre-condition, but the first wonderful effects of approaching revival. The prayers were like the delicate stirrings of the breezes that showed that God was about to come down and visit His people with power from on high. The only privileged part that God gives His children to play is in providing the act of contrition or of *weeping before the altar* that God demanded through Joel.

At the Keswick Convention of 1902, in a specially convened prayer-meeting, there was such a mood of contrition and crying to the Lord that it was decided to set up numerous home prayer circles. Shortly after this, pamphlets appeared called *A Revival Call to Churches* and *Back to Pentecost*. These had such an impact on Jessie Penn-Lewis that she went in search of like-minded people.

She tried Europe and Britain but found that God was ready to respond in Wales first because, she said, its theology and hymnology and pulpit preaching had consistently exalted "Christ the Redeemer and His Atoning Work on Calvary." She then traced how God had chosen women intercessors in West Wales, young ministers in the Rhondda, a band of praying workmen at Pencoed near Bridgend, and a humble pleading Dean of St. David's, all crying day by day, "Revive Thy work, O Lord."

All this had taken place before the first Keswick in Wales was held and before the series of West Wales conventions in 1903-1904. Everywhere, a spirit of anguished longing seemed to rise up until all these spiritual forces converged in the autumn of 1904, and bore much fruit in the moistened soil. Ultimately, saints from all denominations drew together in a call for greater contrition, holiness, and spiritual discipline and for a bolder, more open witness.

After the revival began to fade, Jessie repeated this call to intercessory prayer as the key to overcoming apostasy. In face of the known dangers threatening every revival, she repeated her old argument that safety lay only in the Cross, "Let the Lord's people get right with God first and let them go out with urgent spirits and with love to win souls in the only way possible—bring them to the Cross."

She seized upon Elvet Lewis's most memorable words in his British Weekly report about the Wales revival:

> What seems to me to lie at the heart is the unveiling of the Cross. Unchanging love, as it shone and still shines from the throbbing mysteries of the Cross. The Cross stood unveiled and thousands looked and men and women smitten with the grief and the triumph of Calvary arose.

But Jessie Penn-Lewis's range of vision went far beyond revival in Wales. She was convinced that the waves of passion for God and passion for souls would soon roll over the whole of Britain:

> HE is ready to pour into every soul, and every church, and every town, in answer to united prayer. HE must, and will, respond, as He is honored and given His place among men. HE is the Executive Power of the Godhead, in charge of the Church of Christ on earth. HE will manifest Himself as soon as He is recognized and given His place. OH! Spirit of burning, COME!

Reports of the first stirrings trickled in from various centers in England, and a longer account came in of a revival mission to Scotland conducted by a team from Wales. On the whole, Jessie became very impatient with the slow pace in England and she began to write a different kind of essay about the reasons for this resistance to revival in England and Europe.

"But why stop at Britain and Europe when these springs that have broken out can flood a withered dying world?" she wrote, and in that growing faith, began to report the awakening in Europe and then the world.

13

Interpreting the World Revival

Whereas most professional journalists concentrated on aspects of the revival in Wales, Jessie Penn-Lewis had the privilege of being the first to hear about the spreading of the fire in many other lands. Her famous descriptive essays about the *Awakening in Wales* had been sent all over the world and read out by missionaries to their native workers and to their congregations. The effects were sudden and spectacular. Reports came in about the stirring of the waters caused directly by such essays especially when supported by eyewitness accounts from any staff workers who had come from furlough.

After a while these people began to send exciting reports to her about the different ways in which revival had come upon them. An Armenian pastor told her how revival fervor began to develop unexpectedly out of the prayers of an Orphan Boys' group who were originally asked to support the local Witnessing Band. Just as their impact was losing force, a Spirit-filled evangelist arrived to help them.

One of the staff in the Assiut schools in Egypt, where she had spoken to hundreds of students early in 1904, wrote,

"There is blessing among both Coptic and Methodist congregations and real joy is breaking out like a river over dry land. They are praising God's grace. Meetings are being held among the Arabs now."

From Algeria, in February 1905, came similar news of the wonderful joy caused by the tidings from Wales. A Lilian Trotter, who worked in Algeria and Morocco, said that everywhere there was great expectation of the Spirit's coming.

Similar reports came eventually from South Africa, from those working among the Kaffir people and from those who had fellowship with the Boer people who had so recently been at war with England. One letter from South Africa told of just one young man filled with the Spirit who had brought many people into blessing.

Remembering how Evan Roberts had called upon people to confess known and unknown sin in the early days of the revival in Wales, Jessie was quick to notice similar outbreaks of confession in South India and many other countries. She was told about a sudden upsurge of this "sorrowing testimony" in the Sakai Holiness Movement in Japan. This was interpreted as the literal fulfillment of Joel's words about weeping at the altar.

A Chinese student sent her the story of a spontaneous movement in Fukien province which seems of the same type. The foreign tutors, native teachers, and students of the Anglo-Chinese College had been asked to set up prayer-cover for a mission. Suddenly they experienced the full presence and power of the Holy Spirit. For several days the whole group were looking at their sinful selves, confessing secret faults and asking pardon from anyone they had offended. Then the cleansed students felt able to go to the non-Christian students and bring them in. When the official evangelist at last arrived he said, "There is nothing left for me to do."

A far more widespread revival in China was reported to Jessie at the end of May 1906, and she decided to incorporate several testimonies from converts in her magazine column. In May 1906 also, Jessie included in her *Life of Faith* column a very detailed report on the outbreak of the same kind of confessional revival in Formosa, which began among children, youths, and students. Once more it was a case of coming forward to sorrowfully confess all their sins, and urging others to do likewise.

This kind of revival took even more dramatic forms in Africa. In the third issue of the *Life of Faith* in 1906, Jessie devoted two columns to an outbreak of revival among the Hovas people in Madagascar. Welsh missionaries who had read about the revival in their homeland gathered together for urgent prayer for many days before their yearly meeting. The first signs of tearful repentance and confession of sin appeared among the native workers, and then in the middle of a communion service where the Spirit of God wrestled with many guilty souls. All through the following Sunday, people came in to confess secret sins, and throughout the following week, the cleansed Christians went seeking those whom they had cheated or insulted and sought to put things right. Jessie was particularly struck with the reported prayer of one young Christian leader who trembled from head to foot and then cried out:

> It is I, Oh Christ, who have denied Thee. It is I who have crowned Thee with thorns. It is I who have insulted Thee and crucified Thee. I drove the nails into Thy hands and feet. Oh Christ, can'st Thou pardon me?

From the district of Bongadanga, in the Congo area, the Rev. A. E. Ruskin sent a report in February 1906, on the outbreak of repentance among scores of backsliders. This was followed by a procession of men and women carrying fetishes and charms that they wanted to have burned in a great bonfire, just like the repentant sorcerers in Ephesus in Paul's day.

The brightest of the converts went to the Seekers' Class and then the Preachers' Class. Many made such progress that Jessie declared in her report, "We are convinced that this awakening is due to nothing but the power of the Spirit of God working among the natives in answer to prayer, and that the blessing can only be maintained by unceasing, sustained, and persistent prayer." She printed an appeal from a student:

> Oh friends! do pray for us—continue praying, and then we shall be truly united in Jesus. I tell you, if a light does not shine, how will it guide people into the road? Pray for us, the church at Bongadanga, that our light may truly shine before men, in the name of Jesus Christ. I would also say that when we read the books of the Father we do not understand the meaning of the Word. Pray therefore that we might become the righteous people of God. He who writes this is BOKOMBI. I have a desire that we and you may some day see each other before the Throne of Jesus.

One other area where the spirit of confession came upon the churches was in Jamaica during the summer of 1906. Strong men were felled to the ground by the wayside, and many young people surrendered to the Lord at Christian Endeavor meetings, Jessie was overjoyed to hear that the new Christians in Jamaica were now making intercession for Brazil and other dark lands in South America.

Jessie devoted eighty percent of her magazine column to events in India because she became convinced that it would become the focal point of a world revival. It was through several provinces of this teeming sub-continent that revival forces seemed to be sweeping irresistibly. From his mission station in the North Bengal district, the Rev. Pengwern Jones sent her stories that proved that daily hours of intercession had melted many hardened hearts. When visiting Calcutta, Pengwern Jones also discovered that wherever a group of

Christians were really pleading for blessing in some adjoining room during a meeting, there were wonderful results in the main meeting room. Mr. Jones said, "Now it is time to plead for all of Bengal and all of India because stupendous issues are at stake."

Jessie's next report—January 31,1906—described an unmistakable movement of the Spirit at Ratnagiri when it was visited by one of Pandita Ramabhai's Prayer Bands that were composed of converted widows. Later on, it was the turn of the other Mukti Prayer Band led by a Miss Abrams. There were confessions, restitutions, and agonies of remorse among the hundreds of listening women as the fire of the Spirit fell on them. News of this spread swiftly among other missionaries and Indian workers. Soon Jessie was receiving reports from Asansol and Krishnagar and as far off as Travancore.

Asansol proved to be the entry point for prayer and witness bands to penetrate into Bengal where there was much stronger opposition. Jessie again tended to link any victories with her own prayer-circle activities. Surely this factor alone could not account for the strange events at Poona where an unconnected group of schoolgirls began to pray so persistently, naming each single inhabitant, that suddenly there was general revival in that elegant town.

From Asansol also, Jessie was sent a very moving account of how leper members of the church united in prayer for revival blessing and were clearly thrilled when their prayers were answered. Someone sent from Asansol a translation of a Bengali revival hymn about how to find Jesus:

> If anyone asks in what way
> he shall be recognized;
> Yes—there is a sign—
> nailprints in His hands and feet.

A king, they call Him, but
has He a golden crown?

Yes, yes, He has a crown, but
not of gold, it is of thorns.

How shall I know that He is
calling me?

See Him on the Cross, with
hands outstretched towards thee.

Up to Easter 1906, Jessie's reports about India were entirely optimistic, yet only a little later she began to write about resistance and Satanic attacks and what she called "The long steady battle." As usual, she was convinced that at the heart of the opposition was the group that rejected the presentation of the Cross that she was then proclaiming far and wide. The four essays she wrote in April-May of that year are little classics and may well have been intended for translation.

The Father's Love-Gift at Calvary—God's suffering love.

Throne Life of Victory—God's answer to powers of darkness.

The Victory of Calvary—How churches can hide in the ROCK.

The Battle Is Not Ours But God's.

About halfway through 1906, Jessie wrote four reports about North East India: Extraordinary Growth in Mairang; The Glory of the Lord came down at Pilhibit; one about Lushai; and one about the Punjab. Smaller reports dealt with the "Confessional revival" and with a Telugu upsurge that sprang from the reading of revival extracts from Wales. All India was being quickened. From Khassia came a surprising letter citing a prophetic message—that England's revival was long delayed because of "Pride of race, pride of knowledge, pride of wealth, and pride of Imperial power."

England must therefore experience self-humbling through the preaching of the Cross; then all hindrances would go. From this point onward, her *Life of Faith* essays became a repetition of one theme—the need for churches to face their great dangers by being more aware of conflict ahead. "Awake O arm of the Lord" and "Cry aloud and spare not" were her chief messages. She began to make pointed comparisons with Europe where exciting things seemed to be happening. We must briefly consider her contacts there and see whether this was true before we return to India.

Jessie naturally took a lively interest in those European countries where she had ministered in 1896-1899. As early as January 31, 1905, she was appraising the impact of revival on Denmark and Finland and speaking rather wildly about the chariots of fire that were driving toward her beloved Russia. Wearing her heart on her sleeve, she told the audiences, "Russia is my country after the Spirit." At first, the blessing seemed to fall on various conferences in Germany, such as Wandsbek, Mulheim, Blankenberg, and especially Friedenwalde where "glory filled the Home and the fire fell suddenly." (Letters, May 27, 1905 and October 10, 1905.)

A similar time of blessing happened at Dresden and Dusseldorf. A small party made their way to Keswick and spoke so glowingly that she longed to go back with them. In May, Jessie was invited over to Copenhagen. After visiting several conferences, she wrote to a friend, "God came down in melting fire and did extraordinary things at the Workers' Conference. Not one soul was untouched. It was extraordinary! Marvelous! Pentecost!" Faced with requests to take conventions in England and Scotland, she demanded far more freedom from the usual programming and told the conveners, "God will never send you revival until you are willing to let your program go when the Holy Ghost desires it."

Someone whom she met in the Copenhagen conference must have sent her the eyewitness reports from Norway, which were kept with her other revival records. It contained news from the Methodist chapel at Lillestromme, and a large Sunday school and Bible class at Drammen. There was some kind of a Pentecost at Bergen that made the YMCA and the churches acutely aware of the need to witness—"UP. Let us work for Jesus in the power of the Spirit for there is still in our city thousands of young men who need salvation."

From Christiana in Norway came news of a revival in a prison. Writing about eighty men there, Jessie said:

> [They] take hold of free grace and have peace and joy. When they have an opportunity to write, they seek to bring their relatives and friends to Christ. It is just the same with the jailers and warders. Those who have come to Christ are standing true and resisting temptation. The chaplain is still experiencing that Jesus is the friend of publicans and sinners and that those who are forgiven much, love much. He says he has never seen so many tears and yet such shining faces when Jesus has been received.

One lady who responded wholeheartedly to Jessie's messages was Sigrid Kurck, from the Kvindelige mission, who urged her to visit Sweden as soon as possible and to make sure she stayed with her. Her letter is remarkably emotional:

> Thank the Lord He permitted you to teach such precious words. I praise the Lord but I do not deserve so much, especially to have my Lord's beloved servant in my home. I feel I have gotten wings. In a meeting of thirteen sisters we all testified and then fell on our knees in praise and intercession—with a new vision of the

Cross. Three of these ladies are going to Norway.

In a letter written on July 5, 1905, Jessie said, "My heart is full of praise and joy. The anointing abideth—teaching, equipping, uniting, deepening all the way. What a sweet fellowship—with or without words. We gather at 3.30, to give praise and testimony."

Madame Kurcke eventually returned home to her great mansion in Rynge, Sweden, and found herself opposed by the local clergyman, who said women should not speak at meetings. But she was a true overcomer who kept her vow until she met up with Jessie once more and told her, "I will not compromise our principles. I will be faithful to the power of the Lord."

Gradually the revival reached Stockholm which Jessie saw as the springboard to Russia, the land she most cared for. A worker wrote from Stockholm in February 1906, to tell her how the Lord had visited them with holy judgment in October 1905, and had caused hundreds to cry for mercy. A second letter told how the January "Week of Prayer" had become a time of cleansing and humbling and reconciling that brought entire families to the Lord. At the height of this awakening, Jessie wrote to her prayer partners about turning back the powers of darkness from Russia's cities and countryside also:

> God is preparing to pour out His Spirit on Russia. I have pleaded for the land with anguish. The Lord is watching and His purposes cannot be hindered. He will lift up the standard of the Cross. Pray against all that prevents His working. Be fervent in prayer and cry to God. You will overcome by the Blood of the Lamb.

How she rejoiced when letters began to arrive in June 1906, from Pastor Fetler speaking of revival meetings in St. Petersburg, Moscow, and other centers. His many vivid and inspiring letters would make a miracle story in themselves. One of Jessie's notes will show how she felt about it:

> This, in God's sight, is the greatest remedy for all Russia's needs—an outpouring of the Holy Spirit. Yes, if this is given to all the believers in Russia, they will then be brought into such communion with Christ in God that they will see the temporal need of their country from the viewpoint of the Throne of God. They will be brought into such heart-union and fellowship with God and each other that rivers of life will be poured through them into the sorely stricken land.

By the end of 1906, some of Jessie's reports were sounding like prophetic messages. Some were eighty percent Bible exposition and only twenty percent report. Some readers wanted these articles to be combined in one book. Others asked the *Life of Faith* editors to ration her. Various letters from the editorial board to and from Jessie show she simply refused to separate her reports from her burden messages given directly by the Lord. By the end of 1907, she was no longer a special correspondent for the *Life of Faith*— but she was now a feature writer for *The Christian.* This meant that her new editors had to deal firmly with her when that damaging controversy arose between missionaries in India in 1906-1907.

Long after the last echoes had died away, Jessie said that the sad divisions in India were a perfect demonstration that a great revival is such a threat to the kingdom of Satan that every effort is made to divide its leaders and spokesmen. Jessie had already had problems with the overweening Matron Olebar and had also lost her old relationship with Dr. Rudeshall, the scholarly publisher who complained that he was being falsely accused and harassed by persons unknown. He lost all his enthusiasm for her work.

Really serious trouble arose after Mr. and Mrs. Garr came

hotfoot from the Azusa Street Mission in Los Angeles, California, to set up their own fellowships in and around Calcutta. Jessie was told that even the editor of the South India Prayer Circular, Mr. Ward, had deserted old friends in order to form this "Separated people." It was Mr. Garr who first persuaded these people that, if they tarried, they would sooner or later be receiving new gifts of the Spirit that would equip them to prophesy and speak in tongues. Adverse reports came from missionaries such as Wilson, Kohl, Sandys, Pritchard, and McDonald. A plan was made to separate Mr. Ward from Mr. Garr, who had quite a reputation for tough dictatorial actions. His friends saw that Mr. Ward was becoming a nervous wreck and was wanting to get free.

It was at this crisis point in February, 1907, that Jessie sent the most helpful letter one could imagine. Drawing entirely on experience, she said that the only way of safety for any one of the group was to ensure that the natural mind was kept by faith continually crucified with Christ on the Cross. Even bearing witness to the Cross would not afford enough protection against the deceivers. Speaking of the Garrs, she asked why they lacked meekness and love and why did they make this unscriptural claim that the gift of tongues is "the invariable evidence of being baptized." She asked why they made such a fuss about gifts and signs that could merely excite the flesh or even lead us into the sin of pride.

Mrs. Ward sent a sweetly humble letter thanking her for the "shaft of light into the soul" that made it possible for her husband to withdraw from the rough-mannered Garrs and be reunited with the missionary team. Jessie was persuaded to set out her answer in pamphlet form, but this was regarded as an attack on Garr, T. B. Barratt, and the Pentecostalists. People failed to understand that Jessie was only an intermediary who was concerned with keeping God's people together.

In a way, it was unfortunate that early in 1907, she

publicized some of the stories Mr. Maynard had given her about roarings and screamings, neck-strokings during meetings, and the use of special techniques to stimulate physical prostration. A Mr. Kohl expressed surprise and shock that most missionary leaders showed such unconcern and unwatchfulness about these developments. He claimed that, "Only Jessie Penn-Lewis has been given the light and is the Lord's chosen messenger for this time of crisis."

Missionary George Wilson pointed out that Pandita Ramabhai's witnessing and praising bands had adopted tongues but had forbidden rollings, groanings, and other body movements. No one wished to pass judgment on the revered Lady Pandita Ramahbai, so Jessie simply commended the leaders of that group for using a spirit of discernment.

Supplied with much evidence from the mission field plus good pamphlets against the Barratt/Garr groups, Jessie used her column to ensure that every key worker in India was forewarned against excesses. Far from denying the gift of tongues, she asked only that those who had no gifts would exercise patience, and that those who had received the gift would stay humble: "If we could preach the Cross for weeks from every aspect, she wrote, with no reference to tongues, God the Spirit would lift up the standard and the atmosphere would be purified."

After the Garrs and two female prophets moved on, the various subgroups fell into confusion and hived off from each other. Mrs. Penn-Lewis wrote again and asked all other leaders to help them win a victory over dark forces. She began to speak of love and understanding and humility and the healing of the broken hearts and contrite spirits. When rebuked for moderation, she said she preferred to think of their many friends from revival days as "having a temporary film over their minds."

Even Wilson stopped murmuring when he realized that everything had been quiet and thoughtful for weeks, that the leaders had rallied round the Gospel and that mission stations were completely free of the extremists. A Mr. Foucard had appealed on behalf of the new movement and had freely acknowledged that confusions and errors could have arisen and might arise again. These could always be overcome as long as they all "exalted the Cross and the Power of the Blood in praise and prayer." Here was the other half of the bridge so slowly devised by Jessie Penn-Lewis.

A careful study of all her correspondence in 1907-1908, would silence those who have misrepresented Jessie Penn-Lewis as an uncompromising enemy of all forms of Pentecostalism. In fact, several features that she condemned were removed by Pentecostalists themselves a decade later. What she saw and dreaded most of all was the breach between faithful missionary workers, the separate meals, the criticisms, and the coldness.

Four years later, in a short chapter on revival in *War on the Saints*, Jessie set out clearly her general principles of spiritual unity through wise discernment and love:

> When the true influx of the Holy Spirit into the human spirit took place, there was unity with others in the same spirit; there was joy, liberty and power to witness. But when the counterfeit appears, the supernatural experiences often occur at the same time that a wrong spirit is discernible, such as harshness, bitterness, pride, presumption and disunion. These show either that the experiences are not from the Spirit or that the human spirit is out of co-working with the Holy Spirit. The Counterfeit is marked by inability to recognize and unite with the Spirit of God in others, and a spirit of separation and division on account of not seeing eye to eye on non-essential matters. Union of spirit is possible apart from union of faith.

14

Reinforcing the Revival: Local Conventions

Jessie Penn-Lewis was just as concerned as the Rev. R. B. Jones and a score of church leaders about the best ways to nurture and instruct the hundreds of converts won during the revival. This chapter describes how she helped accomplish this task by means of a nationwide Keswick Convention and, secondly, by the formation of many local or district conventions.

The possibilities of a Keswick-style convention for Wales had been discussed informally two or three times by 1902. But it was left to Jessie Penn-Lewis to make a direct approach to Mr. Albert Head, the Rev. Evan Hopkins, and Dr. F. B. Meyer, all of whom she knew personally. The revered Dr. Inwood also gave his blessing and promised his full support. Her first move was to go down and visit Dean Howells of St. David's Cathedral in West Wales, who told her of his own conviction that Wales needed a channel of revival. He prayed for and spoke in favor of the Keswick Convention but was in Heaven before it was held for the first time. Other Anglican clergymen promised their support.

The first Convention met at Llandrindod in 1903. The speakers dealt boldly with the three truths that were not spoken of much in Wales: the power of the Life of the risen Christ in the Church; the power of the indwelling Holy Spirit in each believer; and the sufficiency of God's promises to fully assure our salvation. Jessie was watching the audiences closely and said afterwards, "All prejudice and doubt fled away as the truths were unfolded."

It took a whole year in the lives and ministries of a score of preachers and pastors before the full fruit could be wholly shared with others. After that year, many preaching festivals and even denominational conferences were transformed and hundreds of the laity got excited about the next Keswick Convention to be held at Llandrindod. If 1904 was rewarding, then 1905 was a thrill from end to end. In her reports, Jessie gave a vivid picture of the crowds of revival converts tasting the Scriptures like honey and going off to the lakeside or the woods around Llandrindod to pray and praise hour after hour.

It was in 1906 that Jessie initiated a special meeting for Christian workers on one of the afternoons, and this became her annual opportunity to open up new truths to such key people. A Mr. H. D. Phillips took over the role of convention reporter and had enough local influence to book a full page in the *Radnor Express* from 1907 through 1912. (It became a four page supplement later on.) From his detailed reports, we learn that Jessie spoke at the "Welcome" meeting in 1907, and played a prominent part in a "Special Breakfast" in 1908. She conducted the Christian Workers' meeting by herself but also gave assistance to evangelist Seth Joshua in his late-night prayer and confession meetings. Then, on a Saturday morning, she chaired a farewell meeting in Albert Hall and called on listeners to consider the possibilities of "Throne-Prayer" and exercising faith in the risen, exalted Lord.

In 1909, there were problems in the meetings for the first time. An undercurrent of restlessness caused a few score people to stay away from the Bible readings in the tent and to hold some kind of open praise and testimony meetings. Without consulting anyone, Jessie announced another informal meeting at six o' clock. Many more converts turned up to testify about their personal blessing during revival meetings.

In the 1910 Convention, Jessie discovered that she had nothing scheduled for her other than the Workers' Meeting, where she introduced the theme which now dominated her thought: "The Christian's Warfare, the Christian's weapons and the Christian's Victories." She was overlooked again in the main program of the 1911 Keswick Convention, and took instant action when a telegram arrived from Evan Roberts saying, "Withdraw at once." It was the end of an epoch.

As we stand midway between the Llandrindod Keswick Convention and the various local conventions set up between 1906 and 1912, it is well to be reminded that in both these developments Jessie played an unseen but vital part as a maker of bridges between two cultures. The crucial debate took place in 1907, at the end of a long and complex correspondence between the Rev. J. Rhys Davies, the Rev. Owen M. Owen, Mr. Albert Head (the chairman), and Jessie Penn-Lewis (joint-secretary).

After much talking, it was decided that five Welshmen would be invited to join the Council of Reference and that there would always be representative preachers from Wales, such as R. B. Jones, both at the main convention and at local conventions if they had been approved by the Council of Reference. In a nice gesture of appreciation, the Council then invited Jessie Penn-Lewis to be a standing member, in recognition of her devoting so much time, energy, and talent to the Convention ideals. Four years later, she found it well-nigh impossible to serve, but the main conflicts of interest were over and the permanent principles had been established.

Apart from R. B. and W. S. Jones' holiness meetings in North Wales, the first fully developed conventions were in the Rhondda Valley—Llwynypia and Porth—and also in Carmarthen. The key to the success of the Llwynypia Convention was the dynamic presence of Dr. Pierson, who had stayed in Wales to witness the revival and its aftermath. His full opening address was recorded in a local newspaper and shows how carefully he developed the theme of the risen Christ sending forth the Holy Spirit who gives us full assurance of our salvation and true liberty. He urged the listeners to give over total control of their lives to Him, "It will not do to let God have some rooms and shut Him out of the rest. He must have the full run of the house."

Dr. Pierson also spoke at Llanelly and at the Carmarthen Convention, alongside Professor Keri Evans. They spoke on such themes as "Evil Spirits" and "The Four Keywords to Holiness of Life." For some unknown reason, at those conventions the interest was diminished and the attendance reduced.

The ministers of Merthyr and Dowlais districts kept asking for top class speakers at a time when poor Jessie and Arthur Morgan the treasurer had no cash reserves. She was forced to accept at least three changes in the list and ended up with an Anglican clergyman instead of the evangelist she wanted. Undeterred by all these upsets, Jessie began to contact more religious leaders in Wales. In one of the boxes containing her papers, there was found a complicated set of denominational address lists for about four hundred clergymen and ministers who were contacted.

In February 1906, they first ventured to hold a large winter convention in the spacious Cory Hall in Cardiff. Mr. De Courcy Hamilton, a wealthy businessman, had offered his sponsorship, though he personally felt that conventions should be held at the Coal Exchange in the heart of the business quarter. The Bishop of Llandaff gave his blessing, too, and Principal Edwards of the Baptist College offered, but never actually provided, skilled support. Jessie found other useful helpers.

Her first full report of the "South Wales Convention for the Deepening of Spiritual Life" appeared in the *Life of Faith* on February 14, 1906. As a result, people came from all over South Wales, using special vouchers for reduced rail fares. Even at this first convention there were visitors from Germany and Armenia, who had read Jessie's reports and were full of expectation that the revival spirit was still there. They were not disappointed.

On the first night, the Rev. S. McCracken spoke on "Behold the Lamb," and the Rev. Evan Hopkins followed with a meditation on the "Holy Presence of God." His Bible readings each morning presented the need of fitness for service, readiness for witness, and equipment for conflict. A third speaker, the Rev. Gregory Mantle, spoke about the work of the Holy Spirit in such a passionate way that people were deeply stirred and responded to the appeal given later that evening.

This Cardiff-based convention worked well in 1906 and 1907, but then began to fade so badly that Jessie wrote, "I have a question whether this convention should be dropped, for we are out of line with God's will."

Consequently, she threw her weight behind the Swansea Conventions of 1908, 1909, and 1910, which dealt with practical themes such as "Intercessory Prayer" and "'The Way of the Cross." There was also an excellent team of speakers: A. C. Champion (Anglican), R. B. Jones, Jessie Penn-Lewis, and the Rev. F. B. Meyer. An unusual feature was the informal "Tea-Time Talk" on spiritual difficulties. The first was led by Jessie herself and was devoted to "Praise, Prayer and Testimony." It was at the next meeting that her dream of a worldwide Band of Prayer Intercessors was first disclosed. This was meant to extend more widely than the intercession list used by her unidentified "Epaphras Band" who always prayed for her own ministry.

Gradually she came to rely more and more on the Rev. Owen M. Owen, who had the same view of converts' needs as herself. She supported the appeal sent in from the ministers that usually met at Dowlais near Merthyr, and wrote, "NOW is the time for conventions to flood the country with the only teaching that can save the church from the throes of reaction. This is surely the psychological moment."

Of course, there were more teething troubles, especially when the well-known Keswick chairman, Mr. Albert Head of Wimbledon, made his own list of approved convention speakers. The fact that these were mostly Anglican clergy jarred the sensibilities of many Welsh supporters who wanted their own Welsh Nonconformist speakers. They had already been upset by reports that F. B. Meyer was claiming that he had some part to play in the first stages of the revival and that Evan Roberts had been present at his meetings. Jessie persuaded him to apologize and soothe Welsh feelings. Then O. M. Owen complained:

> Some of the speakers that are invited here are in every sense inferior to some of our Welsh brethren. This view of mine is that of the man in the seat who was invited there. If Wales is to be reached, it must be through Welshmen. No-one can touch the heart of Wales like a Welshman. The conventions held last winter in different centers have been an immense success and a large number of ministers have been won over. Opposition has been overcome and prejudices removed and very many brought into a new experience. Diolch Iddo.

What exactly was this opposition and prejudice? The pages of *King's Champions* indicated that a number of cruel accusations were made by prominent ministers in Wales and also by a group of church elders and deacons. The Rev. D. Lloyd of Aberdare asserted that the chief convention leaders were not prepared to give one hundred percent loyalty to the Lord because they were silent about believers' baptism and were sometimes substituting baptism by the Holy Spirit for this. Of course, the convention leaders pointed to the large number of their listeners who afterwards sought adult baptism—but the misrepresentation had a long life. Some leaders were also accused of being dictatorial.

The next Pontypridd Convention caused yet another fuss because Jessie had told the local secretaries that they could count on Dr. Pierson coming, but it was found that he had overfilled his engagement book. Everything had to be reorganized and in that process a number of Welsh preachers were set aside. It was not Jessie but O. M. Owen who wrote a spirited apologia in defense of the Pontypridd Convention and praised Dr. Pierson's part in it:

> During the revival the Holy Spirit was heard from every lip and thousands have been rejoicing in that discovery—that this Person in the Eternal Trinity is a blessed reality. Now they want to know more and more about Him. The Pontypridd Convention showed them many things and sent them home with new Bibles. Dr. Pierson convinced many who had anathematized the teaching on Holiness and the Holy Spirit. He has caused many more ministers to teach neglected truths which needed emphasis.

O. M. Owen gave four reasons why more and more conventions were needed, and Jessie endorsed each of these:

> It will lead them to realize how essential teaching is to life, and how the Keswick teaching goes to the very root of moral and spiritual problems.

> It will show them that holiness teaching is in perfect harmony with the evangel of the Cross.
>
> It will show to them very clearly the great difference between preaching and teaching, and help them to realize that fine preaching is no substitute for sound teaching.
>
> It will undoubtedly make a demand for such meetings in the future. Our old preaching anniversaries, with their rhetorical and oratorical displays must be transformed OR ELSE we must have a Convention in each church where an outsider can say things that pastors cannot.

It was Jessie's special task to introduce the conventions to North Wales. Serious new problems appeared as soon as they began to plan the Bangor and other conventions. Welsh speaking preachers declined to come and Jessie had a hard time soothing the feelings of a Miss Leonora Davies, the local arranger, and assuring her that this Bangor Convention was not under the auspices of Keswick. She wrote warmly, "I do so much appreciate the help given us and I am sure that the Lord will prosper the work. I am grateful for all your suggestions and am quite satisfied with your decision that the whole of North Wales should not be worked at present."

Aware of this hostile feeling, Mr. Albert Head stepped in once more and wrote to all the supporting ministers, asking them to talk to church leaders in North Wales and to see what they felt about things. Afterwards Jessie was able to write, "A decision has now been made to restrict the radius of this conference and keep it as Welsh as possible."

In the end, this Easter convention was very well attended, especially when it was leaked that Evan Roberts would be there. At the convention, Keri Evans did Bible Readings from John 14 and 15 on love and obedience. Evan Hopkins was the chief Bible teacher this time—dealing in each session with some aspect of "Life in Christ."

Evan Roberts gave two passionate exhortations based on three words, "Face the Cross," which included his apology for "all my previous unbelief in the power of the Blood."

Letters were sent to Jessie from those who were seeking to know more about Keswick teachings. They asked her to come and explain these simply in local preaching meetings. A North Walian pastor, the Rev. D. Evans, said to her after one such day, "North Wales is ripe for your teaching." But the opportunity was lost as the North Wales clergy rejected all appeals to come to another such Convention. In vain could the Rev. M. H. Jones claim in *Y GOLEUAD*, "The Gospel preached at Keswick is the supreme need of Wales. Blessed are those believers who are now willing to consecrate themselves as worthy servants of the Holy Spirit."

There never was a network of local conventions there so that men like the Rev. W. S. Jones had to use the customary Preaching Festivals to present Keswick-type doctrines. Both W. S. and R. B. Jones preached holiness and surrender and full assurance with such effect that hundreds of Welsh chapel folk found their way to the same position as if they had been in the Conventions.

> The fruit of the conventions cannot be told. We know a little, God knows all.
>
> From many parts of Wales I have heard of men and women whose lives have been transformed so much by the teachings they had had that their names have been dear to all hearts and their lives prolific in fruit.
>
> (H. D. Phillips in the *Radnorshire Express*)

15

The Recovery and Recomissioning of Evan Roberts

About four miles out of Leicester towards Kettering, there was a little village of pleasant country cottages known as "Great Glen." It had a tavern, a few little shops, and a small railway station along a half-mile of narrow country lane. In that lane stood four or five larger country houses and a farm. The local railroad line took bowler-hatted commuters into Leicester banks, libraries, and city hall departments. Every morning, the immaculate Mr. William Penn-Lewis traveled to his City Treasurer's office. Every Sunday, he and his wife went to the city to attend a Society of Friends Meeting or an Anglican service or, sometimes, a lively evangelical meeting, like those at the Melbourne Hall where men like Meyer and Fullerton were popular preachers.

Sometimes on weekdays the villagers would see rather unusual visitors in Great Glen—a sun-darkened missionary from India, or a soberly clad German pastor, or a well-furred Russian countess whom the lady of the house had invited when she was on her travels. There were no children, of course, and seldom young relatives around. The only other residents at the country house were Jessie's secretary, her bookshop manager, and a dedicated housekeeper/nurse/companion named "Mary." After twenty five years of married life—sharing in spiritual ideals and in a number of practical projects—William and Jessie enjoyed total trust in each other's concerns and journeyings. Often they were able to help and counsel those who came privately. To anyone who confessed spiritual defeat and barrenness or a sense of oppression, Jessie would write something like this:

> Come and stay awhile amongst the trees, flowering shrubs and the calling birds. Have no fear of interrupters You can stay even when we are away at conferences. My faithful secretary and housekeeper will see to your needs. The only thing you must accept is that, when I am here, I shall spend about eight hours a day writing letters, articles, and books.

Several times a year, Jessie visited her mother in Rugby Road, Neath, and went with her to the old Welsh chapel where her grandfather had often thundered his messages about the atoning death of Christ as a sinner's only hope. Early in January 1905, she heard that the celebrated Evan Roberts was coming to Neath. She had already written her first impressions of him after a visit to Loughor to listen to him, but now she desired to meet him personally and to help him in some way.

In her first ever letter to a man to whom she had never been introduced, she wrote with holy boldness, "Will you seek the mind of the Spirit and let me know when you would be free to see me. I do not want to come for a few minutes but I have much on my heart from the Lord. I believe He means me to have time to speak to you on things of God. HE will tell you this. I only want to know what He shows you."

At some point Jessie had begun to collect notes and newspaper clippings of Evan Roberts' reactions to what he assumed to be the Spirit's commands. Both her diary and her correspondence book suggest that she was involved in, or at least aware of, the plan made by certain prominent Keswick spokesmen, such as Charles Inwood, to travel down to Cardiff on February 2-3. They intended meeting with the revivalist and discussing how he could be linked up with their movement in order to safeguard the revival. If she knew what they intended, did she and her friend, Owen M. Owen, let the cat out of the bag? If so, then the sudden decision of Evan Roberts to keep away from Cardiff was not a case of bad manners or bad nerves, but a steadfast refusal to be under the direction of any committee or group—denominational or otherwise.

According to her own diary, Jessie managed to get away from other engagements in the Gorseinon area and dash down to Swansea to have talks with Evan Roberts in the Lloyd household a week or two after his "Week of Silence" in February 1905. What she saw and heard about his "Journal of the Week" and his emotionally overcharged return to Blaenannerch, Newquay, and Newcastle Emlyn, (see *Instrument of Revival*, chapter 12, published by Bridge-Logos Publishers) did not reassure her. On March 29,1905, she wrote to a friend, "Evan Roberts is in much need of prayer." She would assuredly have heard from her numerous West Wales connections how Evan had lashed out at the crowds of faithful followers on his last visit to Newquay.

It was not only Evan Roberts who was doing and saying strange things in the springtime revival meetings. Gradually she became convinced that the Lord wanted her to go to each member of this group, all of whom had suffered from stress in those tremendous months when they took part in forty meetings per week. She told her friends that she had succeeded in meeting Dan Roberts, Sidney Evans, and the lady singers at Gorseinon and had told them how following the "Way of the Cross" would keep them free from all oppressions and deceptions. Now she wanted Evan Roberts to accept her ministrations and believe the same message. Seemingly he wasn't ready even then.

After his successful meetings in North Wales in the summer of 1905, Evan again chose to make Swansea his base and to stay with the Lloyd brothers. A few weeks before the Convention season began, Jessie asked him to come over to Neath in order to get rid of his burden. Instead she had to come down to Swansea for brief afternoon sessions

Sometime during or after the visit to the exciting but stressful Llandrindod Convention in August 1905, Evan began to speak rather like Jessie about "entering into the sufferings of the Cross." On August 31, 1905, Jessie tried for a private meeting again and wrote this note to Evan, "Should you need to wire me or my husband, the initial R. or X. will be sufficient to let us know the sender."

Once again, on September, 1, 1905, she wrote to him from her mother's home, and that letter and the others fell into the hands of the secular press. The postscript was mildly indiscreet in that she told him which train to catch and where to book his tickets and how to send a telegram—just as if he were going to a rendezvous. But the true intention was seen in the last words, "If you have no light for future steps yet, OUR house is YOURS for as long as He wills."

The above words echoed his own letters to friends at that time about not knowing the next step and about people urging him to make decisions. William and Jessie were absolutely sure that Evan Roberts was destined for an even higher ministry and that their task was to prepare him, not in Wales but in Leicester. Jessie wrote to him:

> The vision is clearer and clearer. I see you with a trumpet cry to the whole world, and all hell is moved to stop you. It seems to me as if the battle for the world was raging round you just now, and I have no rest in my spirit in crying for you. Ere the trumpet cry goes forth, you must reach The Throne of Victory with the conquering Christ, and see the forces of darkness underneath. God will bring you to Glen and it will be your Bethany when you want to get away with God from the sights and sounds of the world and go forth clothed again from on High.

Still Evan delayed going to Leicester but went instead with good friends like the Rev. Ferrier Hulme to Gloucester and Bristol, and with his Welsh friends to special services here and there. Jessie's fourth letter, dated September 14, 1905, apologized for taking too much for granted and reminded Evan that it was her husband who had asked him to come to the Glen. Now she admitted that she had designed it to be some kind of *sanctuary life*, "shut away from the world outside you." She also told him, "I have the impression that your coming here at this time meant great consequences to God as well as the Adversary. . . . I expect no reply unless God gives it you."

By November, Evan knew that he was off to North Wales once more—this time in the depths of winter. Somehow, he kept going until mid-January. Jessie told *Life of Faith* readers that Evan really wanted to concentrate on one or two areas that seemed ripe for revival. Certainly Evan was completely exhausted by the time he returned to South Wales. Yet he felt there was something more to be done and that he would have to wait on the Lord for guidance. On February 19, 1906, another letter came from the Penn-Lewis household.

> I am waiting for the Lord to show you His will and His time for coming here. Up to last week God kept me

> restrained with you, for it was not His time. On Thursday I found that the Lord had released me and given me permission to speak freely to you. Now He is pouring into my heart so much that He wants me to tell you. I only know that God has a time as well as a plan. I can only wait His time. I do see clearly that He will work rapidly now and that there is a lull for you and me just now. Every step must be in His perfect plan and He has the moment when it will be His will. I need not tell you that my husband is heartily one with me in a welcome to you.

This surely is why Evan Roberts felt impelled at last to turn away from the confusion of South Wales where there were disorderly meetings at Carmarthen, dancing and barking at Llannon, a prophesying curate at Llanelly, a persuasive woman healer in Swansea, and persistent interrupters everywhere.

Just before Easter, he took refuge at Great Glen with William and Jessie and had a first discussion of his difficulties. He insisted on going with her to a great convention organized for the Easter week in Bangor. To the great joy of Jessie, he chose this moment to publicly adopt her teaching about the Cross. It showed up in his passionate prayer-petitions, "Reveal the Cross, O Lord." It showed up in his public appeal to the convention to face the Cross and be delivered. But it was an even greater sensation at the Ministers' Prayer Breakfast, when he announced, "My only aim is to preach Christ and Him crucified, not theoretically but as living truth".

On April 24, 1906, Jessie wrote excitedly to a prayer partner about Evan:

> He is wonderfully coming out and getting right through to the Throne Life. He went to Bangor and you will see how the Lord launched him out. It was an

> unspeakable joy. He was just like a child in simplicity. He has made such rapid strides since he was here and has lost all that self-absorption. He will be here yet a while for we have only just reached the place where he is really at liberty. Now comes the building and preparation for the future.

The Cross was his only theme at one crowded meeting during the Porth Convention where he identified self-centeredness as one of the chief obstacles to blessing . Much of his talk about "Full Deliverance," the "Power of the Blood," "Dying to the World," and "Getting authority over the Enemy" was exactly like Jessie's language in her booklets of that period: *The Way of the Cross*, *Streams From Calvary*, and *It Is Finished.*

In July 1906, Jessie's party took Evan to the parent Keswick Convention in Cumberland, where his four unsanctioned addresses aroused deep emotions. It was his first and last visit, though Jessie continued to serve that Convention for three more years.

Things went better at the 1906 Keswick Convention in Llandrindod Wells, but a new crisis blew up during the Free Church Council's sponsored Mission that followed. Many people were scoffing when Evan again chose to testify, "I am a sinner saved by grace. I can do nothing apart from Christ. All the glory must be His. We are nothing, but He can use us. He is waiting for instruments. Shall we place ourselves in His hands?"

He had already claimed that it was the Father of Lies who had persuaded him not to preach about the Cross. Scores of ministers present, who were also not preaching the Cross, must have seen the implications of this. They didn't like it and they said so and laid the blame on Jessie Penn-Lewis. They were already upset that she had dared to take part in discussions and had made public statements in a land where only the men had such liberty. So now their faces grew longer.

Jessie told the Rev. R. B. Jones, "I know that my words at the 'breakfast' caused much antagonism. I was misunderstood. Some were blessed but several, if not many, were angry. So I fear that I have unwittingly added to the difficulties. . . . I nearly sank during that awful meeting and the Lord has since given me Jeremiah 12:5, about the ministers' attitude to me."

At a meeting of prayer-partners she forewarned people about a "terrific conflict with the forces of darkness." Evan Roberts became overstrained and unbalanced and told loyal supporters, "Hell is raging." Jessie decided that she would keep away from Wales "until every trace of the past strain has disappeared."

In a recently discovered letter to R. B. Jones, she confessed that she had been shattered by the opposition and that Evan Roberts was in an even worse state and would now need months of rest. One of the hostile reporters told his readers that there had been lots of singular activities and excitements. Then he announced wrongly that Evan Roberts and Jessie Penn-Lewis were going down to a South of England resort for "a time of rest."

While all this was going on, devoted friends were escorting Evan by train to Great Glen. He reached the Penn-Lewis house in a chaise and a doctor was sent for and diagnosed "acute nervous prostration." A few weeks later, Evan's friend, J. C. Williams, went to see him and found him lying in "the stillness of suffering." Three months later, on November 19, 1906, Evan was visited by a good friend, Ferrier Hulme, who held out no hope of a return to Wales or to work. Hulme blamed the total collapse on sleeplessness, close stuffy rooms, little food, and the terrible burden of revival meetings and interviews. Evan was anemic and had to use a special diet for weeks. Jessie tried to ration the visitors and cut out as much correspondence as possible. She was very hurt when people murmured about her as "Evan's keeper."

Fortunately, Ferrier Hulme went out of his way to describe how clear-headed and confident Evan was becoming after a few months of such care. There is a lovely letter from Ferrier thanking the hosts and paying tribute to their way of life at the Glen:

> I have enjoyed a restful and refreshing day as if drinking of a well of pure pleasure. The whole day has been a fine tour of all the helpful things you are enabled to do for the Master. There you are doing so beautifully restoring His young servant by such peaceful pastures. I cannot imagine anything on earth more stimulating for one of such a temperament as his.

Friends and family in Wales seemed to think that the Penn-Lewis house was dominating their lost prophet, but that was far from truth. William was a genial host but heavily engaged in local government at a time when most City Treasurers ran the welfare services and planning departments. Jessie was heavily engaged in a round of visits and letter writing as she helped organize the many new Keswick-type local conventions and dealt with tensions and setbacks. At the same time, she was preparing weekly articles, first about revival and then about the "Hour of Peril." Each issue produced a new crop of puzzled or angry or appealing or condemnatory letters in reply, which Jessie invariably answered. A flood of letters came from Europe where Pastor Saillens sought her aid against the forces of Satan, and where her trusted prayer-partner, Sigrid Kurke of Rynge in Sweden, grieved, "You and I are in the mill being grinded into fine white flour."

Under such strains, Jessie soon lost the glowing health and vigor of 1905, and was showing signs of relapse into lung inflammation, neurasthenia, and "oppression." To picture her as dominating the young revivalist in 1906-1907, is utterly absurd.

In the autumn of 1906, her very understanding and caring husband provided another solution, and that was to leave the countryside and reside in a handsome new architect-designed house in Toller Road. It was in a suburb of Leicester where visitors could travel out with ease from the center of the city, and where she could go forth to her endless conferences and meetings. The house was christened "Cartref"—the home. It is quite clear that the intention from the beginning was to dedicate it to the Lord's service. The original plans—still marked with special alterations—show what changes were made to provide workrooms and staff bedrooms, plus a strictly segregated suite of two rooms for the unmarried Evan Roberts. This wise arrangement gave rise to a silly story that he was a prisoner at a time when he was meeting his own prayer-partners regularly, and when there were occasional dinner parties.

"Cartref" was a busy place and yet restful and homely, right up to the war years when the Penn-Lewises grew their own vegetables and Evan Roberts looked after the chickens. This writer was conducted around the house by its present owner, who is an Indian businessman. Oddly enough, he said, "When we first came here from Uganda we felt that we had entered a house of special peace; and the last owner, Mrs. Bates, spoke to us about a sense of happiness here."

In this new residence, Jessie conducted her many and varied home and overseas affairs and received even more visitors. When he had recovered a little, Evan joined her for discussion of the next books or the next round of conferences. Here *The Overcomer* magazine was conceived and the religious classic, *War on the Saints,* was fashioned.

During this recovery period, Jessie's diary enthuses every time she sees Evan in action, but sobers up every time he seems to be under a cloud. No wonder he called her, "My spiritual mother." By the end of 1907, she was encouraging him to give talks to little groups, though the doctors still forbade him to take public meetings. Sometimes he got a little too exuberant and she fretted over this, too. The high spot was his arrival in a very difficult Leicester convention in 1908, which he at once changed into a time of praise and joyously relaxed testimony.

What had led to this complete recovery in spirit as well as mind and body? Jessie had many talks with him in order to show him how to get free from his constant burden of self-consciousness. "Let it be buried with Christ," she cried. Next they reviewed together his experiences of visions, voices, and ecstasies and tried to see which ones had been psychic and which ones truly spiritual.

Next they faced the problem of misjudged and needlessly stressful actions and words that had much troubled his soul. With all her own experiences behind her, Jessie was soon able to convince Evan that he had been wide open to attack because he had never looked for full divine protection.

All this was like a builder removing the damaged sections. The next step, obviously, to rebuild. Probably Jessie told Evan how she herself had been put through all these testings during 1900, and how she had then helped others who had been in the valley of humiliation. By this hard and stony way, they had each been brought to the Cross, broken and humbled, and then raised up with Christ and made ready to co-work with God in fighting and defeating the evil one.

During the last stage of the spiritual crisis, a new helper had arrived. Jessie had written three times to the Rev. R. B. Jones and urged him to come to Leicester because she knew that he had been through a breaking experience a year earlier and because she felt that his teaching and counsel would help. R. B. Jones came to Leicester in May 1907, and possibly in

June, also. When he left, Evan Roberts was a transformed man. In August 1907, she wrote to "R. B." from Davos in Switzerland, expressing her warmest thanks for what he had done and assuring him that Evan Roberts was now ready for battle:

> He has steadily gained and now he is able to think freely. God is pouring light in such a way that I can see the church of God is going to benefit greatly. . . . I see that God is training him as an expert.

Jessie and the other prayer-warriors became convinced that a spiritual war was on the way and that those who had suffered and endured were prepared for conflict. The company of suffering but purified ones, she believed, could co-work with God in defeating all the dark hosts and "binding Satan." The *Welsh Press* talked of Evan's possible return to Wales with a new roving commission, but Jessie felt that all warfare work was to be centered upon the book-room and prayer room at "Cartref" in the quiet suburb of Leicester. Even after Evan made a full recovery, he remained at the side of Jessie and at least four colleagues, facing the same conflicts and sharing the same burdens.

The four colleagues or regular prayer partners were Charles Raven and Arthur Harris—when they were free from other commitments; Henry Johnson—who eventually moved to Paris to pioneer a French *Le Vainqueur* and other publications; Mr. Scottorn—who devoted all his free hours to God's service and later became an Anglican Vicar; and Mr. J. C. Williams. Williams was converted in a revival meeting at Skewen near Neath, moved to London, and was put under the special care and instruction of prebendary Frank Webster of All Souls, Langham Place—Webster was a founder member of the Church Army. After some training, possibly as a Church Army officer, Williams was recommended to be a helper to

Jessie Penn-Lewis. He was responsible for setting up the *Prayer Watch*, the *Prayer Bands*, and eventually a *Prayer and Intercession Center* at Eccleston Hall in London.

One of the mysteries of the second half of the period of 1911-1915, is how Jessie could almost reverence the special role of Evan Roberts as a world-intercessor who spent about eighteen sleepless hours a day in prayer. In a conference in 1908, she had urged the churches to look out for a number of prayer-intercessors, but she was certainly not thinking of just one man. In fact, Evan started off with a prayer-circle that was taught to "pray over and over until everything could be gathered together into one prayer." He personally trained J. C. Williams and others in his prayer-method, and Jessie tended to hand over all urgent prayer needs to this little group. But Evan started to practice solitary meditation and intercessory prayer as early as 1911. Jessie compared this change to the sudden bursting forth of a new spring from the Rock. She encouraged him to pray for the whole church and the whole world. A prophet's chamber was set aside for prayer work, covering all Christian workers night and day. His lamp rarely went out because, as she said, "Gradually his whole being was shut up to the prayer-service."

Departing from all their previous practices, Jessie took Evan to a photographer in Leicester who did an impressive portrait of the revivalist seated in prayer with a Bible in front of him. She was convinced that this intercession was not only helping Christians to meet Satan's attacks, but was helping to bring churches into readiness for the very last days of the dispensation before Satan made his final attack on them. Yet even she was taken by surprise in 1913, when Evan announced to the world his "burden message"—the imminent appearing of our Lord Jesus.

People wondered whether this was a genuine revelation or was Evan sinking back again into the emotional tangles of the breakdown period. Only the spirit of discernment could help Jessie to decide. She shielded Evan from a new influx of visitors and told the Press that he would never converse with anyone who had doubts or unbelief about his role.

In all these ways, Evan Roberts was helped to recover from the great collapse of 1906-1907. He completely overcame his problems and then grew rapidly in stature. It was his close and constant communion with God that gave him such awesome authority when he was moved to speak or counsel. Jessie never doubted his unction and authority. A later chapter will consider the mystery of why the wartime years altered this relationship and why Jessie Penn-Lewis gradually turned to other helpers.

16

Jessie Penn-Lewis and the Earliest "Tongues" Movements

When Jessie Penn-Lewis was persuaded by many letters and reports that she had to attack certain forms of the newborn and fast-spreading Pentecostal Movement, it was the beginning of a vigorous two-year debate during which she became more critical of the movement. All her instincts were hostile to those groups that gave prime importance to "speaking in other tongues" and various forms of body-language. In simple justice, however, this chapter and the next will show that she considered it her sacred duty to guide and warn, but never to condemn Christians who either misunderstood or misused "the gifts," "signs," and other external "manifestations." For that reason, she herself was criticized by strict evangelicals as one who took too soft a line.

Jessie's first doubts about tongues, visions, prophesying, and other phenomena were sown by the essays of Mrs. Pearsall Smith (Hannah Whithall Smith); and by pamphlets written by men who feared that when the next revival came, another army of deceivers would seek to infiltrate those groups who most longed for intimate communing with Christ and for special dealings with the Holy Spirit. This was tragically confirmed by certain events after the Welsh revival changed course in 1907, and when the same thing happened in Europe and Asia. There were many instances where intense new converts were induced to go in for prostrations and trance visions and such manifestations as *guiding lights* and *angelic helps*.

In the Cardiff and Leicester conferences in 1908, Jessie warned everyone that each time a revival meeting moved out from under the control of the Holy Spirit because someone was secretly disobedient, that meeting would always move into the control of fleshly elements—unless someone was there to intercept this and check and warn believers who were "not quick to discern the movements of GOD."

This kind of unscriptural high pressure and excitation during mass meetings took even stranger forms during 1907, and then died down in most of Wales. But there was a great deal of contact with American cousins in Pennsylvania, Ohio, and California; and with those Americans who had visited each revival center in Wales, especially places where Evan Roberts could be seen. So many in Wales quickly became aware that new signs and wonders had begun in the United States. Soon many Welsh converts became convinced that the Spirit had come in power upon Los Angeles, Washington, Ohio, and Winnipeg at almost the same time as the blessing began to pour out through the windows of heaven over Northern Europe and India. At once those old warnings about the likelihood of counterfeiting troubled the minds of evangelists and church leaders who had read about the English mystics, the prophetess Joanna Southcott, the Irvingites, Shakers, and the followers of Prophet Dowie in America as well as certain extremist cults in Europe.

No one had published reports of the Revival more enthusiastically than Jessie Penn-Lewis, but in 1907, she felt led to take a long hard look at all those movements that seemed to be born of the Spirit. It was through her network of private correspondents that she learned of certain new influences that looked to her more like infections. As the fresh outbreak began, she realized that there was as great a need of discernment as in previous generations. Her first evidence came from Germany. Someone gave her a copy of the so-called "Cassel Documents."

This collection consisted of Letters, Essays, and Resolutions to be debated by German church leaders—most, if not all, of them ordained pastors in the Lutheran Church. They agreed to meet at Barmen in 1907. There were to be five themes introduced for debate:

> The Gift of Tongues by Pastor Paul.
> The Cassel Movement by E. Schrenk.
> The Testimonies by Seitz and Ben Ide.
> Satan among the Saints by A. Dollmeyer.
> The Resolutions, preceded by some kind of summing up, by Pastor Dolman.

The Gift of Tongues

Pastor Paul of Cassel, Germany, had originally been a leader of a North German movement for the promotion of scriptural holiness. Somewhere in 1906, he heard people talking excitedly about a new gift of speaking in tongues, which he lacked. "Other tongues" was interpreted as a new kind of spiritual speech that the Lord desired to bestow on all who truly sought it. For this power he prayed every day until, one memorable day, things changed altogether:

> My mouth was being worked with such power that the lower jaw, the tongue and the lips moved quite apart

> from my own volition. I was fully conscious and yielded to what was happening. Later that night this began again as though an organ was formed in my lungs which produced sounds corresponding to the movement of my lips. Each day my lips were moved in a manner entirely strange by a power above me, WITHOUT ANY ACTION ON ONE'S OWN PART.

Convinced that this was the "divers tongues" mentioned in the Bible, he looked for others of like mind. He found one strange thing—that people quite immature in belief had the gift, too; and that people of imperfect life and conduct also spoke in tongues. Therefore speaking in tongues could not be God's reward for mature souls but an initial love-gift to anyone who first received the Spirit. The next statement he made flew in the face of the evidence from the lives of many of God's saints, "If we fail to seek the gift of tongues because it is not desirable or because it appears to be superfluous, the Lord will not be able to entrust the other gifts of the Spirit; e.g. prophecy and healings."

Pastor Paul's parting command to the seekers was that they must convince themselves from the Scriptures that the promise was for them. They ought to stay only with others who were like-minded, to tell everyone that they were seeking this gift, and then obey the Lord implicitly in every detail, renouncing all else and being very attentive to the hand of the Spirit.

The Cassel Movement

The aged ex-missionary, Schrenk, had also noticed that there were many unconverted people in the crowds in the meetings at Cassel. He said at once that a mixed meeting was not the right place for such a Divine blessing to fall. A great number of tumults and extravagances broke out because "the soulish element had got the upper hand and the Holy Spirit was driven out."

Schrenk had discovered that two false prophets had taken control of every meeting by giving out certain catchwords that everyone repeated. At a signal everyone was commanded to pray or sigh or groan together. Whenever the promised baptism didn't come they would demand that the place should be cleansed from elements who had no right to be there. Some of these prophets even decided how long a meeting should last, and they would suddenly terminate a meeting. Schrenk decided that all these new elements were an impure force that had been transmitted "by a restless evil spirit from Los Angeles." The German way was best—holy stillness—in line with the character of gentle Jesus, who never used such soulish methods.

Sincere, godly, attractive Christians had somehow been deceived and then caused many to miss the blessing and to avoid the Gospel so that "great harm has been done to the Lord's work." There was need of repentance, cleansing, watchfulness, balance, discipline, and praying against the corrupting influences. His last words to this conference were, "Test the spirits whether they are of God."

The Testimonies

Pastor Seitz' contribution was to ask for an act of repentance because they had all failed to discern the lying spirit. He praised God that one group after another was escaping "the snare of artifice and evasion." A letter from Ben Ide, a Christian worker, described how groups had fallen for odd experiences such as trembling and aerial voices, all so mixed up with such blessed times that they were convinced that revival was going on two lines—God's blessings and Satan's mingling. Ben Ide's stories were additional proof.

Satan Among Saints

Dollmeyer's paper had already been published in the German magazine *Reichjsgottes Arbeiter*. It included a repudiation of things he had said in favor of the "Azusa Street Movement." He now told his brethren that he realized he had been deceived by a lying spirit who must "want to disunite the children of God and to bring souls into fanaticism." He alleged that in order to delay the final victory, Satan had sent demonic spirits to infiltrate God's host. It was an angel of Satan who was presently offering false gifts, false prophesying, and false visions, he declared. Satan had got in among the saints. He wrote:

> We allowed ourselves to be controlled from the tongue outward, and when the spirit of the tongue is accepted as the spirit of the Lord the individual becomes simply a slave.
>
> Deception, confusion and division is Satan's work since it frustrates the evangelization of the world.

The Resolutions

The last speaker was Pastor Dolman who deplored Dollmeyer's accusations and advised moderation. He said, "I kept my peace because I had no commission from the Lord to judge brethren whom I love and esteem."

Dolman certainly accepted "tongues" as a praise instrument when the heart was overflowing and needed another language. He said, "It is certainly not correct to say that every brother who has had special experiences this last year has been deceived by a lying spirit. It would certainly hinder God's work if we kept on being afraid or if we said, 'We don't want anything unusual,' or if we didn't believe that God could do great new things among us."

It looks as though his calm, irenic spirit prevailed at the conference held at Barmen on December 19,1907, for the members eventually decided on six months of silent consideration. A number felt that they should lay down general guidelines that could be resubmitted and endorsed later. The guidelines were:

> We acknowledge that God might give all gifts of the Spirit in our own day. The church should allow herself to be ready.
>
> We state the solemn fact that in the movement at Cassel and other places, many recognized as believers received a gift of tongues and prophecy which was not of the Holy Spirit.
>
> We acknowledge there has been a lack of trying the spirits.
>
> We confess this lack to be GUILT on the part of large circles of the church and we implore all children of God to humble themselves with us in this matter and to beseech the Lord to have mercy upon us and to heal us.
>
> In deep consciousness of how necessary it is to close our being to every strange spirit, we warn our brethren and sisters not to let themselves be carried away. We advise them most strongly to hold back in holy reserve with watching and prayers. What we need is not sensational experiences and visions but diligent, persevering searching of the Scriptures with sobriety of mind, personal surrender, and a holy walk in the fear of God.

By the end of 1908, the various leaders of the tongues movements in Germany had decided to hold a separate conference that was fully committed to the new teaching. They met in Hamburg and they invited Polhill and Boddy from Britain, T. B. Barratt from Norway, Cooke-Collins from Switzerland, Polman from Holland, and Johnson from Sweden. A new magazine called, *Pentecostal Greeting*, edited by Pastor Meyer of Hamburg and Pastor Paul of Berlin, was to be the channel of their teaching. Thus the evangelical party in Germany separated into two camps.

Jessie Penn-Lewis felt it was important to give these debates and resolutions full coverage in the *Christian Press* of Britain and worked hard to convince the editors. Eventually, she was invited to the 1909 Conference of the uncommitted group whose leaders made one more attempt to come to terms with the tongues movement. Her articles in *The Christian* during the latter half of 1908, show unmistakable signs that she had become far more distrustful of the new movement and more especially about what they called "manifestations" or "signs." She had received a small number of letters from Scandinavia where T. B. Barratt had spread the new message of "baptisms with tongues," but had promised other "signs." Many of Barratt's statements aroused hostility, especially his story of how tongues of fire had come upon him and how he had sung in some language of angels. Several conventions in Scandinavia, Germany and Switzerland were disturbed by claims and counterclaims and the upshot was the setting up of separate prayer and praise fellowships.

The great German debate came to a climax when this public repudiation was made by a much respected leader:

> I have to humble myself because I did not make use of real watchfulness and did not try the spirits but let him use power over me. This spirit revealed himself

> in tongues, prophecy and dreams, pretending to be the Spirit of God and speaking in Bible words. I entreat all those souls who came under the influence of this spirit to refuse him their obedience and then be cleansed in the Blood of Jesus.
>
> We must keep aloof from this spirit who wants to disunite the children of God and bring souls into some fanaticism,

For many months, they followed his advice to test the spirits before they pronounced their final verdict. Jessie Penn-Lewis was able to then inform the world that a large group of respected leaders had decided to distance themselves from the tongues movement, not because there was no such gift but because there had been too many examples of deception and self-delusion, and too many ways in which the powers of darkness could invade and destroy.

Jessie appears to have used this period of meditation and study to get hold of a remarkable collection of the original Pentecostalist free newspapers from the United States. This gave her a unique opportunity to study the various branches of infant Pentecostalism. Each of the twelve newspapers had its pages of testimony about healings, visions of Jesus, involuntary movements of tongue and limbs, ecstasies, prophetic messages, singing in the spirit ,and so on. She saw very clearly that there was a great variety of Pentecostalist and tongues movements, some of which were fierce critics of the others. What Jessie was looking for was not the testimonies but the signs of deception and "soulishness" or " carnality". We need to make a quick survey of these newspaper sources.

> *Pentecostal Wonders*, published in Akron, Ohio, claimed that tongues speaking was God's final answer to the materialists and skeptics. It was the sign of spiritual conflict in the last days since it was always opposed by

"dark forces." This paper admitted that there had been extravagances and unseemly things but it asserted, "Anyone who discourages, disparages, prevents or forbids this speaking in tongues will find sooner or later that they have incurred the displeasure of God. The directors— William Seymour, Miss Campbell, Mrs. Hudson, and Mrs. Mary Davies—held strongly pre-millennialist views and took the same view as Jessie Penn-Lewis on an imminent world-conflict with Satan's hosts.

Pentecostal Witness, published in Illinois, claimed that they had restored and cleansed "Zion City" and made it ready for an influx of people baptized in the Spirit and prepared to renounce property, medicines, surgery, and certain foods. One leader—John Lake—denounced any tendency to hierarchical organization and another—Bryant—made short work of "hissers and shakers."

Pentecostal Testimony was the voice of William Durham of Chicago, Illinois, who rejected formal associations, organized missions, systems and leadership pyramids of any kind. Durham rejected any claims that the Pentecostal experience and truth could percolate through existing denominations. He also denied that there had to be a second stage of sanctification before one could be baptized with the Spirit. The baptism of the Spirit would be sufficient to remove all the inbred corruption and sin-inclinations because of the finished Work of the Cross. Yet those baptized with tongues would not be perfect and would still need to take up their daily cross and live the fully crucified life.

The Apostolic Light, published in Washington, DC, was the first to warn that if those who receive the baptism with the Holy Ghost and speak in tongues backslide from

> that state, they may retain speaking in tongues for a while after the divine love has gone, but gradually this gift will also melt away. There was a clear link between the gifts and the quality of faith.
>
> *The Apostolic Faith,* published in Los Angeles, California, was the organ of many Azusa Street leaders and of the Pacific Apostolic Faith Movement. It offered the hand of fellowship to Atterbury and Ryan of the much older Holiness movement. Like the Overcomer Testimony founded by Jessie Penn-Lewis, it said that no further gifts of the Spirit were bestowed until one had been, "Sanctified through the Cross and called to holiness. In all Jesus' great miracles, the work was wrought by the power of the Holy Ghost flowing through His sanctified humanity. The baptism always falls upon a clean heart."
>
> Months later, in volume 20, one of the articles stated, "God Almighty is not pouring His Spirit on unclean vessels. Some say you have no need of a second work of grace and false teachers are trying to rob children of their sanctification. It wipes out carnality for ever. Sanctified people do not fight the truth."

Jessie could have adjusted to this kind of teaching, but must have been put off when this same newspaper carried extraordinary stories about anointed handkerchiefs, and men cured by tying their newspaper to damaged limbs. Such untested stories traveled far and wide—and still do. On page 4 of volume 1, there was printed the story of a Mrs.Hebden—a story that Jessie would surely condemn because that lady spoke openly about the Spirit seizing and clasping and shaking her hands and causing the hands to strike every part of her body. She said, "Later I was moved to exclaim loudly and on Monday I was made to sing. The Holy Ghost seemed to lift me and carry me."

> *Word and Work*, printed in Massachusetts, claimed to be the mouthpiece of a newly revived movement in Los Angeles that believed that the "Latter Rain " teaching had stopped short of the full truth. One writer, Mr. Otis, damned advanced education, divorce and remarriage, and other moral defects that had marred their movement. A great deal of attention is paid to the sayings of Dr. Lillian Yoakum, whose "Pisgah Movement" had carried out supernatural healings among the dropouts and derelicts.
>
> The most extreme of these North American periodicals was the *Intercessory Ministry*, edited by Mr. Street and published in Fort Wayne, Indiana. The editor was very fond of italics and heavy capital letters for all kinds of amazing announcements. Contributors seem to be working on night shift somewhere when they write. They make a very unusual claim, "Every word of this has been written while we were speaking or singing in tongues. Sometimes even shouting at the top of our voices in joy of praise and happiness in God Himself. It does not in the least interfere with the work of writing or thinking , because it is done in the Spirit."

These are the men who wrote in error that Jesus could not speak in other tongues while He lived in an earthly setting and in a different dispensation. Therefore it followed that Jesus' teaching through the Spirit-baptized apostles was more important than His own direct teaching when in Galilee.

In volume 3, the editor narrated how he himself had received baptism and speaking in tongues after days of determined struggle and many months to reach the lower part of the valley of humiliation. Finally, he was empty in thought, his body laid flat and his speech organs used to start laughter, groanings, and finally a heavenly anthem. He said he was taught to heal by "moving my hands in the air a few inches above the body of the sick until a mighty power of fire and life streamed into the sick." For the reception of the gifts, Street advised all the seekers, "Tarry in confidence, let go all past experiences, stop thinking of anything but Christ, avoid curiosity over what is happening, forget yourself and others and even time and let your body be used in order to destroy your pride. When He takes complete possession of you, He will have your tongue—the last rebel."

Equally controversial was his claim, "There is only one act that any man can perform to prove he has had the true Pentecostal experience and that is to speak in tongues." He added, "To try to solve our problems of work and witness without this gift is an artificial forced condition."

Almost certainly it was this hyped-up, dogmatic form of Pentecostalism that Jessie Penn-Lewis chose to write against in her articles on the American movement in *The Christian* in late 1908. These wrong teachings and practices were fiercely attacked in the United States and some of the attackers wrote to Jessie for support. The greatest scandal was that the main groups denounced each other's views because some were dispensationalists, some were strong advocates of believers' baptism, and some came from Holiness sects. Every attempt to set up some kind of Pentecostal league broke down and there were numerous examples of splinter-groups being formed. This evidence in itself would have confirmed Jessie's view that demonic forces had crept into the Pentecostal movement in order to cause confusion and division everywhere.

Jessie would have done well, however, to approach more moderate movements and magazines such as *The Apostolic Messenger* (Winnipeg, Canada), which pleaded for a suspended judgment. Could she have held out an olive branch to the tongues movements if she had only the moderates to deal with? Was it unfortunate that her missionary friends told her far more about the way-out Barratt movement than about the quieter groups? Were the experiences and phenomena that emerged in 1908 and 1909 the real source of her stern opposition later? The answers to these questions will be clearer after we have studied the experiences of the tongues movement in England.

17

Jessie Penn-Lewis and the English Tongues Movement

In spirit, Jessie was a good deal closer to the English movement centered upon Sunderland where Vicar Alexander Boddy poured out his new truth through a number of periodicals and booklets. The Rev. Boddy had stood with Evan Roberts in revival meetings and had been thrilled by the evidences of the Holy Spirit's work in their midst. But, by the following year, he was seeking something more, and he heard with joy about a new kind of blessing in Azusa Street Mission in Los Angeles, California, and other places. Eagerly he sought the same blessing and found himself worshipping the Lord in "new tongues."

As he testified to this in his church and community, others experienced the Spirit in this and other ways. He felt he should publish their testimonies in the form of little booklets under such attention catching headings as, *A Plumber's Testimony, Testimony of a Vicar's Wife, Testimony of a Lancashire Builder, A Vicar's Testimony, A Carlisle Brother's Testimony,* and *A China Missionary's Witness.*

When Boddy's presentation of tongues as essential to Spirit-baptism blessing was questioned, he defended his position in six booklets:

Manifestation of Truth;
These Signs Shall Follow;
Prophetic Message;
Speaking in Tongues—Is this of God?
*A Safety Signal (*a seminal book of apologetics);
Pentecostal Baptism (a counsel to leaders and others).

Boddy launched his British magazine in April 1908. He called it *Confidence*, and announced that it would bear faithful testimony, whatever the opposition, to the doctrine of, "Pentecost with Signs—beginning with the sign of the tongues." He stated that such a gift had been foretold, had been bestowed upon holy people, and had been followed by the "latter rain" of healings and prophesyings to which the column reports bore witness.

Boddy started gently but soon grew bolder in that he would not permit hostile critics or even waverers to enter their conferences but only those who stated, "I am in full sympathy with those who are seeking Pentecost with the sign of the tongues." After a while, he made links with Welshman, T. Madoc Jeffreys, and with G. B. Studd of Peniel Hall, in Los Angeles. He held a conference and invited the evangelist T. B. Barratt from Norway, whose charismatic personality fascinated them all.

The June volume of Boddy's magazine (1908) has a valuable picture of the early conferences where warnings were often pronounced against people going to extremes or neglecting the elementary task of training before they went about or abroad, or against those who forgot to test traveling messengers who spoke falsehoods in the name of the Holy

Spirit. One conference discussed "The Nine Gifts" on Tuesday, "Prophetic Messages" on Wednesday, "The Unconscious Mind" on Thursday, "False Messages" on Friday and "The Warrior Spirit" on the last evening. These earnest debates were lightened by hours and hours of spontaneous adoration.

On the whole, the magazine *Confidence* was a serious and creative effort. It was a far cry from the magazine *Victory,* which treated both Boddy and Barratt as if they were the only authorized, inspired European apostles of the Azusa Street Mission in California. The editors would not permit any questioning or criticism of the movement. This magazine always featured the sensational healings, the angelic messages, the singing in the spirit ,and other subjective experiences that were the chief objects of Jessie Penn-Lewis's attacks in 1908-1910.

Jessie also had more respect for the more balanced Pentecostalist magazine, *Flames of Fire*, which denied satanic influences and said that the so-called deceptions were due to muddled people, clever counterfeiters, and showy persons who had been given far too much attention at the start. But this magazine also promoted, "Waiting Meeting" or "Tarryings." *Tarrying* was not a passive process but a combination of "struggle prayer" and self-preparation for the entrance of the gifts; beginning, of course, with speaking in tongues. Jessie picked on this process as an example of how fleshly elements had crept in and seduced fine saints. She would have rejected claims that "in this Latter Rain Revival the gifts of the Spirit have all been restored." Eventually, Jessie was receiving and using very hostile testimony, alleging that too many healing stories were unauthenticated.

There was another magazine belonging to a smaller group that was directed by Pastor Cantell of the Maranatha Movement. It strongly emphasized Spirit baptism and Holy Spirit healings but paid scant attention to tongues. It had a definite ethical theme such as anointing and sanctification and the need for Christ-likeness. It may not be accidental that this magazine was also named *The Overcoming Life*. Some of the notes in it are very close to Jessie's own calls to "take the Cross and the Blood."

Turning now from the magazines to the correspondence, one of the most interesting packets consists of notes going to and fro between Boddy, Barratt's disciples, and Jessie Penn-Lewis's friends. A very earnest and loving effort was made to find a middle way, or at least to understand and not despise each other. Vicar Boddy wrote a personal letter to her asking her not to discourage people who had "received the fullness" and not to join with others in "a mighty effort to keep out of Great Britain this sign which the Lord is giving and which He had promised." Boddy believed that Jessie's writings could actually have led people along the way to the full blessing. On the other hand, Jessie never doubted Boddy's sincerity or graciousness, and at one point she prepared a very friendly letter, but it was never sent.

On October 11, 1907, Jessie visited the same meetings at which T. B. Barratt was introduced. At first, she resolved to watch impartially and communicate with the Boddy's in an informal way. However, having met a number of very unimpressed eyewitnesses, she prepared a far more hostile letter—October 28, 1907— that would have put the fat in the fire:

> I cannot be true to God without writing to you in His Name to say how pained and grieved I am to hear of such manifestations being attributed to the Holy Ghost. I feel deep in my soul that you and Mrs. Boddy and others with you are yielding to false supernatural forces.

In effect, she accused the Boddy's of letting their guest preacher, Mr. Barratt, transmit alien powers into the bodies of all those he touched. The rest of the letter is still more severe, and it is hardly surprising that it was scrapped. The letter actually sent was more moderate in that she expressed continuous prayerful concern:

> I know and see in what a terrible position you are. You have committed yourselves to a line of things which is bringing upon you a storm of trouble. I see what the suffering and strain and antagonism must mean to you but if you could only get out of the center and look at it from outside, you yourselves would see developments coming which will prove to you that there are other spirits at work in your midst. I am most grieved for your dear wife.

The "dear wife" was said to be more passionate about the new tongues speaking than her husband, and there is in the box of Jessie's materials a note from Mrs. Boddy expressing her indignation. In November 1907, Boddy wrote to Jessie again to announce that they were all at the beginning of a new spiritual movement that would shake everything that could be shaken. He feared that Satan was making people so obsessed with possible counterfeits and delusions that they had lost sight of the fact that "the Holy Spirit can and does manifest Himself more powerfully and wonderfully. They minimize the power and the care of Christ for His people and they flee from abandonment to God."

A second letter dated November 12, 1907, firmly denied that there was anything carnal or satanic going on. Everything was "under the Blood" and they had resisted all fleshly tendencies and sought that only God should be glorified. Boddy gave her his personal assurance, "I tell you that I have a desire, my only desire, to live and speak for Him. I have known great blessing in those waiting times and great joy when speaking in the Spirit."

The Rev. and Mrs. Boddy wanted an independent private conversation with Evan Roberts and invited him to come and hear testimonies from those who had "received," in order that he could see they were scriptural and that they too desired the "pure center of every revival." Jessie felt it safer to invite the Boddy's to come to her home and to have helpful conversations with Evan Roberts, "who has clear light on the matter and is greatly burdened about you." These were unwise words, and the rest of her reply in her November 1907 letter likewise slammed the door on reconciliation:

> I understand the intensity and reality of your motives and I am praying that God will unveil among you all that is not from Him. I can only write most urgently and pray you for Jesus sake to turn to the Lord. I have cried to the Lord for His will to be shown concerning a way of meeting. But God is giving me a work to do on these dangers.

Whatever was the exact relationship between Boddy and Barratt, there is no doubt that it was the latter who incurred the full wrath of denominational leaders and *Christian Press* correspondents. Sometime during 1907, Jessie received a letter from Norway that pictured a typical Barratt meeting:

> There was an electric surge and the atmosphere clanged and pure adoration was exchanged into a strained expectation of wonders. Eyes flashed and cheeks burnt when Barratt began to sing a "song without words" before he solemnly promised them "the gift." Every person there dropped down and waited.

This eyewitness and correspondent, who was named Anna, told Jessie that she was standing close to Barratt and felt as if she was at the side of an electric battery. Stories like this circulated and eventually reached the national press of several countries. Someone got hold of the fact that he openly encouraged quite young children to be filled with the Spirit and have power to be witnesses. Eventually more stories came in from his overseas journeyings.

The situation reached a crisis point in India, which had known such blessing in 1905-1906. Now the work was in total disarray as some groups honored T. B. Barratt's work and welcomed representatives of the tongues movement, whilst others gathered up stories that discredited the whole thing—not only the exploiting of children's feelings, but the blatant whipping up of hysteria among scores of uneducated people who were ready to overlook the fact that a confident prediction of an earthquake coming upon a sinful city proved to be a myth. To read Stanley Frodsham's account of healings and exorcisms in 1908 in India and China is to walk in a different world.

Many of the criticisms by missionaries disposed Jessie against all such events. A Mr. Findlater, who was closely linked with Indian affairs, confronted one Barratt group successfully at a conference in London. He sent his analysis of certain of their meetings to Vicar Boddy with a request to send a copy to Mr. Barratt. His first doubt was whether the many people seeking and claiming the gift of tongues had even been converted let alone sanctified unto the Lord. Such people could easily fall back into sin and this would invalidate the claim that tongues' were full, absolute proof that they were baptized with the Spirit. His second misgiving was about the constant linking of baptism and tongues with "torturing physical shakings." He definitely rejected Mr. Barratt's methods such as the pressing of heads.

In Barratt's tract, *Pentecost NOT Hypnotism*, he admitted that both phenomena used animal magnetism and automatic movements, but he claimed that he always took great care that each seeker had been cleansed and had not been enslaved or overawed by the ones who were laying on hands and exhorting them. Findlater argued that power through animal magnetism was not the same as power from the Holy Ghost and the two must never be mingled because one was "of man." The tongues movement should not be encouraged, he said, until these things were dealt with clearly. He challenged Boddy and Barratt to give an impartial examination in the light of the Scriptures and history.

A copy of this powerful analysis was sent to Jessie Penn-Lewis, who was not impressed by Barratt's books about *Pentecostal Visions* and *With Signs*. They seemed to her to be pieces of special pleading, but she gave more credit to his booklets, especially the tract entitled *A Friendly Talk with Ministers and Christian Workers*, which describe in glowing terms how a personal Pentecost would transform the ministry of priest, missioner, and church officer, and would restore power and energy and "light" to any church.

Jessie Penn-Lewis could find no fault with Barratt's personality and wrote these gracious prayerful words, "His spirit is most beautiful and the inward man seems very Christ-like. It appears to me that unknown to himself the enemy has whipped up some natural magnetism."

Because of her bold articles in *The Christian* about "perils," Jessie received innumerable letters that ranged from the enthusiastic through the interested, the tolerant, the confused, and the openly hostile. A Mrs. Dresser from South London told her that their leader, Mrs. Price, who was closely linked with the Sunderland group and who had been the first to receive Holy Ghost baptism, was attracting people from all walks of life. She had built up a circle who were looking to her in hope of a greater manifestation than before. In her meetings, according to Mrs. Dresser, there were prostrations, holy laughter, and a form of exaltation that looked like the Transfiguration scenes.

From London also, an Elizabeth Baker reported that even if there were some counterfeits, there was a genuine Pentecost with speaking in tongues and with other demonstrations of the Spirit such as shakings and prostrations and heavenly anthems. As before the plea was, "We must not lose the real thing through fleeing. Just put in your claim for the gift, and then trust God to keep you. Go ahead!"

Someone from Erdington in the Midlands assured Jessie that the experience of tongues had come to those who had never heard of Pastor Barratt and that all they had needed was a kind of cleansing. Yet another correspondent pointed out that the new message of Boddy and Barratt seemed to be a filling out of her own teachings. W. B. Sayers, who was involved in the "Church Revival Mission" in Glasgow, was a strong advocate of praising in tongues. He used the verse, "Cry out and shout, O children of Zion!" to justify allowing the unlettered converts and the slow of tongue to join in "spiritual praise." He wrote Jessie this letter:

> Let those who have realized by faith that they are filled with the Holy Ghost and have received the power to confess Christ and who find themselves freed from miserable chains of convention and self-consciousness, let them burst out in jubilation. If words fail them let them make a joyful noise before the Lord.

On the other hand, many a voice was raised in opposition to the tongues movement in Britain. Support for Jessie's stand came from several mission and prayer circle leaders who had seen their groups divided as the cry for more gifts grew stronger. Most vocal was an Ann Kilvington who alleged that entire churches were deceived as they became charmed with the offer of the gifts. The running after tongues, she alleged, was actually hindering England from a deeper Pentecost. A Mary Lloyd wrote Jessie on February 7, 1908, that she feared that one effect would be that more would resist leadings of God in things of the Spirit and would fall asleep spiritually. A much older correspondent said that he had known many movements since 1875 and that anyone truly baptized of the Spirit would show love, grace, and humility, which seemed to be sadly lacking in the tongues movement. Jessie said firmly at one point that this was certainly not the case with Alexander Boddy.

What eventually made Jessie pause and reconsider her harsh judgments were letters from people like a Mr. Fell of Rochester, who testified gladly about the sense of being delivered from a barren, joyless Christianity. His letter concluded, "The Holy Spirit never does anything rude or unseemly. We have a sweetness of the presence of the Lord that only the Holy Dove could bring. So! Ask God to give you what He has for you. He will not let you go." This was written lovingly.

Exactly the same impact was made by letters from very old friends such as Mrs. Groves, the missionary who had joined in the Latter Rain experience, and testified that it had given her a fuller sight of Christ her Savior as truly the Son of God come in the flesh. Though trying to remain meek and humble, Mrs. Groves said she had no choice but to stand alone for this new revelation if necessary. This letter ended with a loving plea to Jessie Penn-Lewis to receive the new blessing—but Jessie replied by asking Mrs. Groves never to impose her experience on others who have a different understanding. She wrote:

> The important thing is to go deeper and deeper until we reach the very roots of faith down in the Cross, and

> from there ascend into a life of purity and worship, of which "Tongues" could be one expression. Let us pray together for the defeat of Satan and for all the faithful watchmen on their watchtowers.

One has just a glimpse here of a way in which the sad divisions and misunderstandings could have been overcome. But, for the time being, hundreds of sincere men and women looked for more light. Nothing shows this more clearly than the many letters of Yorkshireman J. W. Whiteley to Jessie Penn-Lewis. At first, he had taken heed to D. M. Panton's vigorous words about a pretend spiritual movement that had been spawned by the prince of darkness (Letter dated December 9, 1907). But he had been deeply impressed by a personal meeting with the Boddy's and said that he desired to pray for them because they had such love and courage. Unfortunately, they had made no attempt to stop many questionable effects but rather rejoiced in these. He was sure they were dear children of God intent on following the Lord but unbalanced by certain texts and in need of discernment. He, himself, he said, could not believe that the days of the Apostles would return except in new missionary areas like China, because "where there is abundant testimony of God's saving power, what need of adding physical manifestations?"

At first, Whiteley wanted Jessie Penn-Lewis to sound the alarm more forcefully, but when he had read A. J. Gordon's *Spirit of God,* he became convinced that a present day "personal Pentecost" was a possibility after all. Now he argued that the false prophets were causing the confusion and that if the right tests were used and the movement was really exalting Jesus, Son of God, a great deal of the strange happenings were acceptable and there could be understanding and mutual love.

Perhaps Jessie Penn-Lewis would have moved towards the same understanding long before she and Evan Roberts sat down to write *War on the Saints*. But her intimate connection with the tongues movement in India and her studies in German and American experiences turned her in another direction. The earlier articles on "The Hour of Peril" in *The Christian* in 1908, began with pleas for avoiding all teachings that divided asunder the saints, and continued with a long tribute to the thirty pastors who met at the Barmen Conference and did their utmost to calm things down. In her third article, however, she put together all the statements from California that suggested that the tongues movement had been overrated. Only two weeks later, she was using such words as deception, lawlessness, confusion, and unfruitful experiences. Then came her main attack on the tongues movement. The followers' deliberate passivity was a snare to their minds and a menace to their souls, she said—yet as late as March 1909, she was still pleading for openness and re-examination. Her last message to the leaders was, "Let us aim by every possible means to keep the unity of the Spirit in the bond of peace; then God will bruise Satan shortly."

In the years 1911-1912, when she and Evan Roberts were preparing the manual known as *War on the Saints*, her attitude towards the "tongues and signs movement" was hardening and she was endorsing the severe condemnation of D. M. Panton of Norwich, and the verdict of the Rev. R. B. Jones that the movement and become self-deceived and divisive.

18

Testings and Oppositions

At the same time as Jessie Penn-Lewis was in the throes of a long struggle with the many fringe movements associated with the first phase of Pentecostalism, she was coming under attack from other directions. This was all the more hurtful because it came from former prayer-partners and from prominent men who had once praised her. Pastors, preachers, conference members, editors, and Welsh ministers, were all on a collision course with her by late 1907. Little wonder that, on January 8, 1908, she sent a circular letter to the beloved prayer warriors—telling them, "The conflicts are intensifying and the assaults increasing upon the work of proclaiming the Cross."

The first signs of trouble were some murmuring that the 1906 Keswick was being threatened by the presence of mercurial and over-emotional Welsh people such as Evan Roberts, Jessie Penn-Lewis, and other revival leaders. One writer deplored the crying and the applauding as harmful to the discipline of the convention meetings. Evan Roberts spoke out of turn in the overflow meetings and, despite the startling effects of his exhortation to give themselves to the Master and ask Him to deliver them through the Blood of His Cross, he was asked not to repeat this kind of sobbing and pleading. Now, in the pavilion on that same Sunday, Jessie Penn-Lewis had also spoken about liberty and victory through the Cross, and an observer said that her voice rang through the building and that her tones and the sob of intensity swayed hundreds of hearts. First, she piled up a pyramid of texts supporting her declarations, and then she asked them directly to claim deliverance and demanded a minute's silence. A great hush fell and a great awe. One after the other, each man and woman began to say, "I take the full victory of Calvary today."

This was exactly what certain leaders had feared and they felt worse when they heard that Jessie and Evan Roberts had visited the YMCA camp and spoken to a crowd of young men about this liberating power of the Cross. A correspondent for *The Christian* reported in the August 6, 1906 edition that once again there was a shower of confessions, after which Evan Roberts spoke to them about full surrender and "reckoning yourselves dead" as a sure and certain way to victory.

For months after that convention, the criticisms increased in volume, especially when it was discovered that local conventions inside and outside Wales were showing the same signs of excitement. Some letters to the *Christian Press* were suggesting that Jessie Penn-Lewis's writings also tended to stir up strong emotions. There were conservative gentlemen who queried whether there should be any room for a woman's ministry, except in the ladies' meeting, which ought preferably to be held in some nearby hall. Jessie replied angrily that the trustees had undertaken to give her full freedom in 1906, but were now out to restrict her. Then she spoke out with quite astonishing boldness:

> It will be of very grave importance to the whole Church of Christ if Keswick officially sets its face against women speaking to mixed audiences when, at this time, God is using women in a very marked way. The whole current of life moving through the spiritual Church is towards clear and open ground for women in the work of God. I have been invited to take a service in one of the chapels and I have no alternative but to accept. I cannot stay in line without a sacrifice of principle and a disobedience to God. The Lord has set the seal of blessing on my messages at Keswick, where many have come up to receive the message not the messenger. Out of loyalty I must state the people's wishes.

The Keswick Council saw to it that she had no further place in which to proclaim her message of the Cross. By 1910, she had virtually withdrawn from the movement, pleading pressure of work. Meanwhile her own conventions and workers' conferences and magazine had taken off.

A number of respected Bible teachers had also begun to find fault with the teachings of Jessie at this time. Dr. Pierson, who had worked well with her during the conventions in Wales, was now writing critical letters—enclosing cuttings of her essays and booklets about the Cross that had disturbed him. He wanted to contrast the Keswick principle of cleansing and victory by faith in Christ's finished work, with what he called, "Your struggle theory invoking self-purification and self-mortification." Some of her language, he said, sounded like the mystic cults who also talked of "Entering into the pangs of the Cross." Then he rebuked her more severely:

> We are never told to crucify self but only to mortify what is already reckoned dead. To tell a man in the agony of his conflict with temptation to overcome by the Blood

> of the Lamb is unintelligible unless he takes hold of the fruits of Christ's finished work without further effort and struggle.

In his July letter to her, he pictured Satan as exploiting the search for holiness by making sincere people morbid, self-disgusted and so despairing that they become open to delusions. He called Jessie's ideas "out of proportion or unbalanced." Can one imagine her reading at the breakfast table this letter from one whom she greatly honored? What heartache!

Other people besides Dr. Pierson would certainly have objected to the dark pessimism of certain statements in her 1911 book, *The Conquest of Canaan*. For example this urgent warning:

> The wily foe can wait for twenty years, until he thinks you have forgotten all about something in your character which God dealt with and you thought you would never have to face the matter again. Twenty years afterwards it is attacked by the enemy without your knowing until some occasion comes which causes you to discover that the devil is quietly aiming at the old place of weakness.

Such a statement would surely go against all the divine promises of blotting out trespasses and. cleansing from all sin. Where was her usual emphasis on Romans 6, which offered every servant of God in Christ a full deliverance from the dominion of sin?

Many godly people wrote to the *Christian Press* editors to complain that Jessie Penn-Lewis should never have raised such issues as Satanic deception because most Christians were unaware such things could arise. Others got agitated if she mentioned a few of the "doubtful practices" in too great detail.

Few would have agreed with Dr. F. B. Meyer that she was the only one offering to guide perplexed souls. Writing from abroad, he said, "The watchman should blow the trumpet and warn the people." On January 27, 1907, Jessie made a direct appeal to Mr. Morgan, who owned the journal, to allow her far more freedom to deal with the tongues movement in its variant forms. He replied that he could not allow the tongues debate to dominate the magazine. Jessie explained that she was planning a much longer and balanced article, which task brooked no delay. In fact, the longer article was held back and there was talk of cutting her out altogether, just when she wanted to do her final assessments based on fresh information from India. She told Mr. Morgan, "I shall send all further details from abroad and give out the light God taught me in the cause of their getting into delusion."

Jessie had tried the dove-like approach to moderate forms of Pentecostalism and her only reward was a set of protest letters that charged her with being too keen to give out "details instead of doctrines." One critic said, "Please find us a level-headed Christian who will deal with these matters maturely." Her "Hour of Peril" articles in the *Christian Press* were terminated during 1908.

The editors of *The Christian* and the *Life of Faith* were upset once more by a report of her convention at Leicester. Jessie allowed herself to say in an indiscreet press release, "The chair was empty and the Holy Spirit was the only President." Soon letters arrived from several countries saying that there were local meeting leaders who were copying this as if it were an article of faith to tarry for the direct guidance and control of the Spirit. It was alleged that such meetings went out of control or lost meaning, and that the *empty chair* often led to an empty experience.

Before long, a chorus of Pentecostal prophets and evangelists were also speaking against her. For the next ten years, in one way or another, virtually every Pentecostal journal deplored her interferences and set out to prove that she was not a worthy interpreter or safe guide.

By November 1908, the editors of *The Life of Faith* were also hinting to Jessie that she should have a bi-weekly and not a weekly feature, and that this would save her from "laboring points" and "spinning words." Her reply was an appeal to let things continue as they had been.

> So that I can do the Bible studies when the full power is flashing and pouring and when the Spirit of God is burning my heart with some message. May I not take responsibility for what I write myself? If not, there are other channels ready to print all that can be said by myself and by Evan Roberts, who has the light which souls are needing.

They replied unwisely that she ought not to make Evan Roberts into an oracle, "Let us encourage him to go softly and learn of Christ and of his brethren."

Jessie called this "harmful talk," and the links with the *Life of Faith* came to an end that year. In January 1909, she wrote to her trusted friends all over the world to tell them that she and Evan Roberts would find another way to prepare Christians for revival and warfare. She alleged that both Keswick and the journals had lost the vision—but her own attitude has also changed. Her article, "The Key to Revival" in the June 1911 issue of *Living Waters*, published in Nashville, Tennessee, proves this.

> Many are praying in India and in Wales for the revival to be revived whilst others are so troubled about the excrescences which have accompanied revival that they shrink from asking for such a doubtful blessing as "a fresh revival wave." The adversary challenges every

> revival move of the Holy Spirit and seeks to frighten by his imitations the most earnest children of God. Looked at from this standpoint, it is a most solemn thing for any to fear or shrink, rather than earnestly seeking to know how to co-operate with God and how to check and defeat the workings of Satan by weighing and proving and learning the ways of God.
>
> The outcome of the last three years' fiery trial to the Church of Christ is that the pure work of the Spirit of God is now becoming recognizable, and the fleshly and soulish has grown equally discernible. The past revival can be seen as a training ground for world revival; that's how Mr. Evan Roberts sees it. Do not ask for the revival to be revived, but expect that a far greater and purer movement of the Holy Spirit is coming which will quicken all members of the Body of Christ.
>
> . . . Ask the Holy Spirit to reveal to each child of God all that the finished work of Calvary means in preparation for the awakening, for herein lies the key to a pure revival. A purer revival is possible if the servants of God will but go back to Calvary and in simple faith use—the victor's cry, "IT IS FINISHED"—the final cry of victory over the world, the flesh and the devil. (From the tract, *It is Finished.*)

Had Jessie Penn-Lewis lost faith in the Keswick conventions only because the leaders had sidelined her at a time when so many ministers and laity were blessed that one minister wrote, "Just leave the issue with the Lord Himself"? She had a courageous champion in Dr. F. B. Meyer who wrote from Shanghai on July 9, 1909, "I am praying for you in all this anxiety about Keswick and Llandrindod Wells. Of course, if they give you no door of utterance at Keswick, they have themselves to blame if you promote conventions of your own. I cannot but feel that the church does need those deeper aspects of Romans 6 and Colossians 2, which have been revealed to you. I do hope that Evan Roberts may be led to be with us in living co-operation." In fact, Evan Roberts encouraged her to break with the parent Keswick in 1910, and with the Keswick in Wales a year later.

The situation at the Welsh Keswick in Llandrindod had become increasingly disappointing. As one of the organizing secretaries, she found it harder and harder to balance different interests and she feared a major division. Chairman Albert Head said he was not in favor of nationalizing a convention that was founded upon the spiritual ideal of, "All One in Christ Jesus." Jessie tried to satisfy everyone but at length became rather bitter. "Had we seen clearly the possibility of relaxing a little and giving liberty for open prayer, we could have tided over a difficulty for a year or two," she lamented. At the same time, however, she grew weary of the attitudes of many of the Welshborn ministers and said, "It is beginning to dawn on me that they are naturally touchy." No wonder she felt they would not be prepared instruments of the expected revival.

About 1910, Jessie began to pull back from Keswick in Wales and its branch conventions. Urged on by Evan Roberts' telegram, she resigned and withdrew in August 1911—to the great regret of J. Rhys Davies and the intense distress of Mrs. Albert Head. Her letter of March 12, 1912, speaks of her hope that in the hereafter "all veils of all kinds will be gone forever and there will be perfect instead of partial vision."

Another form of severe trial also came from Wales—this time from Evan Roberts' family and from certain troublemakers. Its pressure became so intolerable that at the end only Evan Roberts himself could save the Penn-Lewis establishment from further insult. It has to be born in mind that in, 1906, a great number of people in Wales simply could not understand why their revival hero had been whisked away and then kept away from the tumult and the shouting. By and by, they heard about his complete nervous prostration (some called it a worse name), and of his weeks of confinement in one room and of the doctor's attendances. In this atmosphere, the Rev. Vyrnwy Morgan published his hostile account of the revival. He represented Evan as someone snatched from Wales and kept under wraps by F. B. Meyer and especially by Jessie Penn-Lewis. It was suggested that the patient was allowed only certain letters and was more or less forbidden to have family visits.

Jessie's private diaries—newly discovered—show, however, that this was not the truth. She escorted Evan's mother three times by train to Leicester; she arranged a friendly pre-Christmas visit for brother Dan Roberts, and she gave Evan a room to meet his friends. Yet rumors persisted until F. B. Meyer met one of the Welsh ministers and told him bluntly, "Mr. Roberts has a perfect right to choose his home."

The earlier stories about possible lunacy and restraint had been demolished by 1908, when Evan Roberts' first beautifully written Welsh booklets appeared. The rumors of captivity died out, but in their place came the malicious whispers that fifty-year-old Jessie Penn-Lewis was "soft on him," as they say in Wales.

A different tale said that William and Jessie were making money out of Evan, to which Jessie replied, "The books are not making a profit, there's no advertising revenue and only a few donations come—and anyway Evan doesn't keep money."

So now the press turned to the third theory, that the Penn-Lewises had come between Evan Roberts and his Welsh roots and had subjected his mind to undesirable revelations and influences. Again the answer was straight and surprisingly frank, "Evan does not want to meet his family anymore because you do not believe his present messages. That was the truth."

In November 1913, the well-known "Awsten," the *Western Mail* journalist, was sent to Cartref, Toller Load, Leicester. His mission was "to lift the veil of mystery which has enshrouded the position and attitude of the man who formed such a prominent figure in the revival." His resulting four-column report killed off more myths. He announced that Evan had his own latchkey and went out to chat with people whenever he pleased, that he often went out on his bicycle or went on trips in Mr. Penn-Lewis's car, and that he had his own guests at meals to whom he talked intelligently.

Awsten wrote, "I found no evidence of a disorderly mind but only of a special vision and a burden message." Awsten also learned that Evan held a Bible class in a kind of converted glasshouse (greenhouse) but that he also had strictly private quarters—sanctum—up above the morning-room. It was he who decided to reject every attempt by the family to take him back, because he now had a worldwide ministry.

The leader of the prayer band, J. C. Williams, also wrote to the South Wales Daily News, which printed his defense of Evan Roberts' right to live according to his conscience and guidance. Finally, in *The Overcomer*, Evan himself publicly acknowledged his benefactors and openly stated his spiritual debt to them before proceeding to describe the nature of his ministry since 1908. Eventually these ill-natured attacks on Jessie died out, but her frail body took the punishment of this and all the other trials. She was shockingly run-down in 1913, and was in no fit state to stand up to the controversy that broke out afresh a month or two after the appearance of *War on the Saints*.

Long before the publication date of this unique "manual," the authors had expressed fears that they would be misunderstood and that the message would be rejected unless it had full prayer-cover. The chapters which dealt with Deceptions, Counterfeits, the danger of attacking "passivity," and even greater danger of "total submission of reason," were widely praised and were printed separately later on. The lengthy final sections on triumphing through the Cross were accepted by many who longed for deliverance and who sent warm letters of appreciation and thanksgiving. There was also considerable criticism leveled at the book, however, not to mention the remarks made in the Pentecostalist press.

Firstly, the psychologists noted that the writers were blaming Satan and his demons for the kind of behavior that springs out of what they called the subconscious. Acute frustration and dark self-disgust, for example, are not to be attributed to an invasive force from outside but are natural parts of the human mechanism. Maybe Jessie and Evan forgot that Jesus had given His disciples a list of the horrid forces that came out of the heart of man.

Secondly, the teachers of pastoral theology and counseling were horrified by the Jessie Penn-Lewis/Evan Roberts thesis that men and women born of the Spirit could be "possessed" by the devil. Readers had not noticed Jessie's broad and too loose definition of the word "possessed" as meaning, "any hold which evil spirits have in or upon a person in any degree." What Jessie and Evan meant to warn against should be called "harassment" or "oppression."

Instead of backpedaling, however, Jessie stated dogmatically in *The Overcomer* that the more a man was in the Spirit, the more he needed to be guarded from the entrance of evil spirits. She even claimed, "IF THEY GET INSIDE THEY WILL MAKE HIM DO WHAT THEY WILL." Large numbers of Christians, then as now, rejected this theory in its entirety. Demon possession is not an option for those who are born of the Spirit, the Water, and the Blood. That which the Spirit has sealed cannot be usurped, or "hijacked," in this way.

Thirdly, there were the Pentecostal leaders who were convinced that everything written about phenomena and about counterfeits was aimed at them.

Finally, there were Calvinists who would have nothing to do with dispensations, raptures, the millennium, etc. In this manual they found a new cause for objecting to such teachings. Both Jessie and Evan had been taught that the prayers of earnest saints could hasten divine events and that the hesitations of saints could hinder and delay them. So the Body of Christ—that is, the entire fellowship of believers—could now delay the dispensation's ending, the return, and millennial age. In reply to this, the critics would say, quite correctly, that prayer-petitions are cooperative acts and not manipulative acts, and that they cannot change God's timings. The whole concept of prevailing prayer and of authority to bind the evil one came under attack in Britain, whereas some American teachers really tried to hasten things on.

The two authors' usual response to the critics was to re-explain each teaching in special columns in *The Overcomer*, and to assert that their testimony was true. A preface to a second edition of *War on the Saints* says, "The test of time has revealed no need for any fundamental modification of the truths set forth." Jessie and Evan gradually built up a collection of supportive testimonies, but there were abusive letters, too, which had caused much pain. There were signs in 1913 that Evan Roberts was disappointed in the book, but Jessie would not modify anything.

The years 1913 and 1914 must have been stressful but, in a little booklet, Jessie explained how she coped:

> Enduring grief, suffering wrongfully, with patience and a loving spirit, is the true spirit-life of one who is joined to Christ, in the attitude towards those human beings who are the visible and immediate cause of the suffering.

By this principle she lived daily and overcame tribulations. There were many testing times also for Jessie in the wartime years, but they were mostly of a physical nature.

Her diaries for 1915-1918 are brief indeed, and there are numerous references to pain and helpless weakness.

Then Jessie came face to face once more with Bible verses such as, "From henceforth be strong!" and "I can do all things through Christ who strengtheneth me." Soon she began to share this glorious secret of victory and not just endurance. In that same little tract, *More than Conquerors*, she expressed her new conviction:

> The devil knows the laws of the spiritual sphere and he whispers, "Oh, you do feel bad today." But God says, "Be strong!" Then you say, "By faith in God I am strong." Satan whispers, "You are going to break down," and you say, "I believe I shall break down," and you find yourself really going down. But now let the weak say, "I am strong." . . . "Be strong in the Lord!" That is a position. Take care that you never stand anywhere else.

Could any trial or tribulation destroy such an overcomer?

Part Four

The Minister to the Christian Workers

19

The Editor of *The Overcomer*

When Jessie Penn-Lewis and Evan Roberts began to plan the magazine that they hoped would equip Christian workers to live holy lives, and would instruct them how to fight faithfully against evil forces, they probably had a very modest project in mind. The first "Circular Letters" or "Cyclostyled Sheets" had been well received but looked amateurish and very impermanent. Whilst Jessie and Evan were jointly founding and staffing *The Overcomer*, other helpers were preparing a Bookroom on one side of the front hallway of Cartref. Jessie's faithful secretaries probably used one room for letters and interviews and the other, nearer the tradesman's side entrance, for the Bookroom.

A few years later, this work was using the talents and energies of six voluntary staff. Mr. Usher was seeing to the Workers' Conferences, J. C. Williams to the Prayer Band's expanding work, and Mr. Perryman to all the stenographic work from the conferences and from the magazine editors. Jessie always checked everything before it appeared in print.

From time to time, visitors would arrive from European countries and would spend a few days correcting the draft translations of her booklets before they were sent to Mullers of Barmen or Kobe of Basle or the Vainqueur office in Paris where the translated texts were published. Some Spanish editions were actually prepared in Argentina.

One presumes there was a business office squeezed onto the first floor where another volunteer managed the donations, bills, payments, and subscriptions. Somewhere, also, room had to be found for efficiency apartments for the secretaries and the housekeeper. This pressure did not ease up until 1914. When Awsten Davies the journalist visited "Cartref" in 1913, he noticed that even rooms near the family suite were adapted for the work and that in one shut off part of the upper hall, at the top of private stairs, Evan Roberts used to pray or write all the day long. Besides supervising translations of Jessie Penn-Lewis's booklets on *Communion with God* and *Spiritual Warfare*, he wrote his own pamphlets for the people of Wales. *Reckon Yourselves* presented his view of dying to sin and the world, and the pamphlet, *Preparation of Peace,* was a call to witnessing. *Why should the Church Pray?* was a practical manual about prayer-preparation, prayer-hindrances, prayer-burdens, and prayer-power.

In many different ways, the Bookroom at Toller Road spun its web over workers in all the world, yet the monthly magazine had to take precedence over everything else. When Jessie cut off all links with *The Christian* and *The Life of Faith*, she had to find another way to keep in close touch with all those in Britain, Europe, and the mission fields who believed in "the warfare." Circular letters were not enough. For several weeks she and Evan and some close friends met for days of prayer and discussion about the best way to bring together and help all those who were wholehearted enough and pure-spirited enough to take part in the warfare. Then Jessie and

Evan traveled to London and entered Stationers Hall and signed documents naming them as co-sponsors of a magazine to be entitled *The Overcomer*. The first edition announced that it was not intended for the general church membership, but for the "workers."

Clearly, *The Overcomer* was both a defensive and a nurturing project. Therefore there were several unusual features. There was no topical news, no branch reports, no devotional leads or sermonettes, no serial stories, and no appeals for missions and other good causes. One section was devoted to the Prayer Watch, with a list of requests. The main diet consisted of two presentations of "Overcomer" teaching and a two-page section for questions and answers, similar in nature to those discussed in the quarterly conferences. The monthly edition was underwritten, not by trade charges or advertisements, but by gifts from workers and covenanted support from friends who provided enough for the printing and distribution of about six thousand copies.

By one means or another, these magazines found their way to Europe, North and South America, India, China, and Central and Southern Africa. At some point, a Mr. Johnson branched out with a French and an Italian edition. The magazines seem to have been carried by angels into the remotest places, even as the ravens brought bread to Elijah. Two missionaries in mountainous West China were amazed to receive a bunch of back issues brought by runners over the high passes from the nearest city. Sometimes missionaries in riverside villages in the Congo would be commanded to catch hold of a bundle of tatty copies thrown from a passing boat—six monthly issues put together.

The two founders contributed about seventy five percent of the contents until 1913, when Jessie fell ill and had to depend on the two men—Evan and J. C. Williams—to provide more material.

Evan's first task was to prepare further notes on current deceptions and on other matters that were set out in full in *War on the Saints.* Then, in 1913, he began his Adventist messages, calling on readers to be ready for the "final translation," which was his term for the rapture of the saints. When this event failed to take place when he expected, he wrote essays about the delay factor caused by lack of full spiritual unity:

> Divisions must cease, disunity must be confessed, hasty judgments must be canceled, warnings against each other destroyed, certain books withdrawn, and tears of repentance shed.

He also wrote articles on prayer for J. C. Williams' *Prayer Column.* This consisted of news from workers in the Americas, Asia, and Europe. Often there were requests for help for troubled workers, prayer-cover for those in danger, and the occasional call to synchronized praying against Satan. Instead of praying for a military victory, they prayed for the destruction of satanic workings and for the "defeat of the armies of the apocalypse."

Many of Jessie Penn-Lewis's essays were intended to comfort and reassure. "Faith—the key to God's Kingdom" was addressed to those who had suffered loss of goods and status, whilst "Dependence on Christ" showed how troubled workers could receive cleansing and deliverance. One essay answered a reader's question about the possible danger of having visions. She replied that it was humbler and safer to rely on a gradual revelation in prayer "until the Lord becomes as real to you as is possible. . . . To understand Him is better than to have visions of Him." In this group of essays was the remarkable "Spear Thrust Power," which showed how truly fearless messengers could be like the first Apostles and sting people to the heart and bring them under conviction, as they spoke in the name of Christ exalted and enthroned.

In this series also was "The Message of Light," which was almost certainly a remake of an earlier convention address. Such was its spiritual impact that hundreds of reverent students of the Word made their own detailed notes and then studied and applied them at home.

Like Evan Roberts, Jessie Penn-Lewis was caught up more and more in the theme of tribulation and the end of the age. On the eve of the Great War, she was still thinking of the conflict in the heavenlies and was telling Christians not to be troubled by the war-fever because these storms on earth were only a prelude to great spiritual conflict. In those days, only those "lifted in spirit to the heavenlies" could stay calm, since they were already "partaking of the peace of Heaven." She dedicated a poem composed by a C. E. W. (probably Charles Warren) to them:

> Borne on the current of His will,
> Nothing but peace thy heart can fill
> From morning light till evening hours
> For Christ is thine Almighty Power.
> Rest and be still! Rest and be still!
>
> Borne on the current of His will,
> To Thee can come no fear of ill.
> The lightnings flash, the thunders roll;
> Nothing disturbs thy peaceful soul.
> Rest and be still! Rest and be still!

Toward the end of that year, she placed in *The Overcomer* magazine, twelve "Songs of the Translation" to be sung at workers' conferences. The song titles bade them to be ready, untroubled, standing, and watching. There is an undoubted feeling of joy and confidence in the song written by G. W. Johnson:

> Who then will follow on in His great strength?
> Whose faith will stand and win victory at length?
> Whose heart is strong in God to overcome?
> Such will rejoice to hear, "Quickly I come."
> Who'll face the straitened way, choosing God's best,
> With not a look behind, conquering each test?
> Whose spirit dares to press through pain and fear?
> For in the midst is felt—JESUS IS NEAR.

When a controversy arose about the end of the age, she decided to make a special appeal in *The Overcomer*, urging readers that unity in fellowship was more important at this point in time. She asked them to pray "that the spirit of watching for the coming of the Lord be not dulled through the minds being occupied with events connected with the return. Above all, let us guard the spirit of unity with all members of the body."

The onset of war in Europe and the parallel onset of deep depression in Evan's spirit and new forms of pain in Jessie's body, combined to put a sudden end to all this. Only six months remained before she felt constrained to announce that publication of *The Overcomer* was to cease, the prayer watch was to be moved elsewhere, and the book production slowed down and suspended. A very difficult six months followed. Without a proper index to *The Overcomer,* it is almost impossible to tell how much other helpers contributed to the magazine during the many months when the chief editor could do little beyond selecting good extracts from Andrew Murray and Stockmayer. Someone who used the pen name, "Fidelis," would sometimes borrow part of a conversation arranged between Evan Roberts and certain visitors. Their topics were acceptance of loss, control of gossiping tongues, managing time effectively and "how to roll your burden on to the Lord." On one occasion, Fidelis asked permission to use notes taken at a mission hall on, "The spiritual effects of trials and afflictions." He could not have known that in only one year's time this topic would be a terrible reality for thousands. Almost half of another edition was taken up with the Evan Roberts' studies of principles of prayer. But this ad hoc system couldn't go on indefinitely.

It seems surprising that during the last months before war began, approaches were made by groups who wanted to widen the magazine's ministry or at least to make it a part of a large organization. In reply to these approaches, Jessie said again and again that she had no commission to found or conduct that kind of magazine or to build up some institute of teaching but only "to minister the truth of God to the spiritual people of God."

Before *The Overcomer* was shut down, Jessie and Evan wrote lengthy essays of explanation and of regret that they could no longer communicate with the many Christian workers and missionaries. They were advised to study back-numbers of the magazine and extract the best of the messages. Jessie argued that the closure was a significant sign of the Advent and Evan also claimed it as a sign, "We believe in the near coming of the Lord. Our course is drawing to a close." A few weeks later, Jessie gave an elaborate interpretation of the closedown. She pointed out that the Bible was full of finishings and fulfilments. No one had any right to go on with a commission once the Lord said, "It is finished," and added that it was not failure nor neglect that has ended *The Overcomer,* but an accomplishment of the work God had sent them to do.

Before very long the letters began to arrive from all over the world—protesting and grieving because, as someone named Annie Wood said two years later, "The magazine has supplied a great and pressing need which no other literature has attempted." A Mary Slater, serving with the Africa Inland Mission, wrote, "The closure of *The Overcomer* was the same as if a dearest friend had been removed. I wept and did not sleep until the Spirit helped me to understand."

Only a year later, Jessie was filling the gap by sending out longer and longer occasional papers on vital topics, such as *The Camouflaging of the Cross*. In 1920, *The Overcomer* rose once more from its last resting place and was given a new task of safeguarding the true believers against any form of falsehood. There was no formal price, but costs were covered by donors and guarantors. Once more it contained full versions of the addresses and discussion topics heard at the Swanwick and other conferences. On only one occasion did a hard-pressed editor reprint some early work of Evan Roberts, who had been quietly dropped from the Overcomer team.

After Jessie Penn-Lewis died, the editorial work was shared around until a Mr. Gordon Watts was ready to take over.

In more recent times, the magazine's editors have felt they should bring together, under a theme selected for each issue, some of the most spiritually uplifting essays that have appeared during the eighty years of its existence. Still the streams of living water flow out to Christian workers.

> Eternity alone will reveal all that magazine meant to those members of the Body of Christ who desired to press on into full growth. (Mary Garrard)

20

Literature for the Overcomers

The various books and booklets edited and distributed by Jessie Penn-Lewis were not intended for ordinary believers or for those interested in religion. Each issue and each new publication was designed to meet the needs of dedicated disciples and witnesses. When these people called at the Bookroom in Toller Road, they were amazed to find a great variety of tracts and booklets, reprinted reports and manuals and new editions of major devotional works. Boxes full of French, Spanish, German, and Swedish versions were available at need. To arrange all these publications in a correct date sequence would be a labor of Hercules because Jessie often incorporated the first booklets into later, enlarged versions. Instead, we can look at the whole range and comment on them group by group according to their scope and purpose. One or two representatives from each group will be studied in detail, but the rest will be found in Appendix A.

Devotional and Mystical Meditations

Four early booklets, *They came to Marah*, *Communion with God*, *The Heavenly Vision*, and *Face to Face* had a general appeal. But *The Throne Life of Victory* and *Much Fruit* were clearly intended for new missionaries as a challenge to die daily in order to bear plentiful fruit.

The longest and loveliest of these meditations is one in which the *Song of Solomon* is not interpreted in the traditional manner but as "the heart history of a soul in its progress in the Divine Life." It was her God-inspired answer to our confusions and disobediences and to our longings to enter that Garden and to seek intimacy with that beautiful Bridegroom standing there. Any failure to find the Great Lover signified a loss or lack of that enriching experience. Even the chapter headings in *Thy Hidden Ones* are unique:

The Soul's Self-knowledge;
The Clefts of the Rock;
The Power of His Resurrection;
The Heavenly Life;
The Blessings in the Heavenlies;
The Hidden Life;
The Shrinking Soul's Reply;
The Victorious Soul;
The Precious Fruit of the Soul;
The God-possessed Soul;
The Soul's Failure in Abiding;
The Soul Out of Touch;
Leaning on the Well-Beloved—The Key to Communion.

Remembering the dreadful, desolate state that Jessie Penn-Lewis was in after her total collapse in 1899, one can only marvel that as she lay on her daybed, with nerves jangled and lungs inflamed and mists of depression sweeping over her, she could still write these words at the end of the argument:

> Oh! Child of God, hidden in His heart, abide in this deep love of the eternal God. Listen to His words—"Continue ye in my love" (John 15.9) and welcome the flashes of fire proceeding from that love, the fire that seeks to purify thee as fine gold. Dwell in the God who is a consuming fire and thou shalt see the King in His beauty, and dwell on high. (page 151)

Jessie came to believe that anyone who wished to get close to the love of Jesus should also be ready to keep close to Him in His sufferings. The book that most clearly reflects her experiences is *Studies in Job*. She announced that the book was intended for all who walked in integrity of heart and obedience and yet were in fiery trials. Drawing on her own experiences of longing to escape, when even her Russian friends had stopped praying for recovery but she had refused to dwell upon her imminent death, she told readers not to seek death nor yield to it without knowing God's clear will. "Choose Life!" she challenged.

The second lesson from Job's life was that the turning point in a pathway of trial comes when we turn away from our own captivity, leave ourselves in God's hands, and pray for others:

> When wilt thou cease to think of your own needs and, in thy emptiness and poverty, give thyself to the ministry for others? Yea! When thou dost desire with thy whole heart the blessing of others more than thine own. Rest content with the will of God whether it be deliverance from the furnace or no deliverance, so that thou mightest shine a brighter jewel in the Master's crown.

Books Centered Upon the Cross of Calvary

First in time and perhaps the most popular of all was the *Pathway to Life*, which spelt out how all disciples could travel towards Calvary and the empty tomb and experience their delivering and conquering effects in their own and others' lives. The concept was illustrated by a diagram or schema. In 1898, Jessie wrote *Message of the Cross* stating with great fervor that the renewed preaching of the finished work of Christ on Calvary was the only answer to the churches' need. After this, she produced Via Crucis leaflets that each dealt with one topic, such as using the Cross as a test of genuine faith. Other Cross-centered books were, *The Climax of the Risen Life,* and *All things New—The Message of the Cross for the Time of the End.* The latter was a patchwork of old essays. All would agree that there were two of her books that were outstanding:

> 1. The Cross of Calvary and its Message (1903). This was written in special circumstances. The publishers later added on some valuable extracts from addresses by Dr. Meyer and Dr. Murray. This book was published in French, German, Swedish, Dutch, and Spanish. Its theme was identification with Christ crucified. In several ways, it explored and applied the verses that stated believers were crucified with Christ, raised with Christ, and exalted with Christ. It contained a number of striking statements such as this on page 122.
>
> The crucial message of Calvary to a man is salvation from himself. If he will take, for himself, the Cross and, accepting the spirit of the Cross as manifested in the Christ who died for him, and if he will deny—or renounce—himself as crucified on the Cross with His Lord, he will in so doing be delivered from the bondage

of his sins, the terror of the law, the spirit of the world, and the powers of the devil.

2. *The Centrality of the Cross* (1925). This contained some convention addresses, the ensuing debate and questions time, more excerpts from godly writers and a superb declaration of faith that was borrowed from another writer. This may well have been the book that she submitted in note form to the Rev. R. B .Jones, who filled the margin with notes of caution and dissent. This book is well worth reading, if only for the majestic and still fresh essays entitled, "The Cross and Revival," and "The Cross and Proclamation."

Books Centered Upon the Holy Spirit Life

The first booklet—prepared some time before 1900 for young converts—dealt with such practical issues as, "The Revelation of the Spirit," "The Entrance of the Spirit," "The Supply of the Spirit," "The Equipment of the Spirit," and the "Daily Leading of the Spirit." About the same time, Jessie published her studies in Ezekiel called *Abandonment to the Spirit*, which incorporated her address given at a Waiting Day of the China Inland Mission's Ladies' Training Home on Good Friday, 1898. A printed version—four editions altogether—became necessary and about seventeen thousand copies were sold. Using the experiences of the prophet Ezekiel, she explained, "How God prepares His instruments," "How God frees people for service," "How God commissions the obedient ones," and "How God cleanses body, soul, and spirit." She applied Ezekiel's vision of the valley of dry bones and the vision of the stream of water, not to community or church life, but to individuals who were in great need of a Spirit-filled soul, mind, and body.

Several short tracts were prepared and the most controversial of these was *Four Planes of the Spiritual Life.* Believers in Christ, she said, all lived on one of four planes: the evangelistic plane, the revival or Pentecost plane, the path of the Cross plane, or the spiritual warfare plane. Each of these had a commencement, a continuation, and a consummation before you went on to the next. That upward process could include times of setback, or testings, or darkness experiences. Keeping in mind her own spiritual journeys, she now claimed that whoever passed through these planes and moved onwards could give helps and counsels to those who were coming behind. Aware of the way that proud people could use this theory, she warned that the planes were experimental and could not elevate or enlarge one's position. That warning was not heeded and other teachers began to speak misleadingly about being elevated or raised into heavenly places. Various sects have taken up this concept since that day, with obvious perils to the oneness of Christ's people.

A little later in date were the reprinted tracts called the *Inner Life* series that dealt with victorious life, risen life, and communion life. These were designed to fit in with a key book titled, *Bible Readings on the Inner Life*, in which Jessie Penn-Lewis had selected choice verses on a great range of topics—such as full deliverance, discipleship, and the joy of the Lord.

There is one major book of a very different kind called, *Soul and Spirit*, which is a study in biblical psychology. Dr. Pike, a visitor to the Penn-Lewis household in 1909, said that he had noticed an entire row of books on psychology in the study room where he had been allowed to interview Evan Roberts. At the time when Jessie was writing this book, few had ever gone into this matter of the complex workings and interrelationships of the body, the soul, and the Spirit. She designated these areas: the carnal, the psychical, and the spiritual.

The book is in three parts, but is so badly organized that arguments belonging to part 1 reappear in part 2, and arguments in part 2 are interrupted by long sections that should be in part 1. The modern Christian reader would be helped most of all by chapter 4, which spells out all the ways in which the human psyche can develop qualities and powers that look as if they were inspired of the Holy Ghost but which, in truth, are the product of the highest faculties of the human mind and soul. Some of those ways are all too obvious in contemporary life and we need to discern the spiritual from the psychic.

With God-given discernment, Jessie next traced the signs of the psyche versus spirit conflict in various world issues and Church issues. Then she opened up a fascinating topic. How far can modern psychical inquiries and movements be seen as fruits of the carnal human race's psychic energies that are, she asserted, most certainly under satanic influence if not under his full control? (Modern Rogerian counseling theory and Zen and Yoga and Scientology and Transcendental Meditation and the movements linked with New Ageism ought to be put under this spiritual searchlight. They will be exposed as either carnal in outlook or psychic in inspiration.)

Instead of cultivating the soul life, Jessie wrote, we should be laying it down at Jesus' feet and waiting humbly for the true life of and from the Spirit. And if we are in any confusion as to which is which, then the best touchstone will be the Cross. Many of her teachings are echoed in the works of Watchman Nee, who acknowledged his many debts to Jessie Penn-Lewis.

Literature for Christian Workers

Many of these booklets were edited versions of addresses given at Workers' Conferences. But earlier books were reprinted by the Overcomer Trust, and one of these was a *Handbook for Workers* that had been written about 1895 for volunteers attached to YWCA branches and various city missions. It is remarkably fresh and could well have been written in 1995

In the book, she gave a number of principles or instructions to those attempting to help others:

> Seek to meet souls on their own level. Give them sympathy and encouragement.
>
> Seek to be only a voice used to direct souls to Christ.
>
> Seek for grace to discern the work of God.
>
> Seek so as to be able to work in patience.
>
> Seek earnestly to know the 'Silence' of Jesus and to enter the interests of others.
>
> Seek to manifest lowliness of mind, never arguing or engendering strife. (2 Timothy 2. 23,)
>
> Do not dogmatize over anything; lead them to the Cross.
>
> Seek to live in unbroken communion with God.
>
> Seek that your interior and exterior life correspond—blending spirituality with practicality.
>
> Above all press on and seek a life hid with Christ in God.

During the five fruitful years when Jessie enjoyed the respect of Mr. Marshall and the open friendship of R. C. Morgan and his son, she prepared a number of booklets called *Words to Workers* and *Words to Warriors*. Both series were steadily expanded and each booklet was furnished with numerous proof-texts. A third series was the product of counseling sessions and debates at Workers' Conferences (see Appendix). The best known were the handbooks called *Spiritual Perplexities*, which looked into various testings and conflicts, and a *Clinical Handbook* that had blank pages in which Christian workers could enter their own experiences of deception and defeat. All these booklets were the best answer to the known fact that many bright and conscientious Christians had been so deceived by *subtle spirits* that they had left the battlefield and lost their strength, confidence, and knowledge.

The key question debated was, "Can the people of God find the basic principles that protect believers—both as individuals and as congregations?" It was answered in a very dogmatic fashion.

Both of the better known handbooks included the views of Evan Roberts, whose close reasoning should dispel once and for all the myth that he became erratic and naive. His work was the fruit of extensive reading and study as well as of a rich and varied experience.

Literature for Warriors

In 1897, Jessie was invited to address a conference in the C. I. M. Hall in London on the subject of spiritual conflict. Notes of her addresses went through two editions under the provisional title of *Conflict in the Heavenlies*. Ten years later, she wrote a more comprehensive study that was published in 1908, under the title, *Warfare with Satan and the Way of Victory*. It is such a frightening seventy page description of the great adversary's resistance techniques, wiles, deceptions, false visions, snares, and further devices invading every part of one's life, that it is absolutely essential to read chapters 6 and 9 first. Only thus can readers have inward assurance that the divine armor is at our disposal, that the mighty sword of the Spirit is ever with us, and that all who have trusted in the Cross will definitely reach theThrone—both now and in Eternity.

Three years later, Jessie delivered seven addresses to the Workers' Conference. In them, she interpreted the first part of the Joshua saga in terms of the whole Church following its divine captain into the battlefields of life. She gave frank warnings about the ways in which the Lord's host could be deceived and defeated. However, there was a new confident note as she dealt with verses such as, "Fear them not: for I have delivered them into thine hand" (Joshua 10:8). She was teaching the workers the secret of aggressive warfare—praying against Satan's hosts and Satan's plans throughout the whole world. Whatever its blemishes, the resulting book, *The Conquest of Canaan*, has proved so inspirational that a ninth edition was issued in 1975 and is still available.

Towering above all other productions of the Overcomer Bookroom was *War on the Saints*, published in 1912. Called a "Manual of Christian Warfare," this book consisted of three hundred pages of closely reasoned arguments against the principles, powers, and deceitful practices that both Jessie Penn-Lewis and Evan Roberts had met with on their own spiritual journeys. But this book had a wider, global, perspective because the daily warfare was viewed as part of the great cosmic battle that had fascinated Christian sects ever since the time of Daniel and of St. John's "Apocalypse."

The first edition was intended for Christian workers only. The revised editions were sold publicly but with a warning, "It is a textbook for believers on the work of deceiving spirits among the children of God. Only those who have experienced the baptism of the Holy Spirit and personally known of supernatural things can understand and benefit."

The two authors affirmed that this book was the product of six years of inquiries and testings of the truth. They had included evidence—sent by European friends—of counterfeit signs, visions, exercises, and manifestations. They had included stories received from missionaries, and testimonies from the Christian workers who came to the "Spiritual Clinics" whenever they felt they had been deceived or daunted. Evan Roberts disclosed later that he had included his spiritual autobiography because he had long since realized that he too had been deceived and harassed by Satan until he was given power to understand and discern.

The authors took the extraordinary step of warning readers against their own likely temptations—such as sudden disinclination to read, reducing the time to meditate, forgetting things just read, and failing to "Lift up holy hands." They advised all earnest students to pray before they tried to transmit these teachings to any circle of believers. The book was furnished with a glossary of terms used to define aspects of the battle, and was also equipped with a six page comparative index to true and false spiritual phenomena.

After two years of debate among the Christian workers—and after much comment from mature, spiritual people—the Bookroom re-issued the three most valued chapters that dealt with:

The volition and spirit of man dealing with *passivity*;

War on the power of darkness: prayer as a destroying weapon ;

Victory in conflict: the Christian's complete armor.

Always the Cross was emphasized as the only way to deliverance, renewal, and victory.

War on the Saints proved to be a thought-provoking book, but it had its flawed thinking here and there, and there were many criticisms and misunderstandings. Only a year after the book first appeared, Evan Roberts was saying that somehow this book was confusing and dividing groups, and that there was now an urgent need for a second book presenting positively the principles of "Life in the Spirit." As we have seen, a number of booklets such as *Four Planes of Spiritual*

Life were republished, but Jessie never combined them into a single book that might have become a spiritual classic.

The onset of the European war must have distracted people's minds from the book, but Jessie made haste to have a French version and a Spanish one printed on the eve of that terrible war. Since then, *War on the Saints* has appeared in several languages and editions, and there is a much abridged and modified version on the market.

The diaries and letter books show that after Jessie began to use a Derbyshire cottage as a writing center, about 1923, she revised several earlier works and did a great deal of re-editing. She also prepared reprints of works by Andrew Murray and Madame Guyon. In 1925, the work was moved into London and the flow of new or re-edited books stopped. Yet Jessie's vision was not lost and the magazine and books are still being published. In a way, Jessie is still seeking to fulfill ,through them, the aims she set out when God called her to the writing ministry a hundred years ago.

21

The Christian Workers' Conferences

About the same time Jessie Penn-Lewis withdrew from the Keswick Conventions, she quietly developed a new type of teaching ministry that was more restricted in its audiences. For as long as she possibly could, she stayed in close personal contact with a network of conferences for practicing missioners and other Christian workers. It was only during an enforced convalescence in Guernsey in 1915, and another on the Derbyshire moors in 1923, that she had to delegate this work to Charles Usher and J. C. Williams or some other helper whom she could trust not to depart from its ground rules. She consistently refused to have a council or committee and announced that she would depend on the Lord for the supply of all her financial needs and for the practical help she needed. She was never disappointed. There were also monthly conferences that were held in Sion College and later in Eccleston Hall in London.

Apart from the one Innovative session, which will be explained later, all the meetings kept to her principles that were probably influenced by the restrictions imposed upon her at Keswick Conventions. In order to give maximum liberty, she refused to have any programs of addresses and refused to appoint the traditional type of convention chairman. If it so happened that the appointed chairman for the day failed to keep the appointment, she had to improvise. That is why she was later accused, quite unfairly, of inventing the ritual of the *empty chair* that was copied far and wide. Jessie was sure that experienced Christian workers needed not Bible readings and addresses by experts, but the kind of exhortation and the kind of devotional input that spiritual men and women could equally give. So there was open prayer, testifying, and singing in each main session..

The first main session consisted of a welcome speech and a keynote address by Jessie, Charles Usher, the Vicar of Crick, or ever faithful J. C. Williams, who was convenor of the prayer watch. Here is a sample of how J. C. welcomed two hundred workers.

> I have asked the Lord what I shall say because, rightly or wrongly, the first public utterance tells the spirit of all that follows. We have come not for controversy but for abundant , victorious, ascendant life. There are two classes of people here—those who have difficulties and reach out for new spiritual openings—and those who have no problems. Let us pray then for those who need deliverance and for those who need to put aside their pride and to be ready to lose what the world calls liberty in order to gain the precious gift of a victorious spirit.

Both groups went to the first and last addresses and took part in the debates, which were usually summed up in a paper or given a column in *The Overcomer*. For those who were mature, there were special interest meetings. One was for the

Prayer Band that was engaged year round in prayer warfare; another was for the Missionary Intercessors who considered problems on the field; another dealt with *The Overcomer* magazine. The London conference may also have dealt with European issues because it was noticeable that men and women came there from all over Denmark, Sweden, Germany, and France.

For the less mature and more troubled workers, there was a very important session known as the "Student Class" or "Soul Clinic." For three hours every Christian worker was liable to be questioned closely about their personal stresses, temptations, and failures. Sooner or later, someone would own up to slackness or barrenness or yielding to the deceiver. At length, Jessie would stand up and begin a winding up comment, judgment, or interpretation. Then she would call them all to earnest confessional prayer. Side-rooms were opened where one could often see some weeping missionary or heartbroken evangelist accepting the loving ministry of others who had passed that way. This was Jessie's fulfillment of her claim in *Four Planes of Spiritual Life,* that those who moved through the planes could help those who were coming behind.

What needs explaining is a peculiar tea-time session, because it originated and evolved in a quite different way. We have to go back first to the Swansea Convention, then to the Leicester Convention of 1908, that was in disarray after the chairman and the principal speaker (they had them in those days) announced that they were not able to take part in the mid-week sessions. Jessie brought in Evan Roberts, who was partially recovered from his two year breakdown. In a morning session, Evan explained how the vital principle of "recognizing the Holy Spirit's presidency" had been manifested in the Book of Acts and how it had been manifested again in the recent revival. What was needed, he said, was not a chairman of the traditional kind, but a Spirit-filled leader who would always act cooperatively with the Holy Spirit whenever He moved among the people. Even this process could end at a precious moment when not even the leader was needed, because all those present would fall at the Spirit's feet and thus become sensitive *channellers*. Then the "chair" would truly be empty. The truly amazing thing was that, on the afternoon of Thursday, this unique spiritual process actually happened—and at the tea table.

"About 80-100 of the Lord's children sat down to tea each day at 4.30. On the last two days it was impossible to break up until past seven o'clock," wrote Jessie excitedly. She said that the themes had been "Prayer" on Monday, "Life in Christ" on Tuesday, and "Revival" on Wednesday. On that third day, the Christian Workers began to give their testimonies and this practice spread. Now, at the Thursday tea-time conference, Evan Roberts called out from his place, "Let all bring out your personal burdens and then we will take them to the Lord."

"A volume of needs-prayers kept pouring forth," Jessie said, "Until all these were taken to God and the meeting felt lightened."

"Now!" said the leader, "Now you are free for others." Then a torrent broke forth for sons and daughters and relatives, for the factories, prisons, and slums.

It was noted at the time that the very next day many conference members went out into the market square to witness fruitfully and that others sat in sorrow, realizing their own failures to witness. A little story in a Christian journal described how one faithful street evangelist had asked Evan Roberts why his words were not heeded. Evan asked him to observe how many times the skilled mason had to hit a stone before suddenly it cracked—"but crack it will," said Evan. The evangelist went on preaching the Gospel with renewed faith.

Evan Roberts was at his best during these tea-time conversations, several of which were recorded in *The Overcomer*. Jessie would sometimes rest during this tea session and would leave the men to handle the tea-table discussions. But she would step in later to comment on the more complex questions.

At one workers' conference an agitated Christian worker spoke on behalf of others, "May I ask in regard to dealing with our own children?—for a terrible anguish and anxiety has driven me to pray."

Jessie replied, "Anguish of spirit would be more effective than the anguish which arises out of natural affection because the former puts the intercessor into intimate touch with the sorrows of the rejected Christ... Sometimes a natural sorrow can even quench the Spirit and hinder unless and until it is lifted up to the Cross where Christ bore them. So he is to be saved as the fruit of Christ's death and not because he is your son. We need to arrive at the universal heart of God so that every soul AND YOUR SON are all alike to God."

This was the way in which a private problem was often converted into a general principle that would be learned by all the workers present, and perhaps put in *The Overcomer* as well. Probably this was the way in which Evan Roberts and J. C. Williams dealt with tea-time questions about stewardship, meditation, and disciplining. Now there was a danger that these findings would turn into binding rules, whereas Jessie was most anxious to preserve liberty in the Spirit.

In 1913 there was a debate about "How best to prepare for Christ's Return' "during which one worker asked, "Should we now spend all our capital on the Lord's work?'

Jessie replied, "Each child of God must have liberty to walk with God in such matters. Do not follow your leader or run after one another."

Then someone else asked whether a specific time should

be set aside for recreation and again there came a surprising reply, "Do not make any standard for yourself or for others for all such exterior things. Seek to know the will of God."

If they accepted this advice the Christian workers would never regiment their missions and converts and would never forget that "the letter killeth but the Spirit giveth life."

One question and answer session took another look at the matter of expecting the Lord's return. Someone asked, "If one is pressed by many duties how can one set apart time to be aware of the Lord Jesus?"

Jessie's reply was arrestingly new, "Do you not think that we might have some control of the distracting circumstances? And that we should absolutely refuse to allow the powers of darkness to drive a lot of secondary things upon us?" She surprised the workers by advising them that, instead of depending on a morning hour with God, they should practice God-consciousness and God-direction at every hour.

In the 1914 issues of *The Overcomer* the report shows that the same question and answer method was used for key Issues.

The question was raised, "If there is a discordant note in the harmony of the Body of Christ, how would you discern it? How could you discern whether the hindrance is in yourself?"

Evan Roberts gave a lengthy and comprehensive talk that was fully developed and printed in *The Overcomer*, together with his personal confession prayer beseeching the Lord that He would take away anything in His own life and witness and teaching which would cause division and misunderstandings.

Another question, "Do you say it is possible that in Christ we can obtain authority over the demons—and more?"

This time it was Jessie who replied and made a number of statements that were perhaps more bold than clear.

Obviously such an important question would not go away. Both Charles Usher and Jessie untypically devoted entire conference addresses to it.

These question and answer sessions were so treasured by the workers that when the full team, including Evan Roberts and J. C. Williams, reappeared in 1923, they were greeted with joy and we are told that a number of workers were there "transformed into living souls."

It is clear from the older biographies that Jessie Penn-Lewis felt that the Matlock Conferences were the most rewarding. It was a great sadness to her when the pressures of the war compelled them to close down regional conferences and meet only in London. Concerning the last conferences at Matlock, she wrote in *The Overcomer*, July 1914, about its great spiritual benefits:

> The Conference was far in advance of preceding ones. The guidance of the Spirit of God from first to last, in leading the conference as an united whole, hour after hour, with no program, yet with no sense of a break in the cable of His leading. All this rejoiced those who watched over the proceedings with jealous prayer. It showed how deepened in spiritual maturity and understanding those present were.

The main conference addresses in 1913-1914 are worthy of some notice. They had become captivated by the warfare theme. That part of her address on warfare that was linked with Revelation 16:13-14—the spirits and the false prophets—has survived:

> The great fight is going to be the liberation of the circumference. The Holy Spirit dwelling in your spirit but the fight lies in getting the mind free and as clear as crystal, filled with the light of God. It will need dealing

with God for sight, riches and healing of the mind. Yea! All I need in Thee to find, O Lamb of God I come.

You will need to watch that there to no strain. A strained mind can see nothing straight but lays itself open to unbalanced views of truth. To set right your memory and imagination and judgment is spiritual work. God has said, "COME! let us reason together." That is not spiritual nor reasonable but the two together.

What about Healing? Well! There can be healing of diseases and in many ways. There is healing to get free and break the hold of the dark powers. There are "possessions" manifested through a chronic suffering, for they delight in our suffering. I knew and proved this 15 years ago. Well! What next? A liberated body is liberated for activity. I am quite open for you to send in any questions about this victory over sin, death and Satan. This means a fight. As your stage of victory ends, there comes your next stage . . . Pray that there be no restraint of truth and nothing nor anyone can hinder.

"Hindering" or "Hastening the First Return and the Final Return of the Lord Jesus Christ" was an issue that troubled almost every workers' conference. On one such occasion, the leader set out a number of *brakes* on such anticipation:

Give up the temptation to want to be raptured in company with others. You may have to be raptured apart from your family in order to be with God.

Give up preconceived ideas and thoughts about the events of the Lord's Coming. Ask God to give you true light. Preconceived ideas may get in your way when the Lord comes. A great deal is written about it which cannot be all of God, so we have to discern what is of Him.

Refuse all demoniacal revelations about the Lord through dreams and visions. Do this deliberately because there will be counterfeit and spurious versions.

Refuse all demoniacal messages of obtaining

> knowledge about the Lord's Coming. Don't let your mind get passive and open to spurious light.
>
> Watch out for fantasies from a fatigued brain and avoid daydreaming. Ask God for a simple revelation to your spirit.
>
> Learn to detect the movements of the Spirit and just keep your mind in the channel of the Spirit.

Workers' conferences usually ended on Friday, although a few stayed on for informal talks with Evan Roberts after he came out from his "Room of Prayer." Just one example of a farewell address has escaped the wastebin, and this was given by Jessie herself:

> When Mr. Usher spoke to you, you knew very well that the warfare was for experimental weapons; but he took it for granted that you used the Word of God. All that the War-Book is for is to put weapons in your hands, but you must see to God's Word. You cannot expect any possible kind of victory if you don't saturate yourself with the Word of God. Your Bible should be your armory. Honestly! If your spiritual life is to be what it ought to be, your Bible should be full of life and power to you, more than anything else. The only food for the spirit is the Word of God and all your fighting will be empty if you do not take food.
>
> I should like to see our speaking nothing else but Bible language. That is the only safe standard and the only safe place. Learn to think and breathe and talk there. Why should we talk so much ordinary language? I should like when we part to say, "The Grace of our Lord Jesus Christ be with you." Why should we say good-bye. Oh! Wouldn't it be glorious if we became a heavenly people! Not because the days of Pentecost were better than now, but because they were special days of dealing with God and of God's dealings with His disciples.

The fragrant memory of such workers' conferences in various London centers has been the subject of many a testimony. A Chinese pastor visited here lately and told us of his grandparents who had been under the ministry of Watchman Nee. That famed Chinese apostle had testified publicly that he had learned many important spiritual truths from the Overcomer Movement via Jessie Penn-Lewis's teachings.

During the 1914-1918 war, Jessie was forced to miss several of the conventions because she was so dreadfully weak. Fortunately, the letters she sent to the faithful ones before these conferences assembled have survived the passage of years and some of these are reprinted in the Appendix. They were intended to be an inspiration and encouragement to those attending and to those who had offered to take her place. But the letters also reveal a great deal about her own experiences of the Lord at that time of enforced separation.

After the war of 1914-1918, Jessie announced that the chief message entrusted to her was, "The power of the proclaimed Gospel to stop the devil's lips and to hold back the tide of unbelief and lawlessness." Instead of meeting at London and Matlock, the *team* went to the Hayes Conference Center in Swanwick. She invited there "all who would hold to the faith of the Gospel and who would be ready to live the Cross as well as preach it." This time, there was a timetable announced in advance so that people could pray for God to give them something to contribute. Each daily topic was to be related to the Cross—substitution, justification, atonement, etc. It was agreed that these addresses by Jessie, together with any valuable comments from conference members, should be printed in a book called *The Centrality of the Cross*. Everyone noticed the remarkable harmony and unity whenever they stayed at the foot of the Cross and gazed at the One who suffered there. Many never forgot Jessie Penn-Lewis's message comparing the workers' suffering witness with the "corn of wheat falling into the ground." It was a message that ended in complete, humble silence.

In 1921, there was considerable excitement because news had come that there were similar conventions in the United States where the Cross had been uplifted in the addresses. These had inspired revival-like enthusiasm, prayer, and praise.

Heartbroken evangelists and timid pastors were reminded that they had been called to be "lonely witnesses to the Cross of Calvary." They were given scores of texts that assured them that they were going to overcome by the Blood of the Cross.

The next convention was almost canceled because of a general strike, but this crisis ended suddenly on Easter Saturday, a few hours after an emergency prayer meeting. The 1922 convention was held in the midst of an outbreak of revival expectations because of events in East Anglia and Scotland. However, Jessie kept speakers focused upon the Calvary theme. "The Cross alone is the center of light as well as of unity," she insisted. Evangelical unity was becoming a great concern about this time.

During 1923, Jessie was far too ill to attend; but the guest speakers, such as F. B. Meyer, kept faithful to her guidelines. No discussions were permitted about fulfilled prophecy or sanctification or healing or any other issue which could obscure the Cross of Christ and divide them into groups. Jessie wrote, "Our ministry lies in spiritual service to the whole Body of Christ, in the unfolding of the unsearchable riches available to the believer through His wondrous death, Resurrection and Ascension into Glory."

One of the reasons for this insistence was that she feared the ongoing effects of two serious splits—one caused by Austen Sparkes, who had over-stressed sanctification, and the other by Charles Raven, who alleged that the Cross-theology was too subjective.

The Rev. R. B. Jones agreed to speak in 1927 on the first eight chapters of Romans: "The Gospel of God for the Believer." Another loyal supporter was the Rev. Gordon Watt, whose addresses have been reprinted from time to time. The new teachings of Sparkes and Raven threatened to disrupt the old "Workers' Conference" in Eccleston Hall in London in 1925 and 1926, but such dark shadows could not overwhelm the organizers.

How to assess the widespread and beneficial impact of these later conventions at Swanwick would stretch anyone's mind. Just one fact alone would amaze those of us who see the little sprinkle of ministers who turn up at the local conventions today. Wrote Jessie:

> One of the most remarkable features of all the Conferences at Swanwick was the attendance, year after year, of numbers of clergy and ministers, many of whom testified that their ministries had been entirely revolutionized. Eternity alone will reveal what the impact of these servants of God has been upon the Church of Christ as a whole.

Another source of humble amazement was that the gathering together of Christian workers had unforeseen but blessed consequences. In an Easter Conference in 1922, a Miss F. Smith received permission from Jessie to have her essays and booklets translated into scholarly Chinese. Moreover, she undertook, with her brilliant niece, the preparation of Japanese versions—these would be ready for distribution by the next year. No one knew that only one year's breathing space was left for this special testimony before Japan would be devastated by a widespread earthquake. In the same year, a Miss Yu sent an appeal through a missionary named Miss Barber—who took back to China Jessie's permission to publish the most useful *Overcomer* essays. The work was undertaken by

Watchman Nee, who printed them in his *Rising Again* magazine, and expounded them and presented their essential teachings in his later books.

So the aging author knew that her books and conferences were bearing fruit in other lands. Who indeed can assess the worldwide effects of such ministries—for only eternity will show the harvest.

22

Changing Roles and Relationships

In my biography of Evan Roberts, *An Instrument of Revival*, it was suggested that somewhere between 1914 and 1920, there was a parting of the ways. Even in the closure letter concerning *The Overcomer,* there were strange words that implied that neither Evan nor Jessie should be clinging to that work or any other, unless they were sure that it was God's will. In 1914, when so much of the partnership work was closed down, Evan Roberts was still an editor and contributor, a counselor, prophet, and teacher.

Within two years, however, he was a sick man just looking after the poultry and doing odd jobs around the house. Sometimes he held interviews with visitors on behalf of Jessie who was also unwell. He still had a part to play in the *Lord's Watch*, but he was not contributing to the coveted *Circular Letters* and was not present at the Workers' Conferences. Though he kept the usual prayer-list, he was not in communication with world Christian leaders, some of whom asked whether he was still alive. When questioned about this strange absence, Jessie Penn-Lewis would make only one rather evasive comment: "It is remarkable that Mr. Roberts has never been able to take part in the work again. His work has been carried on by others."

The first sign of tension was over the results of Evan Roberts' unexpected revelation in November 1913, that he been given an exclusive "Burden Message" for the whole world. God's time for the translation (We would say *rapture*) of all the saints into Heaven was absolutely imminent, he announced. The news spread like a bush fire into the United States, Europe, and Asia. But when nothing happened and when hell on earth spread over the battlefields of Europe instead, the question naturally arose as to the true status of this Welsh prophet. A handful of Americans offered their continuing support, but others fell ominously silent. Jessie Penn-Lewis supported him publicly at first, but she then claimed that she too had been shown that something quite different was about to happen.

What the rest of the Overcomer team thought about it all was not clear until they all went off to Guernsey in the Channel Islands in the spring of 1914, partly to rest and recover, and partly to rethink. One of those present kept a "Journal of the Guernsey Retreat," which shows only too clearly how a rift could happen among the most godly people. In fairness, it must be said that Jessie was heading once more for a physical relapse and that Evan Roberts was also passing through one of his nervous crises and was in need of counseling and medical aid.

It was a pity that Jessie could not be there all the time to prevent embarrassing situations. She had to go back to the mainland to see to the conferences and the literature work. Soon the long shadow of war was looming over Guernsey and the South Coast and this seemed to affect their nerves. They were even worrying about a possible cancellation of the Cross Channel boats as early as 1915.

With the help of the journal we can watch the day to day crisis developing, then fading, and then climaxing. For example, the Russian visitor, Peter Nephrash, arrived at their retreat and Evan just stayed aloof until that visitor learned to keep in the background. In an American book, Dr. Nephrash has told us himself of the mistake he made in taking it for granted that he would be received every time he breezed in.

After the service on the first Sunday evening in February, the group went up to Evan's room and everyone started arguing about the translation message. A truce was made on Monday, but the next day there was such a stoppage that Charles Usher walked off and had to be pacified. They were so exhausted by these tensions that everyone slept right through the sunny afternoon intended for recreation. On Thursday evening, there was another disagreement about *The Overcomer* itself—perhaps because Jessie was telling them she wanted to close it down. Then on Sunday, the matter of dispensational warfare and dispensational prayers came up and there were more profound disagreements. This time it was Evan who acted as peacemaker—talking with Charles Usher first, then pleading with "Fidelis," and lastly clearing things with Jessie. The result was a lovely evening in the drawing room with "Jessie Penn-Lewis in great liberty and Evan Roberts in strong brainpower until tired." They also planned some outings, but these tended to turn into serious talks.

They were all in high spirits by Wednesday and decided to celebrate the end of the spiritual warfare phase. The record in the Journal states, "All went out in raincoats and galoshes to the rocks where Mrs. Penn-Lewis dashed a bottle of eau-de-cologne on the rock, saying, 'In the Name of the Triune God I dash this bottle against the rocks in honour of the finished warfare with the Prince of Death.' " Then they all trooped indoors to enjoy a hearty tea before they went off to a center called *La Blanquette*.

Evan started to persuade the group that he had the secret of casting off the old nature and obeying new spiritual laws. He was misunderstood and rebuked sternly for preaching *sinlessness*. While Jessie was away for the weekend, the others tried to cope with Evan who was bubbling over with joy and shouting about his wonderful new body that had become strong by faith. "Nine years are over!" he shouted. "Glory to God!" Yet, twenty four hours later he was knocked out completely with strain and was going against the rest of the group and even criticizing one of the lady members, who wrote, "Then his voice changed and he said it was all right, but I sobbed and sobbed. He put a cloak on and went out and I followed around the roadways—cursing the evil spirit. I met Evan Roberts and we walked awhile and I asked him gently, 'Why?' In the drawing room he broke down and wept and was very weak at supper, but I talked with the others and got through." What had caused this great rumpus? Simply that the lady had said she did not believe we could ever identify with the physical sufferings of Christ.

Almost a week later, after Jessie had returned from London, Evan was stabilized at last and told them he felt "like one coming out of dream." Just before she went back to London again, she took him aside and warned him about such behavior and he seemed to be all right for three days. Suddenly on April 16, he entered the breakfast room dressed in his going-out suit. When he came back he told them all, "The Translation is very near. Prepare!" One of those present in the breakfast room admitted their own naivety, "We got tickets to mark everything and we each went to our rooms to put all straight!" Then they all thought, when nothing happened, that Evan had been under satanic attack. They waited eagerly for the return of Jessie who seemed to have power to steady him up without bringing in medical aid. The journalist wrote on May 18, "The atmosphere was once more sweet and clean."

Jessie was forced to spend weeks there during the first year of the war and she could only send messages to the mainland.

The incoming correspondence during 1915-1917, probably gave them further proof that these were *days of darkness* before the end. A Mr. Perry wrote from Turkey about bad troubles there, whilst a Mrs. Blodgett of San Francisco described the increasingly forceful attempts by the principal of her Bible college to get rid of all Overcomer teaching. Madame Kurcke in Sweden was also up against stern opposition. Robert Fetler, the Russian missioner, described how pastors and doctors had been sent to Siberia or detained or even sent into exile because they were supposed to be German agents. George Dymock of Birkenhead reported unusually heavy and widespread depression among students who now realized they were under satanic attack, too. Jessie had to deal with this despite her own problems because Evan Roberts was in no state to do anything. All violence and warfare jarred on his sensitivities. Reply letters show that he failed to answer the most urgent appeals for help.

On September 30, 1915, Jessie was told that her lung trouble had now flared up again and that the only hope was to winter away from Leicester. On November 2, she wrote to all her friends and said she was thinking of how near she was to the "heavenly call," and that she was striving "to hold fast the 'Translation Faith.' " Lying abed in some friend's house, she was heard singing, "There'll be no dark valley when Jesus comes."

From that sickbed, she launched a scheme to get all her friends in Britain to send in the names and addresses of workers at home and overseas to whom she could send letters of encouragement. Her favorite themes were, "Faith is the Victory," and "Lift up your heads for your redemption draws nigh." One of the inspirational letters written in January, 1916, counsels them to "ask God to teach you to pray from His standpoint, the standpoint of eternity not time, the standpoint of spiritual not natural vision." Secondly, she advised them to practice perpetual prayer, "PRAY AND DO NOT FAINT! HOLD UP THE ROD."

There are reply letters from far-off places and even from detention camps in East Africa, where German-born missionary doctors and nurses were treated as aliens. This restricted kind of contact created a stronger demand and eventually gave birth to the first *Occasional Paper* that Lucy Butterwick sent out to several thousand people, which freed Mary Garrard to handle numerous letters. Conference work was put in the hands of Charles Usher and not Evan Roberts.

Despite her bodily weakness, Jessie made a brave effort, in May 1916, to stir up church leaders and community leaders to organize a "National Day of 'Crying before the Lord,' " and she tried to set up a new body of "Intercessors for England," if only because it was a base for so many missionary ventures. A Prayer Conference for this purpose was set up by 1917, and the list of speakers and prayer-leaders included her name. Time and time again she urged the grouping together of "people who will pray under the guidance of the Holy Spirit." A typical plea from this period was, "Let us join our prayers with the Watchers and Holy Ones in Heaven, that God will stretch out His hand to prove that He rules. Don't look at the chaos around but look up to God above." One fruit of all these pleadings was a booklet entitled, *Revival of Prayer*, which may have been sent out with copies of the *Christian.* Other pamphlets followed until it was time to relaunch a slimmer *Overcomer* in 1920, to restart her main conferences and to write new books.

Now where was Evan Roberts while all this was going on? This thirty-seven-year-old man, who loathed war and violence in all its forms, found that he could not escape the demands of the State. He had never been ordained and had no grounds for exemption, but Mr. and Mrs. Penn-Lewis acted on his behalf. By May 1918, F. B. Meyer could write, "I am glad Evan is finally absolved from military service." Instead, he had to be registered, like many older men, for national service of a different kind. There is a strange portrait of him in his fortieth year—heavily mustached. By late 1917, he was ill once more and wrote to his friends about "emerging gradually from the Valley of the Shadow of Death, along whose paths I have walked these last few years." When the long war ended, Evan had made no plans to go back to Christian work, but the Penn-Lewis family came to his rescue in 1919, when he was so depressed that he could not even begin to write again.

The recent discovery of Jessie's 1919 and 1920 diaries, has thrown new light on affairs at Cartref, Toller Road. She allowed Evan to advise her as she prepared new drafts of her books and commissioned him to write reviews and to do research for her book on spiritism. But no major work was undertaken.

Year by year after the war, Jessie became surrounded by new friends and supporters. She did not depend on Evan's counsel when she fell into a deep depression in 1919. He did come out of his private world, however, and took over the task of receiving visitors and handling the counseling work at Cartref.

In the first issue of the new *Overcomer*, Jessie again endorsed Evan's prayer ministry and tried to describe its unique scope and to explain the main idea that lay behind his "Prayer-sanctuary." Now, however, his isolation was an embarrassment and she couldn't hide the fact that he was often misjudged and misunderstood. When he shut himself off, Jessie explained, "He was living in another world, occupied with service in an Unseen Realm. He could only have his spirit and mind free for outer things when God released him from this service of prayer. In deep spiritual isolation the work was done, with a crucifixion in the personal life that few could endure or understand. . . . Thus the faithful intercessor ploughed on and he said he had no choice."

In 1923-1924, the old partnership with Evan, J. C. Williams, and Scottorn came under further strain. For months, Jessie stayed at Moorland Cottage near Matlock to do her writing and thinking. In 1924, she was advised to move herself and her husband to the warmer climate of Surrey, and to base her work in London. Evan also moved to Brighton and Worthing, where he did freelance writing. Apart from a brief reunion at a conference in 1924, the men of prayer went their separate ways—Arthur Harris to one mission, J. C. Williams to another; Mr. Scottorn to a pastorate, and Mr. Johnson to full-time work in Paris.

During this period of change, Jessie agreed to entrust some of the work to new men, such as Vicar Proctor from Liverpool. The next announcement amazed everyone—that she had asked T. Madoc Jeffreys and Austen Sparkes to undertake the main tasks. Remember that Jessie had already announced in 1914 that God's planning made it necessary for each servant to be prepared for new commissions and should never cling on to work that had become unnecessary and unfruitful. Now, in the early twenties, she could use this kind of reasoning to justify her change of helpers and partners. She told friends that she had been looking in vain for a man anointed to teach truth: "I labored in delivery of my message, watching with eyes and ears to see whether there was some hidden and chosen instructor to whom I could transmit the burden. A man who would rise up in God's time to proclaim it to the world."

In practice, the chosen men each tried to pull the Overcomer Testimony wherever they wished to go. Then Jessie herself seemed to be moving in new directions.

Part Five
New Directions

23

A Time for Protest

Neither Evan Roberts nor Jessie Penn-Lewis took part in the big controversies in the *Life of Faith* and the *Christian* (1919-1921) over such ideas as Christian socialism, national regeneration, the League of Nations, and the inroads of higher criticism as it affected the faith. Perhaps she said more during the private workers' conferences at Sion College and Eccleston Hall in London.

This reticence is all the more strange because of Jessie's many involvements in moral crusades during the war years, such as D. M. Panton's two crusades against the refusal to recognize conscientious objectors and against the general practice of issuing strong drink to the young conscripts. In April 1917, she began to campaign against *spiritism* because its advocates were putting great pressure on war widows. She asked her 1917 Conference to pray against this and against Satanism and the "dark forces."

Jessie's main concern was with apostasy. At the time it looked as though a new world network of prayer warriors would be formed who would exchange international news. She got a warm response in June 1916, from a group in Colorado who claimed that all the denominations were turning their backs on the Cross and that there was widespread apostasy and idolatry, which had to be protested against and not just prayed about. A similar letter from Stavanger in Norway, May 4, 1918, tried to set up an alliance against all who opposed "Jesus and Him Crucified." In November of that year, Mrs. Karvel of Drobak, Norway, asked for the formation of a fellowship of those who preached "Christ Crucified." From Sweden, Sigrid Kurke told how they longed for the coming of the Lord, because all their work was being misunderstood and rejected. From far off Brazil, in July 1918, Mr. Wootton told how he had discovered proof of something she had warned then about—"imitations of prayer life". Someone had set up an *Esoteric Society of the Community of Thought*, which argued that Matthew 18:19-20 meant that concentrated prayer would work without reference to the Cross and Resurrection.

The warning pamphlet Wootton referred to was entitled, *The Camouflaging of the Cross,* of which a fragment of the French version has survived:

> There is a complete system of religious and theological camouflage within modern Protestantism, amidst the sermons, conference addresses, and writings of a large proportion of its clergy. The camouflage is so subtle that few discern it or suspect the danger. Error rarely has the courage and candor to disclose herself. It is nearly always under a cloak of truth that it enters the spirits of listeners. Error doesn't show itself openly but likes to mix itself with the truth. A fine sermon, with great eloquence and moving speech, is often only a covering under which are hidden errors. From this the natural development and apogee is the mystical "Babylon" of the Anti-Christ. (See Matthew 24:4.)

The "New Theology" is a striking example of this. It puts forwards its errors under a coat of old theology. In its actual teaching there is a complete "technique" by means of which error is sown, heresies are propagated, and the deadly poison of doubt and negation is spread around.

Let us put up against this method some proclamations of God's Word which proves the heart and intentions of men. (See Hebrews 4:12; 2 Timothy 1:13.;Titus 1:9-12.) There are many speechifiers and seducers who are to be silenced for they overturn entire families. You must rebuke them severely; you must say things that conform to sound doctrine. What impeccable purity of motive and method the Holy Spirit demands of ministers of the Word.

Camouflage of a theological kind is to clothe in an evangelical hue those theories which are contrary to sound doctrine. It is to believe an error without saying so, it is to spread error by means of the truth or negation by means of seemingly evangelical statement.

Mrs. Penn-Lewis said that there was a double camouflage that was corrupting the pulpit and emptying the Protestant Churches: "The error secretly disguised under deceptive theological terms is then propagated by men who camouflage themselves under the mantle of servants of God, pretending to have the right to call upon the Lord while they deny the expiatory Blood of the Cross, the only means of redemption. We need to take heed to Paul's words in Romans 16:17-19. By means of flattering words and under cover of a certain degree of affection for the Bible and for the person of Christ, a preacher can seduce a whole audience who are lulled by his eloquence, disarmed from all suspicion of error by his words and terms that appear orthodox. These are indeed dangerous days and God is giving His people a solemn warning by drawing attention to the camouflages of the last days. The devil is laying his

> snares of spiritual and intellectual seduction on the battlefield of the war of Faith."

The *Camouflage Pamphlet* reverberated all around the world. A shoal of letters expressed praise and thanksgiving and several of these accepted the pamphlet as ammunition in the fight to overcome Satan's wiles. This was a new way to be an overcomer.

Meanwhile, a new field of conflict appeared in 1918-1920, concerning the future of the Young Women's Christian Association, whose branches had been the scene of so much soulwinning and blessing twenty five years earlier. As it happened, two letters arrived the same week, both of which deeply disturbed Jessie. The first of these, from G. H. Lang of Weston Super Mare, on July 24, 1918, called on all godly members to secede from the YWCA because it now employed unregenerate workers. The present leaders, he wrote, would make spiritual recovery a hopeless task. The second letter, from Mr. Menzies of Liverpool, spoke even more severely about the worldliness of their YWCA. Two weeks later, a third letter arrived, from H. Walters of Dublin, who said that there, too, the YWCA had become apostate. Finally, on the 24th of August, a strong letter from Armstrong Bennett called the YWCA "Synagogues of Satan." Jessie's first publicized protest made good use of these private letters.

With great skill, she marshaled all the serious charges against the YWCA, and then set them out in a pamphlet entitled, *The Real Issue in the YWCA Crisis*. She stated that the trouble started during the discussions over a proposed new constitution in 1918. An attempt was made to remove key doctrines, such as the substitutionary, atoning death of Christ and the authority of the Bible as the Word of God. This had opened the door, she said, for non-evangelical workers to get into the upper levels so that even writers in the YWCA magazine began to express very broad views. All protests were stifled and about fifty branches withdrew in order to form their own conference. A national referendum was arranged to see if everyone wanted it run only by those who honored the ideals and beliefs of the founders. Inevitably, the breakaway group was forced to consider an alternative organization faithful to the founding documents, but they also needed a good writer to set out their position.

The liberalizers had been giving the impression that all the fuss was about trifling matters, but Jessie Penn-Lewis dismissed this and said that the true struggle was to prevent dry rot from invading the entire system via modernism. They must recognize that this movement had also become a part of the worldwide apostasy. Now the Holy Spirit was urging all of them, in different spheres, to speak against and pray against this subtle forsaking of the truth. So she made a final appeal to the Lord's Intercessors: "The Holy Spirit is the Restrainer, but He must have instruments through whom He can exercise that power, and the restraining is wrought through prayer. Then go and speak clearly the Gospel of the grace of God."

Jessie's book makes no use of the more dramatic laments about doubtful practices within the YWCA. It was more effective to compare present programs with the visions and plans of the self-sacrificing people who had launched the movement. Only a woman of vast experience as well as deep spiritual perception could have brought out into broad daylight the gradual undermining and diluting of the doctrinal basis and the blurring of stated aims and ideals of that movement.

There was one more controversial issue that was surely the subject of lively debate on both sides of the Atlantic. The issue was the status, obligations, roles, and spiritual functions of born-again Christian women. The matter was more urgent in the so-called Gospel churches that belonged to "The Dispensation of Grace." Their story ran back to the day of

Pentecost when the Holy Spirit had exercised His authority to pour out gifts and powers. If these were bestowed equally upon the servants and handmaidens, it surely followed that they should have equal liberty, honor, and power to witness.

Much of the debate took place in America, but in Britain it was crystallized in Jessie Penn-Lewis's remarkable book entitled, *The Magna Carta of Christian Women*. This book appeared just when the British electorate had acknowledged the right of all women not only to vote but to enter into public offices. Perhaps she felt this was the right time to challenge the serried ranks of clergy who held to the hoary tradition that Christian women had no separate status, no right to communicate the truth, and no kind of ministry other than to nurture and train children and see to the needs of the helpless. Probably she had considered the issue for some years, but 1919 was clearly the right time for a book to appear.

There is now enough evidence from her papers that Jessie had been reading up on this subject for about ten years. The only thing that surprises those who have studied Jessie Penn-Lewis's remarkable career and ministry is that she took so long to get around to the subject of the status of Christian women. For many years she had walked boldly through various gates of opportunity and had even spoken from the parent Keswick's platform, until she was sidelined into "Women Only" meetings in 1896. She spoke trenchantly in public about developments in the national and international YWCA movement that was run entirely by Christian women. She also achieved a certain amount of publicity in Germany and Scandinavia, especially after re-interpreting Psalm 68:10-11 and 25-26 as a divine commission for women to preach good tidings.

During that very traditional Edwardian era, when godly convention chairmen tried to restrain her passionate speeches and when Christian publishers tried to modify her prophetic messages, Jessie Penn-Lewis kept her ideals alive. She seems to have been well informed about, if not always in touch with, great Christian women such as Pandita Ramabhai and Amy Carmichael in India, the gifted Carey Judd Montgomery in California, the redoubtable Mrs. Field of New York, and that brave band of countesses, baronesses, and princesses whom she met in Northern Europe. Among them was Baroness Lieven, the Volkoff sisters, Swedish Baroness Kurke, and that unusual Countess Wrede, who obtained a permit from the prison board to live with her servants in a suite of prison cells each summer so that she could minister to inmates' souls. All these experiences must have convinced her that God had a special purpose for Christian women.

From 1905 onwards, a more dynamic impulse worked in favor of women, because as and when the Holy Spirit came like a flood in the revival, everyone seemed to enjoy total spiritual freedom and scores of *handmaidens* took part. Those who have studied the eyewitness accounts of J. T. Job and others in *Voices from the Revival*, will see how important were the spirit-filled women in transforming worship and reinvigorating witness. Consecrated, spirit-filled women not only testified and prophesied, but interpreted and taught, and answered urgent questions. To leave out all reference to Rosina Davies, Flossie Evans, Maggie Rees, Mary Roberts, and Mrs. Jones of Egryn, would seriously distort the picture. Journalists were quick to see the difference and it was they who commented in a variety of tones of voice. No doubt some religious journals also discussed this phenomenon, which was played down later on.

Curiously enough, Jessie Penn-Lewis did not emphasize these changes in her newspaper reports, nor in *The Awakening in Wales*. Yet, when she herself was challenged to take a lesser part at the conventions, and was actually criticized at Keswick in Wales for disputing with the clerical brethren at a breakfast, she felt they were rejecting her spiritual gifts. In 1907, she wrote to the Rev. Evan Hopkins about spiritual retrogradism in the Keswick movement and said, "There must be clear and open ground for women in the work of God." Year by year, her ministry was marginalized either into the ladies' meeting only or into some extra weekend meeting. It was soon realized that whenever and wherever she delivered the message, the multitude came and many ministers slipped in to hear her anointed teaching. She was denied the main platform in the Scottish equivalent and, eventually, in the Keswick in Wales. She slowly withdrew, and then resigned in 1910-1911, and formed her own conferences. She also parted company with the editors of the *Life of Faith* and set up a new magazine under her own direction.

Exactly when she decided to write on behalf of woman's ministry is not known, but she had gathered together a selection of books and booklets that presented both sides of the argument. Pickering and Inglis' *Books on the Ministry of Women,* had long since set out the old argument that prophesyings and tongues belonged to the apostolic age only and that no woman in New Testament times was ever expected to be a preacher or evangelist. A Dr. West, of Washington, openly advocated the exclusion of all women from all the ministries in church life and denied that Psalm 68:24-26 or any other biblical passage could be used to justify women praying publicly, preaching, teaching, and debating. Only pagan systems, he said, gave leading roles to females. Therefore, giving special status to women would lead us either back to paganism and impurity or onwards into Christian Science, spiritism, and other dreadful errors.

A. J. Pollock wrote that the new moves in favor of women expressed the spirit of lawlessness and were the fruit of "Eve's Fall." Mrs. Morrow stated that a woman's ministry was not to be public testimony or witnessing but compassionate service. John Caldwell set out the traditional arguments for keeping women out of teaching, preaching, exhorting, and evangelizing. The law of silence was right, he said, because the free speech of women in churches led to license and disobedience.

The most infuriating book was Peter Easton's, of Chicago, *Does Woman represent God?* Somehow he made the advocates of women in ministry sound as though they were ready to support women's rebellions, false prophetesses, ancient fertility priestesses, and sorceresses. It is rather difficult to picture Amy Carmichael, Mrs. General Booth, Lady Pandita Ramabhai, Carey Judd Montgomery, and Jessie Penn-Lewis as belonging to this sinister sisterhood.

On the positive side of the debate, Jessie made considerable use of Catherine Booth's 1909 book about female ministry. Her case started with the undeniable fact that the Holy Spirit fell upon handmaidens who could pray and prophesy and surely therefore could communicate the Gospel. This act of God, she said, was an open rejection of hoary Rabbinical tradition and a direct threat, then as now, to the official religious leaders who had, as always, tried to deprive women of opportunities for study and training.

Whatever other writers there may have been in the field, Jessie depended most of all on Dr. Katherine Burchell's books. These evolved from the cyclo-styled notes of her Woman's Bible Correspondence Class (1906-1914), which had its own *Woman's Catechism* and its own pamphlets about *Woman Preachers* and *Women in the Gospels*. One complete series studied "Eve and her salvation." Another set provided detailed evidence of how the masculine bias of translators had caused inconsistent translation of the Hebrew and Greek originals. At the end of each study, one feels as if she has swept the carpet from under the opposition.

The Badge of Guilt and Shame is a splendid surgical job of cutting away accumulated myths and the kind of rules invented and imposed by Rabbis. Only once does her seething anger break out: "Why should the male libertine, the male idiot, the male man of many sins, be given headship and authority when the purest and most modest 'Mary' is told to cover her face with veils as a perpetual sign of her vulnerability to the tempters?"

Jessie Penn-Lewis's own book, *The Magna Carta of Women*, was intended to answer a vital question—whether Christian women in their witness for Christ are to share in the general emancipation of womankind. Alternatively, should all believing, born of the Spirit women retire into a far narrower sphere of service as soon as they become Christians. Her clear mind perceived at once that the truths contained in God's Word would point Christian women to their true destiny and true ministries. She adopted Dr. Bushnell's proofs of mistranslation and unreliable borrowings from Rabbinical sources. She agreed that the text, "Ye all prophesy one by one" could not be translated as a single sex phrase and asked why Priscilla, Chloe, and Philip's daughters were commissioned as proclaimers.

Both writers showed what the word *subjection* really meant in the context of Christian married love. Both pleaded for another look at the idea of subordinate roles, especially where mixed marriages of believers and unbelievers were involved. But the main contention was that within the mysterious *Body* known as the Church of Christ, woman is also a partaker of the divine nature, woman is also an heir of salvation and a pilgrim and a worshipper who is entitled to go within the veil.

The concluding pages in her book are Jessie's own contribution and understandably she links all with her main Cross-theology:

> How can the Church, which is the Body of Christ, reach its full stature if it breaks the laws of the Spirit

> and denies one half of the Church the right to speak in the assembly and subjects itself to man-made ordinances, when Jesus took these to the Atoning Cross and slew their force, just as He slew racial laws and all other distinctions and made all one in Christ Jesus—one in worship, work, and witness.

Typically she cast her eye over the many revivals she had known and wrote:

> The Spirit of God has never been poured forth in any company in any part of the world without the "handmaids" prophesying, for this is the spontaneous and invariable result of the Spirit of God moving upon women as well as men. We dare not quench the Spirit in those whom God has moved to proclaim the Gospel, by saying that only men were inspired by the Holy Spirit.
>
> We earnestly pray that through this message every Christian woman who has been called of God to witness for Him in proclaiming godliness will be strengthened to fulfill her ministry, with the empowering assurance that the Word of God is in harmony with the call of God which she has received.

Slowly, she came to a place where she would assert that, in the age of the Holy Spirit, women could be entrusted with prophetic and teaching ministries of the highest kind. Evan Roberts said that this would not happen until the Millennial Age, but Jessie Penn-Lewis wanted that ideal, absolute equality in the Body of Christ on earth here and now. Hence her dignified protest and her final prayer "that the Lord will send forth more witnesses, both men and women, to proclaim the truth before this dispensation ends."

24

Jessie Penn-Lewis and the Healing Movements

In this twentieth century, which is pre-eminently the age of skepticism, it must surely be God's will that each unbelieving generation shall be brought face to face with great waves of divine healing. Once in every generation a series of healing events occur, not in secret, but in very public places. Those healing events seem to defy any scientific explanation, as so many medical experts have had to testify. Ten years before the Great War of 1914-1918, a generation witnessed one such wave. The post-war generation saw another. More recently, the people of another World War's aftermath saw a third great outbreak accompanied by other signs and wonders. Our present generation has once again been challenged, not only with a widespread practice of divine healing, but also with the first fully worked out theologies of healing. In many cases, these have shown the benefit of the study and work done by Christians who are doctors, psychiatrists, and counselors.

Both Jessie Penn-Lewis and Evan Roberts had, at one

time, experienced healings of the mind and body that they liked to call "deliverances from" or "victories over" the prince of this world. Illnesses, they argued, were part of the spiritual warfare; weaknesses were just opportunities to call on the Lord for the grace that was always sufficient. With the strength of the Lord at our disposal, we should surely be more than conquerors.

Some of Jessie's experiences of divine healing were unfortunate. She was sent the free newspapers of a dozen Pentecostalist groups, each of which had columns and columns of marvelous and supernatural healings. Some of the writers asserted that in the age of the Holy Spirit there was no need for Christians to consult physicians—all they needed was access to Jesus. This became a serious issue with her when she was attacked very bitterly by representatives of a cult in Wellington, New Zealand, in 1916, because she had allowed doctors to examine her lungs to see whether the tuberculosis had recurred. To these fanatics, medicine was a network of conjecture, anesthetics were just a tool, and pharmacy was a kind of witchcraft. The only true way to recovery, they said, was by confession and restitution, and a pledge of full obedience to all the Mosaic laws. Jessie rejected all such legalism.

During the Great War, there were thousands of maimed and damaged Christians returning from the trenches. Many had doubting minds and seared souls, but others dreamed of being healed in some totally unexpected way. It was only natural, therefore, that the religious journals should discuss the possibilities of direct divine restoration of physical and mental faculties. Jessie played little part in the public debate but she had certainly read Philip Mauro's book, *Divine Healing*. She had problems with her own affliction in 1915-1916, and told the Christian workers, some years later, that there were times when she could have accepted that some forms of sickness were actually satanic attacks on their power to serve. This was a dangerous line of thought, and one dear lady, Miss Scoles of Bolton, wrote on June 22, 1922, with some urgency and asked, "Is my multiple illness a sign of Satan's bonds?"

From time to time, Jessie received letters of inquiry that led her to search more deeply into the matter. A lady from Wallingford, who had heard about Jessie's ill health, asked now if it really was the Lord's will that His workers should patiently endure breakdown and pain. "I cannot look at it in that light," she wrote, "I have faith that prayer will at last win through."

Another anxious inquirer wrote, "Anything that you can give for the help and for the healing of the saints in the pages of *The Overcomer*, I shall be most thankful for. I have been ready to make intercession for others and I have often received encouragement and blessing." Yet only once did Jessie tackle this subject.

A Birmingham pastor named George Carter wrote and told her about workers attached to the "Christian Healing Mission" who were humble, sincere, and free from doctrinal error. He appealed to her to put this before an Overcomer conference, to decide how far they would go along with anointing for healing and, also, with some kind of casting out of demons. Inquiries were made and Jessie was told that the Christian Healing Mission was too much under the influence of the Emmanuelists, whose leaders believed in intercession for the sick through the Holy Communion and its elements. They also indulged in mental therapeutics as channels for spiritual forces. In the Emmanuelist Hospices in India, clergymen, physicians, and psychotherapists worked together because it was argued that Christ would have us use all means, from herbs and incantations to the prayer of faith. The theology was quite cloudy.

It was stated rather unfairly that the Emmanuel influence had infiltrated the work of a Mr. Hicks of Calcutta. The miraculous effects of Hicks's ministry were fully reported in *The Remembrancer* on April 9, 1921, which was the Prayer Circular of the Bengal and Assam Prayer Union. One of the missionaries described Hicks's Confirmation Class where there were seven cases of healing and sudden recovery. He also laid hands on a missionary who wanted freedom from an impure demon. Hicks attributed all the healings to the living Christ.

In the South West of England in 1922-1923, there was an official movement centered around the Rev. A. T. Dence, the Diocesan Healing Missioner who served under the Bishop of Exeter. The dispute arose over the role of the consecrated oil that he used. Jessie Penn-Lewis got involved only because a very fine Christian lady had come, full of faith, for Mr. Dence's blessing, and had experienced nothing at all. The family decided to write to Jessie asking, "What can be the meaning of this? She is grieved to see such emphasis laid on the holy oil. She feels that God is being robbed of the glory and that is why He cannot respond to her faith."

Jessie replied:

> I am afraid I am not able to give you much light upon the matter. The whole subject of healing is really very perplexing because, in some cases, God appears to remarkably heal, and in others, some unaccountable hindrance takes place. The light may only come gradually for I know that I have gone through different attacks and have sometimes been a week in suffering, with one cry to God perpetually, that He would give me clear light that I may understand His will. I think that the Lord is giving new light to many and a deeper knowledge of the Cross through these physical attacks. There is something deeper than being directly healed

> through anointing—that is, taking the Risen Life of the Crucified Christ to quicken the mortal body.

While she was making up her mind, Jessie seems to have been sent information about variant forms of healing. She dismissed both Pelmanism and Coueism as too man-centered and the Lourdes type of pilgrimage healing as too psychic and "Angel- centered." Strangely enough, she also ignored fellow-Welshman, Stephen Jeffreys, in the early stages of his "Faith-healing" that caused scores of conversions in South Wales. He became a celebrated figure in London until some of the healed people testified that they had not been healed permanently. There *were* true healings, also, but Jessie was too impressed by the findings of the celebrated psychiatrist, Dr. A. T. Schofield, who had been conducting a three-year research project into "Miracle Healings."

In his last report, Dr. Schofield stated that he had discovered that in most cases the mysterious force of auto-suggestion was involved, but there were instances of artificial stimulation. His essay that appeared on December 7, 1921, was a masterly review of Christian healings in every age that had the common factors of total humility and total belief in the Lord's willingness to answer prayer. He categorically denied all claims that sickness among God's people is the result of disobedience or unbelief, as certain cults taught. About this time, Jessie Penn-Lewis was called upon to deal with two difficult cases.

The first case was of a missionary's wife who had been thrown off balance by the death in hospital of one of her children from meningitis in the same year that she was entering her *change of life*. When she later caught typhus fever, she refused to take any medicines, not even the standard quinine, because she was told it was a sign of sinful distrust in God's power to heal. She had learned some new doctrine of complete healing through the powers bestowed by the risen Christ and by the Spirit, although Jessie told her to put her trust in the Blood of the Crucified One for healing. The unfortunate woman went around persuading others to accept these teachings and wondered why she was winning so few converts. Jessie could see only too clearly that this kind of obsession would most likely become an obstacle to all further witness.

Her answer shows the influence of an article on "Spiritual Hypertrophy" that was found in her box of papers. The article stated that many of these healing ideas emanated from an over-stimulated consciousness ruined through too much dissecting of the soul and too much analysis of spiritual truths. This created a craving for the abnormal and the delusive and this was, in effect, a kind of sickness of the soul. This argument appealed strongly to Jessie, especially when she was asked to deal with the second difficult case.

Letters came from a sincere and earnest Mrs. Laura D., from a town in the State of Victoria, Australia, in which she described in fantastic detail all her manifestations, emotional highs, and ecstatic actions, such as holy laughter, roarings, solitary dances, "kissing the Bridegroom" dreams, and obeying strange commands. This went on up to the moment when she took Jessie Penn-Lewis's advice, burned her books that had taught her about such things, and called upon God to "give back my will," and "enable me to cast out all spirits in the name of Jesus." Then she began to recover but, a few months later, asked Jessie to help her get really free. She was told that she would still be at the mercy of deceiving spirits unless and until she "came out into the light."

Jessie asked her permission to record in *The Overcomer* the stages in her deliverance, in order to help others in the same plight. She told Laura that if such public witness caused her pain and shame, that in itself would help her get free. In effect, the testifier would be accepting a kind of "suffering and death with Christ," she said. Recognizing that this was a serious illness of the mind, Jessie still insisted that it had been caused by a demonic invasion of Laura's psyche that could be defeated only by "His Blood and Calvary's work."

Jessie's first treatment of the problem of sickness and suffering appeared as the tenth chapter of a book she wrote in 1917. All around her were churches who grieved over their chronic cases and permanent invalids, many of whom had to cope with broken minds. There were also a number of older people who had lost interest even in the rapture as they experienced the speedy breakdown of their health and strength during their advancing years. Jessie assured them that these experiences were God's way of preparing them to accept, and even welcome, the hour when "our dying nature will be swallowed up in life. You may be weaker and weaker," she wrote, "yet in the power of the life triumphant over death, you will go forward in the Power of God." Such a reply still did not satisfy the average Christian. Meanwhile, she was kept in touch with new healing movements.

In New Zealand, a remarkably earnest and humble Maori evangelist named Ratana, suddenly became a faith healer, not for everyone, but for his own race. Supported by Prince Tupu, the ex-cripple, and by a Council of Chiefs, Ratana astounded his people by announcing that he could offer healing to any Maori who forsook the old superstitions and ways of darkness. This was necessary because bodily healing through the Cross of Christ, the Holy Spirit, and the Angels of Light needed, first of all, an act of repentance and a complete change of lifestyle. The implication was that diseases sprang from inward soul sicknesses such as lust and anger. Jessie Penn-Lewis would have found no fault with this reasoning, as far as it went.

Something very like this was being proclaimed in the American Midwest by the Bosworth Brothers. In 1923, some

American friends sent her a copy of the *Labor National Tribune* of Pittsburgh, Pennsylvania, that told an amazing story under its banner headlines, HEALINGS MANIFEST MIRACULOUS POWER OF GOD. MEDICAL AND SURGICAL EXPERTS SAY, "PHENOMENAL!"

An entire edition was filled with statistics, biographical notes, and sensational testimonies about healing miracles. They also printed Fred Bosworth's famous reply to a pressman who suggested he would get "puffed up" after all this attention:

> If God does more for me than for someone else, it is because I am a bigger beggar. It would be idiotic for me to get puffed up. There is no glory in being a bigger beggar than someone else.

The Bosworths went on to Chicago where twenty-five thousand heard them at the Humboldt Park Gospel Tabernacle. Then they were called to the Toronto Revival Campaign and explained to the press why the salvation message had to be given first and the invitation to be healed afterwards. It was in the Alliance Tabernacle, Toronto, Canada, that Bosworth propounded his excellent "Thirty-one Questions on Divine Healing". A copy was sent to Jessie Penn-Lewis, who must have approved some of the points.

Here are some examples of the questions:

> Question 11. Why should not the Second Adam take away all that the First Adam brought upon us?
>
> Question 12. Since the Church is the Body of Christ, does God want the Body of Christ to be sick? Is it not His will to heal any part of it?
>
> Question 14. Since the "body is for the Lord," a living sacrifice unto God, would He not rather have a well body than a wrecked one?
>
> Question 16. Does not the glorious Gospel Dispensation offer as much mercy and compassion to

its sufferers as did the darker Dispensations?

Question 23. Since "The Son of God was manifested that He might destroy the works of the devil," has He now relinquished this purpose? Does He now want the works of the devil in our bodies to continue? Does God want a cancer or a plague?

Question 27. Is not God as willing to show the mercy of healing to His worshippers as He is to show the mercy of forgiveness to His enemies?

Question 31. Could the loving heart of the Son of God, who had compassion on the sick and healed all who had need of help and healing, cease to regard the sufferings of His own when He had become exalted at the right hand of the Father?

After many successful campaigns, F. F. Bosworth became even more committed to the concept of God preserving His people from all ills. A tract published at Dayton, Ohio, entitled, *Why Many Die Prematurely*, put together all the Bible expositions and all the testimonies that would prove that the Blood of Christ, shed on Calvary, can provide healing from all diseases. He even claimed that "you can be healed when you put the bread of communion in your mouth, if you are discerning the Lord's body as broken for you." Bosworth said that the chief reason why a healing might *not* occur was that the spirit of disobedience and unconfessed sin was still in the seeker's heart. He stated, "Christ continues to heal all who meet the conditions because what the Atonement did for those who lived in that day, it does for us in our day."

One other healing movement attracted the notice of Jessie Penn-Lewis. It was associated with a poetess, Carey Judd Montgomery, who had a ministry based on the Home of Peace in Beulah Hills, Oakland, California. She was one of those anointed women whom Jessie had foreseen in her famous *Manifesto*. The Home of Peace catered to stressed missionaries and there were daily prayer sessions that were often blessed with healings. From this center, Carey sent out many testimony tracts and other books about divine healing. Her magazine, called *Triumphs of Faith*, told stories of spiritual healing from covetousness and bitterness and other diseases of the soul. A colleague, McCall Barbour, taught that deliverance and victory over the soul's imprisoning passions was a part of Christ's victory on the Cross, which is what Jessie believed also. The essay, "Christ's Healing Touch Today," which was reprinted in *The Life of Faith*, expressed the full teaching of the House of Peace.

> The miracles of healing were not something optional; they were an essential and necessary part of Christ's atoning work. His work was salvation from sin and deliverance from the physical consequences of sin. The healing of the body was external evidence of the truth and reality of forgiveness of sins. We are meant to have wholeness and perfect health and we could reword Acts 4:12 as "Neither is there Healing in any other name than Christ's." The blockage to both blessings is unbelief.

Unfortunately, they went too far in interpreting Mark 16:17-18 as an undertaking to preserve health, protect from all evil, and provide power to heal all sickness. They claimed that, in most cases, failure was "probably due to defective faith or unrepented sin or a rebellious spirit, or an unwillingness to surrender all to God."

It was this kind of dogmatism that was denounced in an article by Dr. A. T. Schofield in *The Life Of Faith* on December 7, 1921. He wrote that this false doctrine "takes away all blessing and comfort from the sick bed and brands the sufferer with unbelief." It is doubtful whether Jessie could have accepted that believers have the right to claim from God a perfect protection, in exactly the same way as one asks pardon for sin. The very idea tortured the unhealed into imagining that they must also be the unforgiven and lost, whilst it inflated those who got healed or never felt sick. What a temptation it was, when results did not correspond with hopes, to think up some explanation, such as secret failure to believe or obey or repent, which would cause more agonized self-examination. One of the group even claimed that for anyone who grew old and weary, God would renew them; so "the Lord has left no excuse for anyone—He has a promise to fit every case." How did all this sound to Jessie Penn-Lewis who had known various sicknesses for forty years and who admitted freely to a growing tiredness?

It was obvious by 1922 that such a wide spectrum of healing movements needed critical examination by good biblical scholars in the United States and in Britain. Dr. A. B. Simpson, founder of the Christian Alliance movement, entered the field in June 1921, with six studies. In the first essay, he interpreted the word "quickening" in Romans 8:11 as a present work of the Holy Spirit—not a raising of the body one day but a renewing, stimulating, and uplifting in the present. The indwelling Spirit can unite us with the risen Christ in such a way that new strength and energy can enter an exhausted servant. But healing is not automatically granted because the Lord will be calling home those who have completed their service.

> Faith for Divine healing is not mere abstinence from remedies or a submission to the ordinance of anointing, but it is the real spiritual touch of Christ, much more rare than many suppose.

Like the Bosworths, Dr. Simpson argued from the Old Testament that both chapter 33 of Job and Psalm 103 bring salvation and healing very close together, and that these are united in Isaiah 53:4-5, where it is stated, "He has borne our sicknesses and carried our pains (see Matthew's interpretation in Matthew 8:17) . . . and by His stripes we are healed." This should not be restricted to soul-healings, Dr. Simpson wrote, for that would be bad exegesis. He believed that the removal of the curse (Galatians 3.13) by Christ's substitutionary act included removal of the physical effects of sin. Thus the Cross furnishes solid ground for claiming divine healing in His name through simple faith. It is God's grace and is a costly gift. It should be returned to the giver in living sacrifice and consecrated living.

All his teachings were summarized in the October 8, 1921 issue of *Alliance Weekly* (New York), and were published in pamphlet form. A final essay on December 31, 1921, was an attack on those healing cults that demanded strict asceticism and hard disciplines that were the very opposite of sympathy and compassion. Christ has taken all the pains of diseases into His own body, which was made like unto human bodies. Now He can revivify and heal each of us.

Our duty is to discover what position Jessie Penn-Lewis finally took up. Apart from a few scattered references in reply letters to inquirers, there exist two major statements.

First is a reply to a question at a workers' conference. This was recorded in a report book called *Experimental Difficulties*. The questioner at the conference asked, "Can you give us some light about sickness?" The reply covered four main points:

> If you can bear and endure pain but it becomes necessary for your service that you are delivered from any attack on your body—on that ground you have a claim for deliverance and healing.
>
> "In His healed wounds there is healing for us'," operates when we share in His wounded and crucified life and death. The same life-power that healed and

> restored His broken body can heal and quicken my broken body.
>
> Healing is part of the finished work of Calvary, but the Spirit has to apply this individually and at the right stage. If your will is not fully united to the will of God, then healing the body might strengthen self-will.
>
> Do not force any believer, or yourself, into a blessing the soul is not ready for. Do not get into bondage through impatience etc. Take this attitude, "I take into my inner being all that the Lord wants me to have." Then wait patiently for Him and He will work.

Second is a booklet published about 1917-1919. The booklet dealt with the proper interpretation of Isaiah 53:5. She agreed with all those who had said that the work of Christ on the Cross had a direct connection with the cure of sickness and pain. But it was not a question of instant miracle cures, nor was it only a question of purging the soul first and healing the body afterwards. If Christ had borne our diseases, as part of Adam's fall and curse, to the Cross, and had destroyed them through His death and resurrection, then our only way of deliverance is by dying with Him and rising with Him. At this point, the Holy Spirit will take over our consciences and will cause us to hate and reject such destructive things as envy, jealousy, pride, wrath, and malice. This will break the power of the old nature or old Adam life, and will clear the way for the new life to be poured into our souls, our minds, our affections, and every other part of our mortal bodies. Then comes that new strength and energy that will affect us physically. Sometimes God will do this work speedily where He knows that the person will not be puffed up. More often than not, He gives this renewing energy in a slower, more patient way.

In the case of God's servants who are called to special duties, God will set aside a kind of reserve spiritual strength that He then gives to His servants when under special strain or attack or oppression. Whichever way it is done, all believers should know that there is a sure and certain victory.

This was a more convincing and satisfying line of reasoning than that earlier statement, sent out in letters, which had argued that a portion of pain and sorrow was a necessary part of a Christian's mental and spiritual preparation for the rapture of the saints. The new notes of deliverance and victory could be heard many times among her closest friends as their times of testing came and they saw loved friends and beloved husbands and wives endure much pain of body and yet still live victoriously. Looking back over her own darkest days, Jessie could still see how God had performed a wonderful work in and through her frail body. His grace had been sufficient for her, His strength had been manifested in her weakness, and she had been able to do all things through Christ her Lord.

25

The Second Advent Debates

Even when Jessie Penn-Lewis took no direct part in a debate, she would still assemble a number of reports and relevant books in readiness for question time at the workers' conferences. She accepted the current dispensational theory, including the millennial reign of Christ, but her main interest was in the manner of His return to this world. That interest was intensified by the burden message announced by Evan Roberts in October 1913. It was made all the more urgent when Europe fell into chaos and violent war whilst the entire task of evangelizing the world and overthrowing the principalities and powers was delayed. Jessie was by no means the only one to revise her views during her lifetime—it was a time when vigorous new sects were also sharpening up their Adventist doctrines.

Second-advent teachings seem to have passed through cycles. The nineteenth century Adventist movements were stern and judgmental. They focused on the social disorder, the political upheaval, and the general wickedness of what they called the "Last Age." Only a few looked upwards into the skies and rejoiced at the prospect of the Lord coming from heaven, first to rapture or translate His own people.

The editors of *Living Waters* in Nashville, Tennessee, promised that during the forthcoming tribulation, Israel would rediscover its spiritual gifts and recover its special role. A more striking presentation of these ideas appeared in a magazine called *Friend of Israel,* which published Thomas Chalmers' teaching that Israel under its present *curse* was always a source of moral corruption, dead tradition, and every kind of anti-Christian philosophy from Spinoza and Hegel to Trotsky. But in the last days, this poisoned source would be replaced by pure God-centered wisdom as soon as Israel was back in its own land and its true faith.

Towards the end of the century, the evils of the present society and the certainty of a final Day of Judgment figured in the fiery sermons of a score of celebrated evangelists in places like the Midwest states of America.

The various doomsday themes continued to thrive in the *Morning Star,* which was published from Sion House in London. Their concept was double-edged in that the "The Evil Hour" or the "Day of the Wrath," which would come upon the world, would also be the "Day of Vindication" and the "Waking up time" for all the children of the Day (see 1 Thessalonians 5). They wrote, "It would also be the Day of Reward for all who had kept themselves unspotted from the world." The main emphasis was always judgment and final catastrophe. Like the magazines of the Seventh Day Adventists and the Watchtower Movement, this journal and its contemporaries spent a great deal of printers' ink in condemning war-fever, strikes, socialism, spiritism, and suffragettism as the typical symptoms of a doomed world.

It may seem a surprising thing to say, but Jessie's announcement in 1897 of a final aggressive warfare against the kingdom of Satan, and her call to get spiritually and morally prepared for the last fight, was more positive than any that went before it. There were to be prayer bands and a prayer host, and this was formed about 1910. Usher and others claimed that a strong prayer movement could still control events on earth and bring wars to a halt. Williams and his friends had close links with missionaries in Baltic lands whilst Jessie tried to maintain contact with a faithful remnant in Russia. From both these areas came messages claiming that the Lord was going to return and intervene soon and take His people before the ultimate terror came. Everywhere the cry rose up, "O Lord return."

Those words were already on the lips of hundreds of Pentecostal believers who said over and over, in tongues or otherwise, "Jesus the Lord is coming soon." No doubt that was why worldwide publicity was given to Evan Roberts' burden message that called people to instant readiness for the great event. At the same time, many were inclined to accept the claim put forward by Jessie and Evan in *War on the Saints*, that intensified prayer by God's people could speed up the day of the rapture and perhaps the day of final judgment, whilst a spirit of doubt and unbelief could well hinder or retard the coming of Christ and all else.

The curious thing is that there was a teaching in Mary Baker Eddy's Christian Science magazine, *Active Service,* that sounded very like this and yet was utterly different. She said that any united, earnest, purely motivated group that engaged in meditation could shorten the European war and bring violence to an end. One advocate wrote in the magazine, "You can bring about permanent peace if you together eliminate all pride and jealousy and greed and if you all think only of the good and if you all work against evil." It was the humanists' answer to the Christian's conviction that no man-inspired effort could do this but only an act of God in Christ Jesus. Jessie repudiated this teaching and that of similar cults.

Meanwhile, she had at last been putting on paper the results of her study of biblical prophecies. She focused on Revelations 12, where the great dragon makes desperate efforts to wipe out the man-child before the end-days come. She reinterpreted the war-lust, industrial strife, and social disorder in Europe as the last works of the "beast from the abyss," who was making a last attempt to destroy the true Church. To Jessie's way of thinking, apostasy was far more serious than any catastrophe or tribulation. So the only defense for the true Church in the last days would be the prayer and testimony of the faithful remnant. This form of Adventism was more practical and militant, and more sure of the prospect of a final deliverance.

When the great post-war debate began, Jessie was already committed to the pre-millenialist position. Between 1916 and 1925, there were notable modifications in her thinking about the Second Advent. One change may have been caused by her editorship of the magazine, *Friends of Israel and the Time of the End*, which brought her into contact with a group who believed that the fulfillment of all prophecy and of all the promises to Abraham and David would have to precede the coming of the Messiah-Savior. The other modification was almost certainly caused by her post-war links with American millennialism. This same movement exercised powerful influences on Welsh Bible teachers such as R. B. Jones and T. R. Williams.

Because of the arrival of hundreds of soldiers and civilians in Bible lands during the Great War, and their excited reports that highways were being made through the desert and that new water channels were flowing wherever Jewish settlements formed, the students of prophecy had to take on board what was actually happening in Palestine. Popular encyclopedias and travelers' sketchbooks had always showed ancient forms of Jewish and Arab life whilst others showed ancient artifacts that had come to light for the first time since the days of the prophets. Now there were new public lecturers equipped with good slides about the "Promised Land" becoming a "Land of Promise." One of the best was Mark Kagan, who showed how biblical prophecies about Tyre, Bethel, Hebron, Gaza, were now already fulfilled. He then showed the exciting evidence of the re-gathering of thousands of Jews from many lands. Kagan predicted a spiritual re-gathering with multiple conversions, a cleansing of the repentant nation and the restoring of the city of Zion. Said he, "Although today the land is polluted by the unbelief of Israel, by apostate Christianity and by Mohammedanism, it will yet be under God's good hand and become in the near future the praise of the Glory of God."

The old theme of tribulation was switched to Israel itself, which must endure affliction before at last it will yield to Jesus and become His witness to the world. Kagan's last book, written a while after the Balfour Declaration, which made solemn pledges to the Jews, focused on Ezekiel's vision of the valley of dry bones being reunited and reclothed with flesh. But he added one more detail—the valley would be a place of a terrible shaking before the cleansing and reunification of Israel is complete.

Two generations after Moody, Sankey, Torrey, and Alexander brought new spiritual vitality into American Baptist and Methodist movements, and their scores of breakaway missions and fellowships, there arose a generation that resolved to bear witness to ALL the doctrines contained in the Apostles' Creed, and that *all* included "From whence He shall come to judge the quick and the dead." By and large, they adhered strictly to the biblical text, and thus took literally the passages about the thousand year reign of Christ and about the great assembly of the redeemed meeting "in the air." They were not all agreed about dividing human history into dispensations, and they were not all agreed that the great reunion in the air was the same thing as the mysterious rapture described by the Lord in Matthew 24:29-31.

Two Americans of high international repute were Philip Mauro and Henry A. Ironside. In 1913, Mauro's *Looking for the Savior* started the excitement, and his 1923 book, *The Seventy Weeks,* completed the details of the case. In between those dates, H. Ironside had produced *Lectures on the Book of Revelation* and his smaller book , *Not Wrath but Rapture.* One can safely say that the Philadelphia School of the Bible, the Moody Bible Institute, and the directors of the Loizeaux Press were all committed to the pre-millenialist position. These were not Pentecostalist prophets or "Second Comers"; but cautious, knowledgeable Bible teachers.

What they were unanimous about was that the seven signs, given by the Lord in Matthew 24, would be totally fulfilled. Some of their preachers turned the spotlight on the bits about false messiahs and false prophets, etc. Others paid urgent attention to the verse, "First of all the Gospel must be preached in all the world." There were also numerous gentle souls who saw the coming of Christ as a longed-for deliverance from the evils of this world. In the words of D. Whittle and May Whittle Moody, the coming of the King Jesus was:

> A lamp in the night, a song in time of sorrow;
> A great glad hope which faith can ever borrow.
> To gild the passing day with the glory of the morrow.
> A star in the night, a beacon bright to guide us.
> An anchor sure to hold when the storms betide us.
> A refuge for the soul where in quiet we may hide us.

In Jessie Penn-Lewis's vision, this process of cleansing and restoration and reunion was equally applicable to the Church. In 1923, she set out her position in two pamphlets, *The Time of the End*, and *Signs and Wonders at the Time of the End.* The first was based on the letters to the seven churches where each part of the Church needed renewal and cleansing. Soon the thousands forsake the faith during the terrible conflict with the beast, the dragon and the antichrist, who is the great deceiver and counterfeiter. In that day, the mere churchgoers would be led astray—all except the overcomers who trusted in the Blood. In her opinion, instead of expecting to be rescued by signs and wonders, those saints would expect to lay down their lives for the One who died on the Cross.

> There is no promise for the Last Days of any God-given movements of signs and wonders, or even of rapid gatherings in of masses of souls for Christ. Neither is there any ground for expecting a visible triumph of the saints . . . Yet God will still have His witnesses, those whose lives will show all the fruits of the spiritual life. Set firmly against the mass of false witnesses there will stand God's "Pillar-souls."

How strange that this interpretation by the overcomers was directly opposite to the triumphalist view of the last days that has taken over many Christian movements today that regularly chant hymns of victory.

Jessie would reach that same refuge for the soul in her last days on earth, but at this point in her life she was receiving the witness from the two groups who wrote to her and shared with her their view of the Second Advent.

A Mr. Wootton wrote to her from Brazil to tell her that he had felt compelled to use his holidays to go and preach to some Indian tribes because he realized "so many tribes had not yet received the Gospel and it seems there is a lot to be done before the Bride can make herself ready. . . . I believe that God is hastening the work and is going to give revivals and awakenings everywhere in order to complete the church for the Lord to come quickly. Amen."

What Wootton believed was also believed in a great circle of young men and women who formed the spearhead of new missionary advances into remote parts of South America and the Pacific islands and into North and East Africa. "Two thousand tongues to go," wrote one inspired scholar. "The whole wide world for Jesus," sang a hymnist. It was all preparation for the coming of the King.

Another viewpoint is well represented by evangelist Charles Taylor, who preached to tens of thousands of people in the great cities of America. He shared his thoughts with Mrs. Penn-Lewis.

> I often wonder what those church members think now in England about the world getting better. Numbers of churches closed their doors against me because I preached Christ's coming and the state of the world before He should come. I had to suffer more through that than anything else in England. Surely the present state of things have opened their eyes to the truth of God's Word. I have been asked not to speak on that subject in some churches in this country, but I take no notice and go straight on with my message. God has given me great boldness to preach the truth and we value your prayers and also the prayers of Evan Roberts and your praying band. We shall always be in the thick of the battle.

We are almost back to the mood and outlook of the mid-nineteenth century. The same pessimism returned like a black cloud over Britain during the twenties, which was marred by social discontent, bitter strife, and a deadly despair. Christians in public life were deeply discouraged, whereas certain preachers—such as R. B. Jones—were inclined to say, "I told you so," and refused to take the League of Nations or the peace movements seriously.

Jessie Penn-Lewis was quite unlike many aged Christian writers and leaders in that, in her final years, she had very little to say about the end times. Naturally enough, she discussed the eagerly awaited rapture or translation after she lost her beloved husband and a large group of old friends. But it was now a settled hope to be enjoyed rather than a belief to be proclaimed. As for the other theme of tribulation, we have the one letter preserved by Mary Garrard, in which Jessie said, "We are increasingly moving on into the shadow, if not having a foretaste of the great tribulation. God is shaking all that can be shaken. Such a shaking by the hand of God, so that things that cannot be shaken may remain, has meant that the foundations are being laid bare. . . . I am deeply persuaded that never was the Message of *The Overcomer* as to the 'identification' aspect of the Cross more needed."

In the years 1924-1926, a number of Christian leaders were having a new problem. Nantlais Williams told his friends that he couldn't find any guidance on whether he should expect revival or the return of Christ. R. B. Jones also went rather quiet about these issues during the late twenties, and so did some of the English Bible-expositors. Therefore, it was only natural that the matter should be raised at the Swanwick Conference, and that Jessie Penn-Lewis's answer should be included as a footnote in the book based on their discussions:

> The question may be asked whether, in view of the Lord's return, we are to pray for or expect revival. There is undoubtedly at the present time an awakening of prayer for Revival. But "The Coming of the Lord draweth nigh." Whether revival will precede or follow

> that glorious event we do not know. . . . In either case we can pray for it, and prepare the way for it, whether we shall be in it, or out of it by being absent from the body and present with the Lord.

Another fruit of one of these conferences was a little book entitled, *Dying to Live*. Its main theme was deliverance, and the last chapter was titled "Always Delivered to Death for Christ's Sake." It was not about martyrdom as such, but about the harsh experiences of *the elect* who get no credit or honour or even recognition for what they do in the service of the Body of Christ. It is these *elect ones* who have a special role to play in the closing of the age when so few will be found faithful. Wrote Jessie:

> Right over the land there are true souls who are learning the power of their lives to be in suffering for the Body of Christ. All over England in her darkness at the present time, God is maturing in a furnace many souls who will shine as gold in the day of His appearing.

Was this her final understanding of the return of the Lord Christ—to identify Himself with all who were faithful unto the end of the age and eager to hear those words of hope, "Well done, good and faithful servant; . . . enter thou into the joy of thy Lord"?

26

Last Valleys–Last Victory

The year 1920 was the last year of peace and progress for the Overcomer Testimony. The magazine was re-launched in that year under Jessie Penn-Lewis's sole editorship, but with multiple sponsorship. Its stated aim was to challenge spiritual apostasy, proclaim the Cross, and remind believers of the return of Christ. These themes were shared with the workers' conferences in London and with the more structured conventions at Swanwick, where famed Bible teachers spoke. The Cross of Calvary was kept at the center.

It was in the spring of 1922, that the first signs of trouble started when sub-groups pressed Jessie to focus more on adventist prophecies, while others wanted more upon higher forms of sanctification. Her letter book for 1923-1924, shows that Charles Raven and Evan Roberts were already holding special "Prayer Warfare" meetings whilst the Austen Sparkes group was already promoting what they termed, "How to live in the heavenlies."

Jessie wrote rather waspishly about spiritual men who were holding endless prayer-sessions and holiness exercises while she and her helpers were doing all the necessary practical work for the Bookroom and the conferences. Her secretary-biographer, Mary Garrard, hardly mentions men like J. C. Williams, Charles Usher, and Evan Roberts, who could have been used to shield her from numerous critics. Johnson, the Paris editor of *Le Vainqueur,* wrote a great deal about this "flood-tide of calumny, prejudice, and contumely which she endured immovably," and he said he would never desert her.

Mr. Johnson, who wrote that first tribute to her sacrificial life, never forgot that moment long ago when he himself was in deep anguish of soul until he was helped by Jessie Penn-Lewis. For many years afterwards, she conducted, on his behalf, a "ministry by correspondence—a personal dealing which was saturated with the grace of God." He was only one of many that she so helped.

This may be the right moment to tell another story about sixty-year-old Jessie Penn-Lewis acting like a twentieth century Philip entering the chariot on someone's desert highway. There was a young Mr. and Mrs. Bennett, of York Place Baptist Church, Swansea, who left all their loved ones and were on their way from Wales to New Zealand. They were feeling very lost and troubled when, suddenly, the frail-looking Jessie came into their carriage at Swansea Station, sat praying for a while, crossed the aisle to hold and comfort the sobbing wife, and somehow turned that compartment into a little sanctuary. Prayers for their lives rose up like incense from time to time, until they went their separate ways at Birmingham. They went rejoicing on their long journey, and Jessie gave her message of victory at a weekend convention.

Because of a serious hemorrhage in April 1922, Jessie was persuaded by J. C. Williams to make as much use as she needed of his cottage on the Derbyshire moors, where the bracing air was supposed to help her labored breathing. Eighteen months later, she finally decided to hand over more responsibilities to others before her planned removal to Surrey. In March 1924, she wrote to all donors of the "Overcomer Thank-offering Fund" to tell them how her own frailty and her husband's deteriorating health had led her to accept, from the sympathetic Lord Radstock, the tenancy of Eccleston Hall and an adjoining flat as a new home for the Bookroom. Clearly, she hoped to be within easy reach of their own new home in Surrey. She said she had consented to the release of Mr. J. C. Williams, who was to become full-time secretary of the North East India General Mission, but that she could not dispense with the services of Mr. Scottorn, who had taken a small country pastorate at Kegworth and was still able to supervise the daily working of the Overcomer Testimony. All this led up to an appeal for a continued generous financial support to cover all expenses.

The second circular letter was an invitation to a "Council of War" at Swanwick in May 1924. The invited persons were Charles Usher and William Raven; J. C. Williams; J. Rhys Davies; Rev. C. E. Proctor from Liverpool: two generous supporters—Mrs. Parker and Mrs. Cullen; R . M. Richards of Cardiff; and T. Austen Sparkes and T. M. Jeffreys, who were now designated as the next joint secretaries of the Overcomer Testimony.

"It is most important," wrote Jessie, "that those who are taking an active part in the Testimony in different parts of the country, should confer together, to compare notes and to consider various ways in which we can spiritually co-ordinate." She made it quite clear that she did not want to set up an organization or society or sect that would divide the overcomers from all others and would threaten the fellowship of all who preach and follow the Cross.

"It should be an organism rather than an organization," she wrote, "knit together by a bond forged by the Spirit of God alone, with each one free to act under the leading of the

Spirit of God whilst remaining in close cooperation with each other."

At first she thought *The Overcomer* magazine itself would still be a pivotal and coordinating center. Now she felt the need for the whole team to be knit together very closely:

> I'm asking the group to remain, if possible, over the weekend, for an all-day of prayer on the Sunday over matters decided upon at our Saturday meeting. There will probably be many others remaining at The Hayes for the fellowship and rest, but we must not be diverted by the sweetness of fellowship with others, from the object of our remaining. Let us not fail God in this crisis hour. . . . May I ask each of you to write to me freely beforehand regarding any subjects you think necessary should be considered. Let us face the greatest difficulties frankly and bravely so that we may know how to strengthen each other for the warfare.

Whatever was decided in secret talks that crucial week, *The Overcomer* and the conference system were firmly reestablished and a call went out to find new workers, including someone who eventually retired from his career post and offered to administer all the office work at Eccleston Hall.

Throughout the rest of 1924, Jessie was forced to leave everything to her helpers because her husband, William, had serious heart trouble and complications. In letters to friends, she expressed the view that he had shortened his life span by overwork during the war because of staff shortages. It became worse in the post-war years when the city treasurer was expected to run the housing and welfare services as well as finance. Several senior officers of the city council had taken retirement in September 1924, but William was asked to go on serving until March 1925. He had promised that he would always be ready to serve if ever there were difficulties because he felt such a strong loyalty to the city of Leicester.

Altogether there were three public presentations to this dedicated local government officer—a cabinet from his fellow officers in September, a silver salver from the Mayor and corporation, with an address expressing their appreciation of his considerable services over twenty-eight years. The third present was a purse of two hundred guineas from the "gentlemen of the city" from which he bought an elegant clock. The *Leicester Mail* reported all these events but had to eat its words a month or two later when it was discovered that the next city council, composed of "new boys," had decided to cut officers' retirement pensions from 50% to 33%. A private letter that Jessie wrote to a woman named Molly, said that this move had been caused by political pressures, but had the same effect as a satanic attack in that it caused them intense mental and physical suffering.

Letters to the *Mail* spoke very angrily about this meanness that left Jessie with a small weekly pension. This was all the more embarrassing because the doctors had already persuaded William to move from Leicester before winter set in, and they had already bought a house in Kingswood, Lapworth, in the Surrey Hills, which they renamed "Cartref." By the time they had sold the Toller Road property, relocated the lady secretary, and moved all the Overcomer Bookroom and administration to Eccleston Hall, Jessie was almost too worn out to feel any joy at the Lord's provision. Mary Garrard stayed on to help her, and a little flat was fitted up for her near the new Eccleston Hall base.

Just a few months after this, the faithful William Penn-Lewis went to his eternal abode, and Jessie, now a widow, didn't know where to turn so far off from Leicester. Eventually, it was arranged to have his funeral in the Friends Burial Field at Reigate (now a wilderness at the rear of a residential home). Dr. F. B. Meyer and other old friends were soon at her side in this new crisis. During the funeral service, he drew attention to William Penn-Lewis's quiet service, which included a ministry of encouragement for Russian friends during the revolutionary years. Then he mentioned that Jessie had written a little thank you to William in the preface to her book, *The Cross of Christ*:

> To my husband who has so freely given me to the service of the Master and who has encouraged and strengthened me in every step of obedience to the heavenly vision.

Jessie deeply missed the quiet, warmhearted man who had kept in the background and had given her devoted love and total support for her ministries and faithful prayer intercession. Few knew about his gifts of generous resources, nor did they appreciate how unusual it was for a husband to give such freedom to serve the Lord in those days. A nice tribute in the *Life of Faith* said, "At the back of Mrs. Penn-Lewis's God-given ministry in public service, there was his unobtrusive presence."

Their friend, George Morgan, said a little more to Jessie, "To return from a strenuous absence and find in him an always sympathetic listener and informed admirer must have done much to dispel your physical weariness. Now yours is the Cross and his the crown."

A small group of condolence letters said over and over that she would be given fresh hope because the Lord was coming soon. Miss Soltau reminded her that at that time a great number of their companions were "entering before us" in readiness for the rapture. Jessie had often written and spoken about the way Christian workers could cope with suffering, loss, and grief by looking at it in the light of the soon return of Christ. Her brief letter to the Ministers' Prayer Band has a genuine ring of assurance:

> The Lord mercifully took him [William] out of a short but terrible suffering. He was a miracle of mercy and grace from the Lord. I have proved that Death is swallowed up in victory and my heart is full of triumphant praise. Now I must be poured out as never before to hasten the Lord's return.

Surely, not even she could have anticipated that within a few months of her bereavement she would have to cope with and endure desertion as well. The full story was not told until after her death, but it seems that she was warned gently that all was not well in that part of the Overcomer Testimony that she had entrusted to two men—Sparkes and Jeffreys. By August 1925, she was hearing fresh rumors, from people who attended Keswick, that Sparkes was now setting up his own movement—it was linked with the name of Honor Oak, a church and college in South London. Having been set ablaze by the outbreaks of revival fire in 1922, Sparkes associated with and gathered together the fervent new groups. He created his own magazine and his own prayer band and held his own convention, which proclaimed their entrance into a new dimension of power and joy known as "living in the heavenlies." By the end of the 1925 season, it had become so obvious that even Jessie had to see that her new organizer had diverted a good many workers into his own movement.

Among the obituary letters from friends following her death, there is one that alleges that this broke her heart, but she assured friends that she could bear this misunderstanding and separation. The fact is, that she had enough energy to visit the Continent with Mary Garrard in 1926, and also to visit and persuade two prominent evangelicals, Meyer and Holden, to become guardians of the Testimony. About this time, the Lord provided her with a new and faithful secretary for the Overcomer Conferences—a Scotsman named Gordon Watts.

Once more her body let her down and she received a very stern letter from her physician, Dr. Johnson of Richmond, who wrote:

> You cannot afford these risks. Your lungs have been weak ever since I have known you—now 30 years or more. The years are mounting up, so that in any case, year by year, you must relinquish some of your strenuous work. I would advise you that you cut down your public speaking to a minimum and certainly those engagements which are away from home and involve long journeys. But your platform work at home should also be kept within very narrow limits. If you could live out in the country for part of the time it would be an advantage. London air and surroundings are not the best for you. I am sorry to be a wet blanket but you must admit it is part of my duty to point out what may happen in the future and how you may set your house in order so as to live as long as possible and as fit for work as possible.

For three months in 1927, Jessie did cut down her travels because of a recurrent flu, which had put extra pressure on her lungs. She concentrated instead on sending encouraging letters to workers such a Mrs. Brunel, of Metz in France, and a very earnest Japanese student named Kimura, who was already being described as the Spurgeon of Japan. One of her advisory letters went to J. C. Williams out in California, who had discovered that some members of a West Coast sect had been making very injudicious use of *War on the Saints* and needed steadying.

All through 1926, she was using her energies to counter the Austen Sparkes rift. Finally, she assured her friends that the atmosphere had been cleared, and that she still had the loyalty of a "steady remnant who hold to the Cross and who have never been caught away by aeroplanic experiences and flights." The Eccleston Hall Conferences had also freed itself by "dropping off that spurious ruling line of things." To a friend she wrote:

> I feel now as if walking in a pure atmosphere, such as we knew at the very beginning years ago. I feel in very deep rest of heart in that peace and rejoicing which keeps me low at His feet. It is the only place for us. I can well afford to wait, like you and others, as to whether He will ever judge me worthy to share His Throne.

That letter was written in May. Three weeks later she had pneumonia once more and was just a shadow of herself after that. One more cruel blow had come upon her, and this time from people she most trusted. She said it was this last blow that shattered her. She felt as though she was holding on to the Overcomer Testimony as if "tied to a stake in the flesh."

> Alas! What has nearly broken my heart has been what has occurred the winter since you went, that is, that Mr. Raven and two or three with him, have joined up with Evan Roberts for what I think they call "Intensive prayer for the Translation." This seems to have required their withdrawal from active service in every way. Miss Campbell has closed down all her meetings at Southend and they meet at her house, with Evan Roberts the center of this prayer move. As far as I know this is confined to Southend and Reigate and they meet for days at a stretch. Worse than this, Mr. Raven has got hold of the idea that all subjective teaching on the Cross is error. Numbers are crushed and in confusion. Enough! I do not want to say more.

An even sadder letter went to Mrs. Brunel in June 1927,

telling her that there had been a satanic onslaught on the work, and that "the burden and anguish connected with all that has occurred in connection with so many of the Lord's children being really diverted to other things, has told upon me heavily. My only comfort is that I can see Paul's last days as very similar."

Knowing all about these desertions and wondering whether she should directly challenge the new movements, Jessie spent a few days at the parent Keswick where more than one friend noticed a special light of joy. This mood of peace and light and mellow sweetness went with her to the Keswick-in-Wales Jubilee Convention. The Cardiff businessman who had helped her launch local conventions back in 1906, was her "minder" at her last Llandrindod convention. In a letter to Miss Mary Garrard, he spoke of those remarkable last days:

> I met her at the Llandrindod station. She was very frail, having to wait on the platform to take breath before proceeding along the platform. But she went to the Gvalia very happy. On the Sunday afternoon she walked to the tent, very anxious that there should be no hitch in the afternoon meeting, after which I drove her back to the hotel. The evening meeting at the Friends' Meeting House was packed and many turned away. Her voice was clear and her message distinct and strong. I tried to persuade her to rest but she again went to the tent at 8 o' clock.
>
> She hardly missed a morning or evening meeting all that week. When she spoke in the tent on two afternoons, her voice was strong enough to fill a tent four times the size, and her message powerful (the theme was removing the schisms from the Body of Christ). Then each morning she spoke to the students of the Rev. R. B. Jones' school—about sixty. On Friday she must

> have spoken for an hour and a half. Then on Saturday she spoke at the Friends' Meeting House in connection with the North East India General Mission. On Friday evening she spoke to a group of farmers who had formed a prayer group since the Welsh revival. Such a program would have killed people much fitter and younger than she.

Returning to A. L. Morgan's house in Maesycvmmer near Caerphilly on Saturday, she was quite bright and cheerful, having refreshment at Brecon on the way. Then "she was about the house and taking tea with us all. Sunday morning she rested and joined us at dinner. In the evening she went in the car to Treharris and took part in a service there. It seemed as if God allowed her to give a ringing testimony in Wales before taking His child home. I never saw her more happy than she was at Llandrindod; she saw her Lord in everything, every step of the way."

Mary Garrard had the task of composing a letter to the Overcomer fellowships, explaining how Jessie Penn-Lewis struggled back to London on August 9 and became weaker and weaker because she had seriously over-strained her heart. Yet, somehow, she found reserves enough to draft letters to the Rev. R. B. Jones about publishing his Bible readings. She told her old friend that she was hoping to grapple with a new syllabus for the winter months and that she had got a few things ready for the next *Overcomer*. She had already made advance plans for the Eccleston Hall Conference and had chosen the "Keynote speech".

On her last Sunday evening she was singing hymns about the Cross. This was written about her last day:

> On Monday afternoon about 4 p.m. she appeared to fall asleep. Then her breathing became easier and growing more and more gentle. At about 9 p.m. it quietly

> ceased as she slipped out of the tired body of '"Fragile clay" into the bosom of the Father. We who were with her shed no tears as she entered into the glory, for the presence of the Lord with us in the room was something beyond the realm of faith. It was almost "sight" in its reality. The Prince of Death appeared to have no part or lot in the matter, and death was swallowed up in victory.

Mary had to arrange for people to write tributes for various Christian newspapers, but found that several friends were abroad. All legal matters were dealt with by Gordon Logan, Matthews of Parkstone, and a Christian solicitor named Robbins. Dr. Tydeman Chilvers agreed to conduct the funeral service with the help of the Rev. George Harper, and the theme was once more, "Death is swallowed up in victory". Nantlais Williams said she went into the company of the conquerors, and that, as they stood by the shared grave of William and Jessie, they sang, "There is a fountain filled with Blood, drawn from Emmanuel's veins."

Many felt that they should print Dr. Tydeman Chilvers beautiful tribute at once and should also print Jessie Penn-Lewis's last essays, "These All Died in Faith" (Hebrews 11) and "The Throne Life" in the next issue of *The Overcomer* magazine. Meanwhile a great friend, Mrs. Spencer Johnson, the editor of *Life and Liberty*, wrote a noble and moving essay about the dear friend of over thirty years:

> She was the first one who taught me in those early days what it meant to be "crucified" and "buried with Christ" and then to take by faith my union with Him in the resurrection life. Again and again, at the parting of the ways, dear Mrs. Penn-Lewis would be my "interpreter" and she would give me encouragement and a fresh vision of what God was doing in, and with me. Many a time, when her heart was torn with grief, like

> one who had been wounded in the house of her friends, she would gather those of us who were part of her Prayer Group, and plead in loving tones for God to open the eyes of those who had misjudged her, and reveal to them the fullness of the Death of Christ which alone would bring "life more abundant."

Amongst the hundred or so letters of condolence that reached Mary Garrard from all over Europe, one could see heartwarming words such as "unspeakably blessed," "still near to us in spirit," a "bulwark of our faith," a "lighthouse lamp burning in waters swirling around the Church of Christ." Some either expressed grief over the recent breaches or asked that the two years of conflict and anguish be forgotten. Men writers called her "our Mother in Israel" and "the Handmaiden of the Lord." Mr. and Mrs. Edward Parker wanted to remember her as a "Great Heroine of the Faith," a present day St. Paul who fought the good fight. They felt that she resembled the prophet Elijah who fought against apostasy and kept a faithful witness by the power of the Spirit. Therefore the best tribute anyone could give to her was the willingness of others to be equally faithful in witness.

Here, lastly, is the thanksgiving letter of Mr. A. S. Richings of Berachah, Claygate in Esher, Surrey, who unashamedly names her "My mother in the Gospel—who nursed me in her prayers":

> I owe almost all to her physically and spiritually. It is 18 years since I first came into contact with her and all those years she has watched, prayed, corrected, chided, guided, encouraged, and comforted me. I have brought her perplexity but these latter years much joy in that her sowing in my life has meant fruit. I have letters and notes received from her of a personal nature all these years, which I treasure next to my Bible. Her

buoyant, victorious, spirit was always stronger than her frail body. Me thinks she is very busy doing more for the fulfillment of God's purposes and hastening His return, because now free from the limitations of the body.

. . . Dear sisters, I do not feel that Mrs. Penn-Lewis's place can be taken by anyone. Her work was unique and she was specially chosen of God, raised up, entrusted and equipped with deep spiritual truths in these last days for the Church, truths that no-one else held. All others are borrowed rays from the light that God gave to her. To me she always stood as an example of one who was completely abandoned to the Lord in everything and utterly yielded to His will. We do not idolize her but we do thank God for her love, life, influence, service, and patience.

27

Epilogue: Still Overcoming

Mary Garrard remembered that somewhere during those last weeks, Jessie Penn-Lewis had made plans for the next Eccleston Hall Conference and had even decided on the keynote speech. She had worked out a rough plan for the next issue of *The Overcomer* and had drafted her next essays for the magazine. It seemed obvious to everyone that Mary Garrard would have to continue the work along the same lines and even edit and print her friend's other convention addresses. Few would have guessed that Mary would serve as general secretary and magazine editor for sixteen years.

Before the year 1927 ended, a meeting of supporters was convened and these people made a number of important decisions, including the choice of Bernard Matthews, a retired shipping agent, as acting chairman of an interim council. A special trustees' meeting reaffirmed the policy of continuing *The Overcomer* as a free issue to workers, the costs being covered by gifts. They also resolved to set up a separate trust to undertake overseas distribution of their beloved founder's translated works. They went on publishing and distributing

Jessie Penn-Lewis's writings and they also determined to maintain the Bookroom. More importantly, they resolved to bear witness to the same doctrines that the leader had defined long ago, without modifications.

It was not until the memorial service in 1943, that the chairman of the council disclosed that Mary Norman Garrard had taken the role of correspondent, sending hundreds of letters to readers who were in spiritual perplexity. She probably left questions of doctrine to others whilst she dealt at once with cries of pain and need. Mary also helped organize the conferences but always sat quietly below the platform. She also processed thousands of tracts but received no financial reward. Another member of the council recalled that it was this unassuming woman who had preserved all the Penn-Lewis messages about the Cross of Christ, and that she had shared with Jessie in a wonderful vision of the magazine and the Bookroom—that they were like the "living stream" flowing out from the sanctuary of God (Ezekiel 47). But Mary was not just a dreamer—she was a balanced, good-humored, and highly practical woman.

Whatever her gifts, Mary Garrard had no desire to be the next leader of the Overcomer Testimony. The sad truth was that in 1927-1929 there was no man who could fill the gap. Meyer and Holden were veterans; the faithful Mr. Scottorn was mentally battered by his experiences in Poland in 1923, and his friend, J. C. Williams, came back white-haired and restless after seeing the awful effects of the Red Revolution in the Baltic States. Williams eventually accepted secretaryship of a missionary society; and so did another potential leader, Arthur Harris. The only leader-type woman available was Miss E. M. Leathes, who was content to run and organize the prayer force (1928-1952). She wrote to Mary Garrard and to the acting convener, Mr. Proctor, saying that it was essential to have a male leader. Apparently Jessie had already expressed admiration for the Rev. Gordon Watts, so Mary asked Mr. Matthews to make the long journey to the north of Scotland to meet him. All the leading people in the Testimony were very wary of inviting some charismatic figure from outside their fellowship after the fiasco of 1923-1924. At that time the Rev. T. Austen Sparkes had suddenly opted out of his office after only one year—pleading that the Lord had told him to disassociate from the Overcomer Testimony and to start up an independent ministry. Despite this example, the special meeting decided to nominate, as Testimony leader, the Rev. Gordon Watts, who had handled annual conferences well and could also write well. But, he too resigned after one year, pleading pressure of engagements. The truth was that he had wanted to introduce additional aims and may not have agreed with Jessie's resolve never to found a distinct movement but simply to feed these teachings into mainstream Christianity.

The council told the next conference that there would be no change or addition to its message. From 1929 onwards, the Testimony was directed by an executive council under Bernard Matthews. He was a natural chairman who was noted for practical concern and warm sympathies rather than deep spiritual insights. He was a great traveller—like an ambassador.

Mr. Matthews' special interest was the Literature Extension Work and the overseas distribution of *The Overcomer*. This had begun very simply in 1923, as a vote to supply spiritual literature to Japan, China, and India. A few years after this, the ministry was extended to Jamaica, Mexico, and other Caribbean centers. Then in 1929, the Free Distribution Fund sponsored more translations of Jessie Penn-Lewis's works into Swedish, Russian, and other Baltic languages—also into Yiddish for Polish Jews. One unforeseen effect of this expansion was that hundreds of USA citizens got to hear about the extension work and asked to subscribe to the magazine that seemed to meet so many needs. Later on, Mr. Matthews visited as many countries as he could.

During the thirties, new ventures in *The Overcomer* included the "Helps for Teachers" series and the Missionary News paragraph. Interesting and challenging articles came regularly from Miss Leathes on behalf of the Prayer Bands. But the chief feature, especially In June, was still the very detailed report of the main conference addresses and of the important debates at the "Clinic Hour" that involved so many field workers. The conferences dealt each year (1935-1941) with a Cross-centered theme. The Revs. Thomas, Harpur, Baughen, and Ellison preached on "The Victory of the Cross" (1935), "The Cross as the Gateway to Life" (1938), and "The Cross and the Reigning Life" (1939).

Interestingly enough, the 1936 conference, aware of the four terrible dictatorships at work in Europe, became a very solemn this-world discussion as J. Metcalfe spoke on "The Shadow," I. C. Williams on "The Battlefield," B. S. Fidler on "Suffering and its Purposes," and Miss Leathes on "The Watchtower," from which she begged everyone to denounce television as thought control and preparation for the Antichrist's dictatorship. In 1937, Gordon Watts preached about "The Coming Conflict," whilst John Metcalfe spoke about the "Judgment of God" and urged everyone to pray for "a lost and distracted world."

This sense of urgency affected the Overcomer Testimony in three significant ways:

> The Clinic Hour, held during each conference, spent far more time considering the great invisible dangers caused by psychic powers that polluted the cultural and community atmosphere and corrupted the inner personality.

> Steps were taken to sharpen up the several sectors of the Prayer Force. The ministers, the young people, the evangelists, and the ministers' wives all had their own Prayer Bands linked by Miss Leathes—who also ran the Prayer Host from her London home. This unique body specialized in aggressive prayer against Satan's wiles.
>
> The stream of literature, sent to an ever widening circle of missioners and other workers in every continent, was accelerated. One dedicated lady in South Africa kept hundreds of *Overcomer* tracts in a storeroom and asked the Lord to help her give each one to the right person. It would not be difficult to find other equally dedicated helpers.

On the eve of the tragic Second World War, Mary Garrard felt led to put in the January issue a little anthology of Jessie Penn-Lewis's letters in which she advised a childlike dependence upon the Lord and an absolute confidence in His guidance—come what may. She said that if the future path included suffering, then they were to regard it as sharing in Christ's travail over the birth of the Church (*The Overcomer*, January 1939).

Next, Mary ventured to include her own essay on "Seed Corn Believer," calling for a moving on towards more intimate knowledge and deepening fellowship with God and closer cooperation with the Spirit:

> The Church needs those who have been filled with Christ's life and have matured and become overcomers. God is looking for men of full age who are going on unto maturity. May it not be that the sifting that men are passing through in these days is permitted by God so that they may discover whether or not they are living on second hand experience and the spirituality of others. YOU must know Him yourselves. . . . Become seed-

> corn believers willing for the pathway that leads to fruit bearing.

The outbreak of the Second World War put a sharp check to the European work. Here in Britain the conferences got suspended one by one, though *The Overcomer* continued to appear. When John Metcalfe began his long service in 1943, the Hayes Conference Center was in military hands and the Eccleston Hall premises was in a perilous part of much-bombed London. For a while, they used Slavanka in Bournemouth and the High Lea Conference Center nearer London. Their own new center and bookshop in Bournemouth suffered grievously from a torpedo bomb. All contact with branch offices in Europe was lost and the posting of literature abroad became a kind of lottery. Settlement of accounts was disrupted as postal packets went up in smoke or went down in torpedoed ships.

Fortunately, Chairman Bernard Matthews was still able to travel widely and to be welcome at many overseas conventions. About 1938, Bernard Matthews went to reside in Hamilton, Bermuda. Despite his advancing years, he opened his own Book Center and offered hospitality to Christians. Each year, he sent comfort messages to the suffering saints in Britain and Europe, advising them to take refuge in Christ when they felt their strength waning. A paragraph from his 1951 letter shows why he was able to enjoy such wide fellowship:

> Each believer has come by various and diverse ways to the Savior's Cross and, for these, eternal life has begun. Perhaps, years later, we hear His voice saying, "Ye have not chosen Me but I have chosen you." We can but bow in worship at the Grace that found us at the beginning and will be with us to the end.

Acting with considerable courage, a new body of trustees, which now included D. N Carr, Cyril Chilvers, A. R. Boughen, George Harpur, Gordon Thomas, Sam Turner, and B. S. Fidler, decided to reissue their literature in German, French, Russian, etc. Financed by the Extension Fund, numerous books and tracts were sent out for the help of hundreds of broken Christian workers who had experienced intense oppression. The whole intention was to overcome the evil powers, released by the devastation of Europe.

It was quite possible for John Metcalfe to introduce major shifts in the Overcomer Testimony and its literature. But he was well aware that in 1938 the chief supporters had once again affirmed that they would add nothing to the special teaching and message of the Testimony. He did not accept the more extreme forms of the satanic warfare concept, nor the fashionable dispensationalist and millennialist views, but he held fast to the presentation of the Cross as the "Touchstone of the true faith." From time to time, he produced a good, sound book such as, *The Net is Spread* and *Studies in St. John*, and another dealing with *The Bible and the Human Mind.*

Without his informative letters to the readers, which were not exhortations but sharings, we would not know how *The Overcomer* magazine slowly changed its format. A much reduced section was devoted to items for the Prayer Bands, but there were excellent new essays on intercession itself.

For some years, the April and Junes issues of *The Overcomer* were dominated by addresses at the Swanwick and other conventions, but this gave place eventually to a different system in the sixties. All addresses that focused upon the Cross and the atoning Blood were printed on separate broadsheets and were distributed free of charge to those who were starved of sermons and essays on this vital truth.

The editor chose one theme for each issue of *The Overcomer*—such as: following, guidance, endurance, separation, buried seed, or perilous times. This system has continued up to the present. He would write a connecting article and would also reprint any relevant essay or part of a book written by the late founder. This ensured a degree of continuity between her teaching and the later expositors. In the late seventies and early eighties one can still find such essays of hers as "The Message of Light," "See that ye be not troubled," "No uncertain sound," "Spear-Thrust Prayer," "Faith is the Key," and "The Vision of the SON." In that context can be found a very timely warning that even many true Christians are going to stumble and be led astray and that their love would grow cold at the time of the end.

Metcalfe and his successors would also fit in long extracts from the great spiritual teachers of his day—such as the E. W. Moore, Handley Moule, Ryle, Tozer, Boreham, S. D. Gordon, Jowett, R. B. Jones, Griffith Thomas, W. W. Clow, F. B. Meyer, A. B. Simpson, Ruth Paxson, and Dinsdale Young. Gradually new names were introduced as essayists—Huegel, Unger, Joe Church, Rainsford.

Because of its international readership, John Metcalfe took care to invite good quality essays from men such as Poonen of Bombay, Pastor Appere of France, Stewart Dinnen from Australia, and Oscar Hirt from Pennsylvania, USA. This policy was unchanged when the D. N. Carr took over the work and chose his own team of writers, with the full support of a new body of trustees who took the place of the seven appointed in 1952. The new men had to be ready to deal with new demands, but were clear that they should not change the founder's aims, ideals, and teachings.

Some of these men attended the Swanwick and Eccleston Hall Conferences and afterwards recommended such devices as the Ministers' Prayer Band and the Clinic Hour to their own Overcomer conventions. Each year there was progress on the international front and close links were formed with groups in New York and Philadelphia; in Alberta, Canada; in three of the Australian States; in Singapore; and in Kenya. Mr. and Mrs. Metcalfe also visited Israel and made valuable friends there. This aspect of their work took primacy over the convention and conferences, which lost ground.

During Metcalfe's twenty year secretaryship, other significant changes took place in the Testimony's outreach and communication. For many years, he and his wife, Margaret, had filled the gaps left by the shut down of conferences by traveling many miles, without benefit of a car, to speak at scores of Overcomer Prayer Meetings or Overcomer Bible Readings. The writer remembers him speaking at a Pontypool fellowship, and a friend recalls his impact on a Barry group. As John and Margaret entered their seventies, their work became burdensome, but the loving Lord provided a part solution. Around about the mid-sixties, they began to prepare sound tapes and then the modern cassettes on which the essence of the Overcomer Testimony could be recorded. About five years later, it was announced that there would be video cassettes available for use by the local groups. In support of these, a number of booklets were sent out to each group who were then asked to give these to interested attendees at coffee mornings and suchlike. The number of orders increased so rapidly that they had to hand the distribution to Ian Melville, who also visited Christian bookshops. In the same years they received requests for Jessie Penn-Lewis's booklets to be published once more in French, Italian, German, Hungarian, and other languages. The Trustees were pleased that the message was reaching the whole world.

This increased work needed professional help, however, and it was announced in 1988 that all distribution would be handled by the Christian Literature Crusade in Britain and America. Demand has slacked off more recently and the

Bookroom that was transferred from Poole to Bristol has now closed down.

Some have expressed the view, not shared by the writer, that the Overcomer Testimony has served its purpose and that the special doctrines to which it has borne witness are now heard in the holiday conventions or read in the magazines of later movements. Can this be true? Where does one hear a thorough presentation of holiness, or of full deliverance through our identification with the crucified Lord?

If the literature of this movement has continued to be a blessing, what about its special testimony? Has the message fallen upon deaf ears? Jessie Penn-Lewis certainly had no thoughts of becoming a theological teacher or of setting up some new sect or cult. She provided young Christians with booklets and she provided *Readings in the Inner Life,* which broke down essential doctrines into lessons. It is perhaps significant that at least two Christian publishers in the United States have made a start on reprinting this type of book, seeing them as very relevant to our present situation.

It is just in four areas, however, that Jessie Penn-Lewis made a permanent contribution to Christian thought and piety:

> An extended interpretation of spiritual warfare to include not only cosmic conflict and social disorders but that hidden inner conflict within the soul whenever oppressed and harassed by deceptions, counterfeits, and sudden despairs and doubts. In such books as *War on the Saints* and *The Conquest of Canaan,* it was made clear that victory in such warfare was to be achieved inwardly before it could be manifest outwardly.
>
> The deep teaching about prayer and intercession and its relationship to spiritual warfare.
>
> The crystal clear teaching about the principles of Christian living summed up in two books, S*oul and Spirit* and *Four Planes of Spiritual Life.* A discerning

eye saw that the inner man would always be in dire need of a continuous supply of life and power brought by the Holy Spirit. Only those who knew and used these resources could go deeper into God.

The comprehensive presentation of every possible outworking of the Cross of Christ in both cosmos and community, in both church life and individual life. How the Cross affected Satan, sin, and death; and how it related to our salvation and others' judgment, were dealt with in five major books. Readers are shown how being crucified with Christ and risen with Christ can touch and transform their daily living. At her next to last conference, Jessie took the workers through "The Plan of Redemption." Then she arranged for her recent essays and speeches to be collated and re-edited in a final work entitled, *The Centrality of the Cross*. One of the key-verses used was, "And they overcame him by the Blood of the Lamb, and by the word of their testimony; and they loved not their lives unto the death. Therefore rejoice, ye heavens, and ye that dwell in them" (Revelation 12:11-12a).

Appendix A

Booklets

Titles of booklets not analysed in this text.

Note: Jessie Penn-Lewis was prone to re-issue her earlier studies with partly or wholly new titles or as components of another production. This can be confusing. Some copies have been placed in the National Library of Wales. A full set is stored at the Donald Gee Resource Center, Assembly of God College, Mattersey, near Doncaster, England.

TITLE
SUBJECT
All Things New
Union with Christ in resurrection life.
Bend us O Lord (Plyg Ni)
Call to surrender.
Be of the Same Mind
Call to use powers of reason.
Buried Seed

Change Your Attitude
Challenge to cope with harassment.
Communion With God
Call to more consecration.
Deliverance Unto Death
How to manifest the life of Jesus.
Dying to Live
Christ's death related to believers.
Fruitful Living
Hill-Top Prayer
On power of the uplifted rod.
How to Walk After the Spirit
Tract about gifts of Holy Spirit
Illuminated Vessels
Based on a Andrew Murray sermon.
It is Finished
Unusual look at Jesus' statement.
Liberation of the Mind
Attack on passivity.
Life in the Spirit
About true and false baptisms.
Life Out of Death
Opened Heavens
Life of union with Christ.
Overcoming the Accuser
Special appeal to despairing workers.
Pathway to Life in God.
Account of Holy Spirit's dealings.
Prayer and Evangelism
Tract—includes binding the strong man.
Power in Prayer
Prayer power.
Prayer and Evangelism
Revival in Prayer Needed

Types of prayer burdens.
Satan Under Your Feet
Our potential to be victors.
Spiritual Conflict
Clear teaching for missionaries.
Spirit of Truth
About discernment.
Take it Patiently
Right attitude toward persecutors.
The Blessed Unoffended
An answer to detractors.
The Climax of the Risen Life
The Heavenly Vision
Printed and published in Bombay, India.
The Pot of Oil
Sermon given as speaker at YWCA.
The Silence of Jesus
Call to meekness and patience.
The Throne Life of Victory
Call them to a different life-style.
They Came to Marah
Morning meditations.
Translated out of the Power of Darkness
Promise of final victory.
Victorious Life
Plea to take every failure and defeat to Calvary.
Work of the Holy Spirit
Fruit within new believer's heart and life.
Why the Tree
Application of atonement.

Appendix B

(Photographs of Penn-Lewis letters)

Great Glen.
Nr. Leicester.

Dear fellow-intercessors.

I doubt not you have rejoiced with great joy over the ever-increasing tokens of the working of the Spirit in Pentecostal measure in many lands but your hearts must be correspondingly burdened with a great yearning over our own land, for with the exception of the mighty manifestation of the Spirit at Keswick we have not yet been able to record any such outpouring of the Divine Spirit as we have read about already in India and in some parts of the Continent.

As I have watched from the beginning the movement in Wales and the manifestation of the Spirit in various centres in India, the conditions necessary for His working, and the means whereby the "fire" spreads, are growing more and more clear to me.

In Wales, in India and elsewhere, it is invariably found that the Spirit-movement reaches others by the telling of the wonderful works of God, and when the workers in India were praying and expecting blessing, even before the blessing actually came, they made arrangements in faith for the quick communicating of the joyful news from one to the other all over the land. It is a growing conviction, pressing upon me again and again as I pray, that this lack of the telling of the works of God is one reason why the longed-for blessing does not come upon us in England. In India the medium has been a prayer-circular, drawn up monthly by a Missionary, recording the special prayer needs, and the answers as they come. Such a link is needed in England, for many shrink back from writing "accounts for a public paper" who would willingly write a private letter from which the records of the work of God could be gleaned ~~and flash it on like a torch-light~~ to others, with no brought ~~[illegible]~~ prominence.

As the Lord has maifestly committed to me the privilege of this service in connection with "The Life of Faith", I am writing to ask if you will co-operate with me in seeking to pass on the glad tidings of the Spirit's work in England. I have found that He is working in many quarters, but the story is not passed on; the "electric wires" are not laid over the country and so the light is not communicated until it becomes the blaze of light from heaven we yearn to see.

It is suggested that at the end of my weekly paper in "The Life of Faith", I should follow the example of the India-circular and record the various indications of the Spirit moving in quickening power in Great Britain, but to do this I must have the help of the Lord's people all over the land.

May I ask you then, if ~~any of~~ you will write to me (in any sort of fashion) telling me of any work of the Spirit you may see around you. It need not be what we call "Revival", but it may be tokens of awakening which will lead to Revival as we continue faithful in prayer. Tokens of the children of God being drawn together in unity; united prayer-meetings for Revival; special marks of blessing in freedom in prayer; and souls being won for Christ. The Spirit of God will guide you what to write me as you seek His leading, and I will assure you again that the wording of your letter will not matter, for I shall only use the knowledge and not the words, unless the Spirit of God sends some manifest message given of Him.

Committing this now to the Holy Spirit to lead you to co-operate wit' Him in this service.

Your fellow-servant of the
servants of Jesus.

Jessie Penn-Lewis

48, SPRINGFIELD ROAD,
LEICESTER.

Apl 27

Beloved -

I forgot to ask you let enclosed go to housekeeping with loving thanks for your freely given help to the Master's little messengers.

I was struck by your words yester morning & it seemed as tho' a flood of light flashed with them for yourself & me - it stood out so clear "all things are yours" - & the walk of faith & power is not asking - seeking or wanting - but believing we have & acting upon it - I am not to ask for healing - HE says "By His stripes we are healed" & I take the position of unbelief in asking - instead of walking upon His calling the things that are not as though they were! It flashed on me that it was also so with you. I saw that you had come to the place where you were to let go past attitudes of wanting a fresh vision or a fresh touch - if we are NOT & HE is our LIFE - how can He be giving us a fresh touch - it is no longer Him separated from us & "touching" us - but we taking our place "NOT" - & HE working through us as He wills - I saw it all with a flash as you spoke - and beloved one this is the secret of authority & power - not you being touched by Him - but Him in authority speaking through you to the mountain "Go & it goeth" - God is & we are not - this would put you in another place altogether & it would mean much to Him & His work - it would mean "irresistible subduing power to others - HE spake & it was done - your own personality as a separate identity merged in Him - I saw it all & your need - & the need of the world you are in - God in power through you - & you lost in Him - not seeking but ABIDING.

- This is a wonder on me to tell you - So I do - I did not see so clearly before - I start at my new book now - so no letter for a few weeks - Shine in Him JPL

There was a strange pain of straps in my leg - and then Yours in Him

Yo[ur] OW[n] + en route to Berlin – Tuesday Feb. 22. 1898.
way back from Russia –

Beloved – dearly beloved in the Lord
My heart has turned to you & then to our God for you – continuously during our journey.

Somehow I longed for a quiet time with you on Sunday, but it was not to be. It wd have been a great joy to me had the Lord brought you right out into His full life ere I left – but first He had to still you & it was very sweet to me to see you so held in His calm yesterday. I cannot doubt but that He will take deep – deep – deep hold of your whole being during these days when you are alone. As you wait upon Him, His life can gently flow into, & permeate spirit, soul & body until there shall be a great calm & you enter into the rest of God.

My soul cries out to Him for it for you. It is my heart's desire. I feel that I cannot rest short of His very fullest life for you. God has knit us together very deeply – I am conscious of a oneness in His life which makes me deeply yearn over you. I cannot take from God less than His best for you – beloved one – beloved in God the Father & kept for Jesus Ct – He will do it. How wondrously He has worked that you & the Baron are the two He has shown Rom 8. 11 to! It is on that stage that the real oneness of the glory is known. How glad I am.

And now He – our wonderful Designer, has planned for you to be alone. I feel that in these quiet days the work will be done – & all the tired look go out of your dear face & you shall know your God & the life of His Son as never before. As you wait at His feet day after day – just wait & say "Breathe into & through every department of my being, Thy breath of life" –

"Come O breath & breathe upon the slain that they may live" (Ezek 37. 9.) – He has slain your old life & now into the framework of y. mortal body, He will breathe His Risen life. What you ask He will do – what you trust for, so He will fulfil – then just trust that now, now, now that life from heaven

shall flow gently through every nerve
& every part – then henceforth
reckon upon Him to maintain it &
reckon upon it for all thy need.
Beloved it was a pain to me to say
all I did Sat night – but if it means
that now He will pour in the oil
of joy, I shall indeed rejoice.
It was hard to me to do naught
but use the "Knife" but I cannot bear
to have you come short of all He
has for you. The little vessel in
its human side you will forgive.
Sunday night dear one, I felt
sorry I spoke as I did abt Baroness
N. I was so tired. I should
only have thought of the love & kindness
that she has shown & which prompted
her interest & questions. Forget it.
I am sorry. I do appreciate in
deepest thankfulness to God all the
love of the many hearts you know
of. Only you see the walk of faith
makes me not dare to waver or I
sh'd sink – & it is so much harder
not to waver with so much poured
upon one of loving questions & care.
God will make me stronger by & bye
to be able to endure both.
Now to our God I commend you – Him
to thank for all His loving care of
me through your faithful stewardship.
– unworthy, oh, so deeply unworthy
I feel in my inmost soul as regards
myself. But blessed be God – I shall
be found in Him & He is all in all.
Our journey has been so smooth. At
the frontier not one thing opened!! All
so calm, so restful, that I have quite
regained my freshness – & all the testings
of the past 10 days are like a dream.
Yesterday morning I was so weak that
I was shaking from head to foot. I
felt I could scarcely bear to see any
one – tell the loved ones how much
it helped me – their not coming to the
station – it was kind because I was
so shaky.
I could not forbear weeping a little
while. The loved ones in Russia are
very precious to me. My life seems
bound in theirs now as much as
if it were my native land. Strangely
bound I am to you all.
Will you tell Benedict – I could
not find a translator at the
moment of my saying goodbye to

My beloved Countess sends her love. She wept at leaving you – dear one – leaving you alone when she was coming with me, she said.
How my heart turns with tender gratitude to you both.

Please give Countess Stackelberg my note privately – not send it.

Beloved you will see how entirely spiritual the whole has been, that I am to-day perfectly well – fresh, no cough, no weakness, no tired. – tell P— G. & Baron N. for them to see how conflict with the enemy wages now through the body – when we have learnt to live inwardly in the heavenlies! –
Will you please put enclosed in envelope & post or send

him to tell him how deeply I have felt his kind attention & care – & how I know my Lord Jesus will not forget it – read to him from me Matt 25. 40.
I want you to read that verse also to the girls & tell them that I know the Lord Jesus takes it as done unto Him.
I would have liked to have said a word to them about taking Him into their hearts & knowing Him. I can at least pray for them all.
My love to all the warm hearts, – Mdme Galitzyn is joined with you in heart understanding with me. I thank my God upon the remembrance of her.
The Baron – Yes – it is "alright"! – give him Luke 11.36 & 1 Cor 6. 19.20. with 2 Cor 4.10, "day by day" – (give him all this privately please)
Yes dear – farewell –
the Lord Himself will now make up to you all you have been to me. – & be to you these days "the God that is enough" – Thy loving Jessie Minisha –

Appendix C

(Photocopy of Overcomer Conference program)

10

The Overcomer Conference at Swanwick, May 2 to 9, 1922.

Theme: "THE CROSS OF CHRIST AND THE VICTORIOUS LIFE."

" At this supremely important hour, then, we invite Ministers of the Gospel and Christian Workers to assemble at Swanwick for our Third Conference on the Theme of the Cross, for the purpose of renewing and deepening our experience of its power, and for such united intercessory prayer that the windows of heaven may be opened over our whole land in "abundance of rain."

Many of our old friends purpose being with us as heretofore, Revs. H. J. Andrews (London), J. Rhys Davies (Leeds), F. E. Marsh (London), J. A. Morgan (Birmingham), E. Parker (Leeds), H. W. Thomasson, Mr. C. H. Usher and others. We shall miss the Rev. Gordon Watt, who sails for a preaching tour in America on April 1st, and Mr. J. C. Williams, and Mr. Scottorn, who are now in Warsaw, Poland, but we shall give a hearty welcome to Mr. & Mrs. Watkin Roberts of Calcutta, who will bring *India* and its needs before us, and Rev. S. J. Nabney, of Ireland, who will tell us of that troubled land.

TIME TABLE (Open to revision.)

DAILY. Wednesday to Saturday. May 3—6.

8 a.m. Family Prayers conducted by Revs. F. E. Marsh, H. J. Andrews, H. Thomasson, J. Rhys Davies, E. Parker, J. A. Morgan and others.

10 a.m. Series of Addresses by Mrs. Penn-Lewis on the Cross in relation to the Holy Spirit, from the new birth to the full growth of the believer. Union with Christ Crucified, Risen and Ascended, the secret of effective prayer and service. The "Royal Priesthood" of prayer for all Nations.

Followed by open meeting. Speakers limited to 5 minutes.

11.45 a.m. The Preacher's Hour.

Wednesday. Rev. F. E. Marsh, on the Message of Substitution.

Thursday. Rev. C. E. Procter, on the Apostacy and the Atonement.

Friday. Rev. J. Rhys Davies on The Cross and Revival.

Saturday. Rev. E. Parker on The Faith of Jesus Christ.

3.15 to 4.15 p.m. The Prayer Outlook.

Wednesday. The Outlook in Europe: Russia, Poland, and other lands.

Thursday. The Outlook in India, and the Overcomer Literature work of countering the Apostacy. Mr. Watkin R. Roberts of Calcutta.

Friday. The Outlook in Ireland. Rev. S. J. Nabney (*Ireland*).

Saturday. The Outlook in Great Britain in 3 directions:
(1) The apostacy in the professing church;
(2) The revolutionary danger in the Nation;
(3) The hope of Revival.

5.15 p.m. Sectional Meetings.

Wednesday. Gathering of members of Prayer Warfare groups (London and Country), in charge of Miss Leathes, Hon. Sec. *Walnut Room.* Ministers' Prayer Bond.

Thursday. *Conference Hall.* General "Clinic" for dealing with spiritual and other difficulties.

Friday. *Conference Hall.* Demon Possession and allied themes. "War on the Saints" as a Text Book.

Saturday. *Conference Hall.* The Prayer Warfare.

8 p.m. Devotional Meetings. The "Why" of Defeat and the "How" of Victory.

THE LAST TWO DAYS.

Sunday, May 7.

8 a.m. Family Prayers.

10 a.m. Prayer for All Nations.

11 a.m. Devotional Meeting, followed by the Lord's Supper.

3 p.m. *Open for the need of the hour.*

6 p.m. Prayer Meeting.

8 p.m. The Missionary Outlook in all lands, and the Lord's Return. Psalm ii. 7-8 & Rev. xi. 15-18.

Monday, May 8.

THANKSGIVING and FELLOWSHIP DAY.

After Family Prayers at 8 a.m. it is not proposed to announce scheduled meetings, but to spend the day primarily in fellowship, group meetings, and personal interviews, preparing for return to the battlefield, not only to triumph in personal victory, but to be used of God in "Revival." Opportunities will be given to workers to freely ventilate their need, and to link them up with "prayer warfare" groups for help in the conflict.

In the afternoon (weather permitting) it is hoped to arrange a motor drive.

8 p.m. The Conference will close with a praise and testimony meeting in the Conference Hall.

GENERAL NOTES.

The Conference will open on Tuesday evening, May 2nd, with a Welcome meeting in the Conference Hall, for Praise, Prayer and Fellowship.

Room X will be set apart for the exclusive use of the Ministers' Prayer Bond for fellowship and prayer.

Room Z, for members of the Prayer Bonds of Lay Evangelists and Women Missioners, and the "Overcomer" Prayer Groups.

Meal Hours. Breakfast 8.30, Dinner 1 p.m., Tea 4.30, Supper 7 p.m.

It is specially asked that no meetings be arranged other than those on the Time Table, without consultation with the Convener or the General Secretary. Every endeavour will be made to meet the needs of all, and special requests will have fullest consideration.

All who attend the Conference are earnestly asked to come with the prayerful purpose of meeting with God, and to continue in "Prayer without ceasing" for the Conference as a whole.

NOTE.—The above copy of the circular of invitation to the Conference, is here given that those of our readers who cannot be present may give themselves to prayer and follow the meetings day by day.

Appendix D

The Father's Love at Calvary

by Mrs. Penn-Lewis

(Printed in *The Life of Faith*, April 11, 1906.)

Once more we reach the season when Christians commemorate the solemn tragedy which took place outside the city wall of Jerusalem some two thousand years ago, when the Son of God—God manifest in the flesh—laid down His life as propitiation for the sins of the world. We have thought much of the sacrificing love of the Son, but how few of us have apprehended the sacrifice and suffering of the Father in thus giving up His only begotten Son to atone for the sins of a guilty, fallen race. What wondrous light falls upon Calvary as we gaze upon it from the standpoint of the lover of God to sinners. "God so loved the world that He *gave*. . . . " How familiar the words are to millions of people! Yet how wondrously they glow with heavenly light when read with their context, speaking of the lifting of the serpent in the wilderness, and the *"must"* of the Divine counsels, which said, "even so *must* the son of Man be lifted up. . . . " And "God so loved that He gave" His Son thus to be lifted up at the place called Calvary, so that out of His lifting up on the Cross in death might flow the healing stream of life to serpent-bitten sinners looking unto Him.

"God so loved that He gave"! Yes, but it was a definite gift of His Son to death—the death of the Cross. The Father's heart to the lost, fallen race of man is to be seen and measured in His gift of His Son. The heart of God towards a world sunk in sin is to be known best at Calvary! Love must *give*. Love must spend itself for the loved one! Love, true, pure, love, yearns but for opportunity to be poured out, and asks nought in return, unless it be response of a like kind. "God so love the world that He gave." It is written of the condition of the world in the days of Noah, that "the Lord saw that the wickedness of man was great in the earth, and that every imagination of the thoughts of His heart was only evil continually. And it repented the LORD that He had made man on the earth, and it grieved Him at His heart" (Genesis 6:5-6). And yet—"God so loved the world that He gave His only begotten Son."

Oh! the great ocean of yearning love in the heart of the Father toward the sin-blighted inhabitants of earth. An ocean of light and life which is vast enough to swallow up in its immensity the dark millions of India, and China, and Africa: for "God so loved the world that He gave. . . . " The ocean of yearning love could only reach the world through the channel of Calvary's Cross. There the God-man must give His life, and as the Representative Man carry to the Cross the fallen race of Adam. God loved and gave His Son, and God the Son loved and gave Himself. Sacrifice on the part of the Father and sacrifice on the part of the Son! "He shall see of the travail of His soul, and be satisfied." Ah! Who can fathom all the travail of the Son over a lost world? *Suffering*—not so much in the exterior tragedy of the driven-in nails and the soldier's spear, but in the travail of His soul.

Thousands weep in sentiment over Calvary, and at the very same time crucify the Son of God afresh by remaining in the bonds of the sins from which He gave His life to redeem them. The travail of His soul in yearning love to redeem a lost world it is beyond our finite comprehension even faintly to understand. We only dimly see that there is an element of suffering in love which makes love a pain until it has brought about the highest good of the loved one. Glimpses into this inner yearning love of the God-Man may also be found here and there in the Scripture. "I have a baptism to be baptised with; and how am I straitened until it is accomplished" (Luke 12:50), He said to his disciples one day. And later at the Supper-table He said again: "With desire I have desired to eat this passover with you before I suffer" (Luke 22:15)—the words dimly showing to us intense depth of travail—yearning to accomplish the work for which He had come from the bosom of the Father.

Later in the Garden of Gethsemane, the Lord "began to be sorrowful and very heavy." Then He said to those with Him, "My soul is exceeding sorrowful, even unto death . . ." In just a few hours the Lord would hang on the Cross on Calvary, and the thought of taking upon Himself all the sins of the world fills His soul with such aversion that it sinks into despair; it is the figure of wax melting before the furnace. And "exceedingly sorrowful" means to be caught in a very cyclone of grief. These are sacred unveilings of the mysteries in Gethsemane; and the same word is used of the grief caused to the Holy Spirit by children of God whom He indwells, when they sin against the Christ who died for them, or hinder or resist the tender workings of the Spirit in them—the same word chosen to describe the sufferings of the Redeemer in the garden—lifts the veil a little from the *love* and the *sacrifice* of the Spirit of God in fulfilling His office of communicating to the redeemed the fruits of the death of the Son at Calvary.

Let us bow in worship as we reverently open our hearts to these Divine mysteries! The love of the Triune God in sacrificing and suffering for the redemption of fallen men;

the Father delivering up the Son; the Son giving Himself to the Cross; and the Eternal Spirit—the Spirit of *Holiness*—loving, pleading, bearing, drawing, indwelling all those who yield to His power.

And what shall be said of the Christian? The ocean of life in the heart of God for a world sunk in sin and death could only find entrance into that world through Calvary. The same life in the Son could only find entrance to the dark world of men by His life laid down at Calvary. And—oh, solemn, solemn fact!—that ocean stream of life from Father and Son can only find entrance into the world now through the channel of the Church—the souls redeemed and joined to Christ their Head—and at the same place and on the same condition—CALVARY. The sacrifice of the Father in giving the Son, the "travail" of the Son in giving His life, the "travail" of the Holy Spirit in begetting the redeemed one for Jesus, must be "filled up" by the "travail" of the believer, in fellowship with the sufferings of Christ for souls. The Church will only reach the Throne by this same "travail" of fellowship with Christ. "I fill up on my part that which is lacking of the afflictions of Christ in my flesh for His body's sake, which is the Church" (Colossians 1:24).

Led Astray

by Mrs. Penn-Lewis
(Published in *The Overcomer*, 1920.)

"There shall arise false Christs and false prophets, and shall show great signs and wonders, so as to lead astray, if possible, even the elect" (Matthew 24:24, R.V.m). The discourse of the Lord Christ from which these words are taken was one given privately to the disciples, in answer to their question, "Tell us . . . what shall be the sign of Thy coming, and of the consummation of the age" (Matthew 24:3, R.V.m). Four times over in the midst of other details He uses the express "lead astray," showing that one of the clearest characteristics of the consummation of the age will be the going astray of many after delusive imitations of the real Christ.

Without touching the prophetical aspect of our Lord's discourse, it is enough for our present purpose to point out the one main characteristic of the "consummation of the age," spoken of in our title. It may be briefly summed up as a deliberate and deeply planned onslaught of the powers of darkness upon the very elect, in order to lead them astray. The Lord's discourse depicts a time of severe testing for the faithful followers of Christ. Suspicion and betrayal of each other— "then shall many stumble, and shall deliver up one another"—through inability to bear suffering on behalf of others; the love of many "waxing cold," because of abounding and increasing iniquity, alongside of a marvellous proclaiming of the "good tidings" of the kingdom for "a testimony unto all the nations," would be some of the signs of the "consummation of the age"; but also such an expectation of the Lord's appearing as to give the Prince of Darkness his opportunity to "lead astray" even the elect. There would be no use at all in Satan inspiring men to say, "I am the Christ," and thus lead many astray, unless there was first in the hearts of the children of God a keen seeking for the Christ, and a longing expectation of His appearing.

It seems, therefore, clear that at the time of the end there will be such earnest, intense awakening in expectation of His coming, that Satan will have his opportunity, and make such a subtle onslaught upon the most devoted followers of the Lord, that their desires after Christ would be used by the enemy to draw them astray. Such an onslaught of the adversary upon the "very elect" we now appear to be slowly but surely entering, and a time of severe testing seems to be just ahead of us, which will prove to the utmost, not only the loyalty to Christ of His redeemed, but their loyalty to one another. That the "love of the many" will wax cold we may sadly anticipate, for the "many" have never been ready to follow Christ when they find it means a cross. It was when "there went with Him great multitudes" (Luke 14:25-26), that the Lord turned to them and spoke of the cross as inevitable for all who would come after Him.

There are many forms in which that appeal may be made. Some utter the name of the tempted—the succouring—High Priest: "Jesus! Jesus!" Some cry in the triumphant assurance of victory, "Jesus saves me." Some do better still, and claim that grace in Him, the lack of which is hurrying them into sin; so that temptation becomes a positive means of grace to them, by showing their deficiency, and leading them to strengthen the things which remain, but which may be languishing to death.

But whichever method you adopt, reader, be sure you do it in one way or another. Swift as the chick to the shelter of the mother's wing, so do you betake yourself to the ever-offered protection of Jesus Christ whenever menaced by the Tempter. The LORD God is not only a sun but a shield. "The name of the LORD is a strong tower; the righteous runneth into it and is safe." He will "cover thy head in the day of battle." (Psalm 84:11; Proverbs 18:10; Psalm 140:7.)

It may be that you have tried to do this, and have failed. You have entered upon the day's life, fully intending to make Jesus your shield of faith, and to hide in Him when threatened by the Tempter. Yet you have found to your dismay, that you have been overcome before you have bethought yourself of your refuge and deliverer. But there is an easy remedy for this, in the aid of the Holy Spirit. He is the Divine remembrancer. It is His office to maintain the spirit in a state of holy recollectedness; and, if the attack be as a thunderclap,

He will be as the premonitory lightning flash, crying, "Beware! Beware! 'Turn to your stronghold, O prisoner of hope.' " (Zechariah 10:12.)

Be sure of this, that Satan cannot tempt you beyond what you have power to sustain or resist. Powerless in yourself, you can do all things in Christ that strengtheneth you. The Lord Jesus has bought you; and you must trust Him to keep you. "The LORD is thy keeper," "He will not suffer thy foot to be moved," "Surely He shall deliver thee from the snare of the fowler." (Psalm 121:5, 3; 101:3.)

The Spiritual Life

Gleanings from Letters by Mrs. Penn-Lewis
(Published in *The Overcomer*, 1927.)

God can afford to throw us into the tempestuous sea, for HIS LIFE must swim—it cannot sink.

"All things are yours," in Christ, and the walk of faith and power is not asking, seeking, or wanting, but *believing we have*, and acting upon it. I take the position of unbelief by continuing to ask instead of going forward upon His Word—His calling of "the things that are not as though they were."

You have come to a place where you must let go past attitudes of "wanting a fresh vision, "or a "fresh touch." If we ARE NOT, and He is our life, how can He be giving us a fresh touch? We are at the place where it is no longer Christ separated from us and "touching" us, but taking our place as "not," and Christ working through us as He wills. This is the secret of authority and power—not our being "touched" from the outside, but Christ Himself in authority at the centre of our being, through us saying to the mountain "Go," and it goes! God is—we are not. God in power through you, and you lost in Him. It is not seeking, but abiding.

Take heed that, for all you give out, you go deeper into God, or your messages will only add to the mass of "words" that is already like a mountain, sinking the English Christians further away from the true life in God. They know too much, and their knowledge is keeping them from the child attitude to their Father. Beloved, may He so concentrate His work through you that one sentence shall quicken into life the needy hearts before you. "He spake, and it was done"! So may He speak through us.

There is danger lest we become more occupied with the *guidance* than with the Guide. The real secret of guidance is, a personal transaction with our Guide. Like a little child, looking up to our Almighty Lord and saying, "Lord, Thou seest my perplexity. I desire only Thy will and Thy plan. I commit the matter to Thee, and trust Thee to block every step not in Thy plan, and I count upon Thee to put Thy hand on my shoulder and guide me by the skillfulness of Thy hand into every step of the way."

So far as I am able to discern, I am under the impression that you are not yet *childlike* in your dealings with God. You are apt to be too much occupied with your part—you want to grasp things too clearly, instead of trusting more absolutely, to be carried safely through in the Father's bosom, without understanding the way. No "light" from others can take the place of this childlike dependence upon the Lord. No one can see all round a situation as He does. No one can understand as He does.

You still see things too much from your side, instead of from God's side. You say, "How can I obtain the knowledge . . . ? i.e., you want to obtain it, whereas I find it easier to take the place of a child, and say, "Father, I am so foolish and ignorant, I don't understand—You show me what I need to know." Friends cannot help you here—their impressions are more likely to blur the simplicity of the agreement between you and your Father-God.

I do not mean you must never consult others—the Corinthians wrote to Paul, because he had wider experience. We certainly should seek light, but *the conclusion* must be arrived at with God alone.

On the practical matter of taking a particular step—you can trust Him to give your heart a "draw," one way or the other. He can work in so many ways, that it is best to stop looking at the "leading," and cast yourself upon the Leader! The Lord's way of showing us that He is pleased with a step is generally a deep settled conviction that all is right, and a blessed heart rest in the steps we take.

You can trust the Lord, you say, but not yourself! I thought you had dropped "self" into His grave! I feel, dear child of God, that you are not quite free yet—you cannot *drop yourself*, and let the Lord look after you and keep you from making a mistake. Your fear of making a mistake is causing you to look all round for light, instead of being His little child, and dealing only with God. It is so simple—so very simple. Trust your Father, and then peacefully and trustfully take the step that looks to you right. He holds you accountable to act only so far as you know.

Appendix E

The Message in Other Lands

The Overcomer Literature Extension Work

(From the back cover of *The Overcomer*, 1924.)

Germany

In response to the "S.O.S." from Germany, given in the April number, we rejoice to say that a German lady, resident in England, has undertaken to meet the entire cost of the first edition of "War on the Saints" in German. The translator writes that the whole of the matter is in the hands of the printer and it is hoped to have the book ready for the Autumn.

In a previous letter she writes: "It is rather a favourable moment for spreading writings in Germany. Literature is simply dying in our poor famine-stricken country. Books have become so expensive that they are a luxury. Printers have no work, and everything that could be given freely would be seized upon with thankfulness."

Will our readers pray much over the issue of the book that nothing may hinder its reaching completion, and the blessing of God rest upon its circulation.

France

Madame Brunel writes, on her return home from the Swanwick Conference, "I never had such a deep sense of help and Christian love as at this Conference. I found here many letters waiting. One from Brazil, in which the writer speaks very highly of 'The Cross of Calvary' and 'God's Plan of Redemption' in French, and says he would like these books widely read and known over there. . . . I have begun the translation of 'Soul and Spirit' into French. . . ."

Will our readers pray for the supply of all needed funds for the valuable literature work being done at great sacrifice by our sister. France truly needs this ministry of truth.

Jamaica

Rev. T. I. Stockley writes: "I am grateful for the copies of *The Overcomer* and other Booklets which you kindly send me. All such parcels are of great value here, because the officers and members of our churches get so little good reading. They receive eagerly any papers or booklets I am able to take them, as I go from church to church preaching the great message of the Cross and the Spirit. . . ."

Japan

A Missionary writes: "Thank you for the book *Soul and Spirit*. It is a book for times, especially calculated to be of help in a nation like Japan, which has had a phenomenal development in soulish spheres. . . . After many delays the translation of the little booklet *The Word of the Cross* has been finished. It has been done with explanatory notes which bring out clearly the Japanese meaning. The translator is a true child of God who has caught the vision of the Cross. . . .

Owing to the earthquake, printing costs are rather high at present, and I do not know just how far we shall be able to go on with the production of the pamphlet. . . ."

Editor of "The Overcomer."

Index